Glimpses

Seeing God in the Ordinary and the Extra-Ordinary

Ed Schwartz

First Edition - 2016

Oak Creek Media
Bluffton, Indiana

ISBN: 978-0-9907862-4-5

Introduction

As unique individuals, we are inspired by a wide variety of things and people. Inspirational stories can move us to emotional and spiritual growth as we pursue excellence in our daily lives. Personally, I receive special inspiration from real life stories that challenge my thinking and status quo.

The daily devotions in this book focus on several topics:
- God's creation
- God bringing good from bad situations
- Successes and failures of people

All of them are geared to stimulate life change and a positive outlook on life that can spur us upward.

Inspirational stories can be found in the ordinary things of life, as well as the extra-ordinary things. God encourages us to live our lives with eyes open, ears tuned and hearts ready as we view life lived out around us.

Most daily devotional books are written for particular days, however I chose to write this with no calendar in mind. You can begin on any day of the year. Though designed for everyday use, there is no reminder or guilt in missing a day or two or ten.

It is my prayer that this book can inspire, motivate and encourage. After all, that is what Jesus was and is all about.

This book is dedicated to the thousands of people who have inspired me throughout my life, as I've observed their faith in the God of the Universe.

A Bad Choice

Truth for Today – 2 Chronicles 20:15

The sea was relatively calm and the three men decided to spend time cruising the Indian Ocean. It was midnight when they noticed the dark outline of a ship ahead of them.

Cranking up their outboard motor, the three Somali pirates headed towards their shadowy quarry. They were quite confident they would soon be in negotiations for millions of dollars. As they got closer, they began firing their rifles at what they thought was a treasure-laden freighter.

Imagine their surprise when a 50 caliber deck gun opened up on them. Their boat was sunk and they were taken prisoner aboard the USS Nicholas, a U.S. Navy Guided Missile Frigate.

The USS Nicholas is a 453' warship, displacing 4100 tons, and is capable of speeds up to 34 mph. The armaments on the ship included 50 and 62 caliber deck guns, torpedo launchers, guided missile tubes and launchers for anti-ship missiles.

After the three men were captured, the frigate then captured two more men from the mother ship. Final score - five Somali pirates captured and sentenced to life in prison!

What adjectives can we use to describe the Somali pirates? Arrogant, ignorant, self-confident, over-confident, uninformed and blindly oblivious? Then I think about myself. Are there times I am ignorant as I try to do battle with satan?

- 2 Chronicles 20:15 - *Thus saith the Lord unto you, Be not afraid nor dismayed by reason of this great multitude; for the battle is not yours, but God's.*
- Deuteronomy 20:4 - *For the Lord your God is he that goeth with you, to fight for you against your enemies, to save you.*
- Exodus 14:14 – *The Lord shall fight for you, and ye shall hold your peace.*

A Bag with Holes

Truth for Today – Haggai 1:6

She was about four years old and it was obvious she was a very happy little girl. I watched her walking with her family and soon saw the focus of her happiness. She was carrying a bag of candy and eating from it. Though while she was reaching inside for a piece, others were falling to the floor through a small hole in the bottom of the bag. She was oblivious to what she was losing as she concentrated on what she had.

Haggai 1:6 says, *Ye have sown much, and bring in little; ye eat, but ye have not enough; ye drink, but ye are not filled with drink; ye clothe you, but there is none warm; and he that earneth wages, earneth wages to put it into a bag with holes.*

The verse prompts me to think about what types of waste or luxuries I have in my life. In a U.S. culture or society that is wealthy by world standards, we tend to take many things for granted. Where do we spend our money? The annual spending statistics challenge me.

- $96 billion on beer
- $4.14 billion on St. Patrick's Day
- $1.4 billion on teeth whitener's
- $16.8 billion on Easter
- $10 billion on romance novels
- $11 billion on engagement and wedding rings
- $1.7 billion on Valentine's Day flowers
- $16 billion on chocolate
- $4.2 billion on perfumes
- $34.6 billion on gambling
- $11 billion on coffee
- $500 million on golf balls
- $11 billion on bottled water
- $25.4 billion on professional sports
- $5 billion on ring tones
- $40 billion on lawn care

A Blessed Bass

Truth for Today – Ephesians 1:3

Jeni and I were having a relaxing time at a friend's condo in Florida. It was a great place, warm weather and a peaceful getaway. Being a bass fisherman, I loved the small lake outside the back door.

I didn't have any fishing gear, so I "borrowed" the absent condo owners gear from his garage. Walking the shoreline, casting and retrieving, I pulled in several largemouth bass. Then I hooked a nice 16" bass. About two feet from shore, he was suddenly gone. Reeling in the line, I noticed the lure was missing. As I headed back to the garage for another, I felt a bit of remorse for losing my friend's lure.

Tying on another, I headed back to the lake, cast, and almost immediately hooked another bass. Reeling it in, I noticed something unusual. Hooked in its mouth was my friend's lost lure!

The experience reminds me of how God loves to amaze us with His surprises. I hadn't prayed for the return of the lure, nor had I expected it to happen. But I do know God loves to leave me flabbergasted with His goodness.

How often do we notice Him working in our lives? Do we give Him glory when He surprises us with blessings? Do we consider the surprises as being a coincidence, or are they truly miracles? Does the Bible give us indication as to God's heart in surprising His kids?

- Ephesians 3:20 - *Now unto him that is able to do exceeding abundantly above all that we ask or think.*
- Jeremiah 29:11 - *For I know the thoughts that I think toward you, saith the Lord, thoughts of peace, and not of evil, to give you an expected end.*
- Psalm 37:4 - *Delight thyself also in the Lord: and he shall give thee the desires of thine heart.*
- Ephesians 1:3 - *Blessed be the God and Father of our Lord Jesus Christ, who hath blessed us with all spiritual blessings in heavenly places in Christ.*
- Philippians 4:19 - *But my God shall supply all your need according to his riches in glory by Christ Jesus.*

A Calming Effect

Truth for Today – Psalm 127:3-5

I was never one to enjoy school. We all have our experiences, some good, and some bad that create a love-hate relationship with the education process. In any case, a minor stomach ache could get me a day of respite from going to school periodically. But, there was a price to pay for that brief vacation. I remember the cure.

Mom would open an upper cupboard door in our kitchen. Behind that sinister door, we could find all types of medicines from the 1950's. But the nightmare began when she would grab the small one ounce brown bottle of Paregoric. She would heat a few ounces of water in a small pan on the stove and put in one to two teaspoons of the dreaded Paregoric. Then the horrible cure for stomach ache along with the subsequent gagging would follow. The cure was indeed worse than the malady. School began to be more attractive.

It was only recently I found that Paregoric was an opiate made from opium poppies. Finally in 1970, it was identified as a Schedule III drug by the Controlled Substances Act. It was no longer available without prescription.

Other liquids in the early 20th century were given to babies, infants and children to calm them before bedtime to assure a night of rest for parents. Today we know opiates and alcohol provided the desired calming effect.

Though my mom knew nothing about opiates in those early years, education and research has now taught us many things about how to care for children. Sadly, there are still many tragic things happening to children and some of those are done with malice and knowledge. The issues of exploitation, abuse, trafficking and cruelty to children is widespread in developed as well as developing countries. How does God look at the tragedies that befall the young of His creation?

Mark 9:42 - *And whosoever shall offend one of these little ones that believe in me, it is better for him that a millstone were hanged about his neck, and he were cast into the sea.*

A Clenched Fist

Truth for Today – Isaiah 42:8

Most are familiar with the travels of Christopher Columbus. Though Italian, he was commissioned by the Roman Catholic church to explore the New World and claim lands for Spain. Beginning in 1492, Spain began 300 years of the colonialization of countries in the western hemisphere.

Ultimately expanding over half of South America, virtually all of Central America, nearly all of the Caribbean Islands, and most of North America, Spain's reach was extensive.

The motivation for their colonization was trade, a hunger and passion for gold, as well as the conversion of indigenous populations to the Roman Catholic faith.

I was reminded of that recently as I read about a Soviet submarine. In 2007 they dropped a titanium canister with a Russian flag into the depths of the Arctic Ocean near the North Pole. That act and subsequent legal maneuvers with the United Nations is highlighting their claim to 463,000 square miles of untapped oil and gas reserves.

It seems human-kind has an innate desire to "possess". Many wars have begun with the desire of one country to possess another. Domination, envy, jealousy, hatred, control and power lead to exploitation.

As we look at history, we learn about the inclinations of mankind. We can use the Bible as a character study on the subject, beginning with satan's desires and lusts in the early chapters of Genesis. Nothing has changed.

As we acknowledge the existence of a supreme, universal and comprehensive Creator, we must ultimately give Him ownership of His creation. It is easy for me to cast judgment on Spain or Russia for their aggressiveness in land acquisition. It is less easy for me to acknowledge that I likewise desire to "possess".

Lord, help me to hold things loosely in my hands. Help me to remember that ultimately the grip on "my things" will end as I face death.

A Dog and God

Truth for Today – Esther 5

His name was Rip. A fitting name for a snarling German Shepherd belonging to my two friends. Rip dove into a pile of boys wrestling on the ground consisting of my two friends and myself. His fangs singled me out. That was the beginning of my lifelong fear, distrust and hostility against God's canine creation.

Fear can overpower reason and logic. Male machismo and courage cannot suppress fear. That encounter with Rip left me asking a question. Can anything good come from personal fear?

There are a hundred things I have little or no fear of. Fear of heights, water, spiders, dirt, germs, public speaking and the list goes on. But, over the course of years, I've come face to face with people who are deathly afraid of tiny spiders, unseen germs on doorknobs, social gatherings, darkness and cats.

However, over the years I've found my personal fear has taught me empathy and compassion for others with fears. I try not to make light of the fears of others, though they may seem trivial. Nor do I want people poking fun at my fear of a dog, though it may be as small as a 5 lb. Chihuahua. I've walked in those shoes.

The worst thing fear can do is cripple us, become our focus, or cause us to miss opportunities to serve Him. Is it possible to find ways in which our fears will help us walk alongside others? Is it conceivable our fears can actually become a tool for God to use? The bite of a dog 55 years ago and the associated fear has become a gift.

> Romans 8:28 – *And we know that all things work together for good to them that love God, to them who are the called according to his purpose.*

A Face Full of Nothing

Truth for Today – Ecclesiastes 4:12

I love taking walks with my grandchildren. Invariably wherever we walk, I get the brunt of the spider webs that are adult level. They walk under them and the webs catch me in the face.

Did you notice how the webs stretch and cling to your face? It prompted me to do research on spiders and spider webs to better understand the mechanical side of things.

First of all, the silk is liquid inside the spider. It is a combination of proteins, sugars and lipids. The silk solidifies when hitting the outside atmosphere. It is not squirted, squeezed or pushed out of the spider, but rather pulled by the spider legs, or by the spider falling while attached to the thread.

The tensile strength of a spider web is stronger than that of high-grade alloy steel.

A web strand is generally 1/10,000 of an inch or roughly 30 times smaller than a human hair. In other words, a web strand is compared to a human hair in the same manner that a sewing thread is compared to a rope.

A spider has six orifices to extrude web material. The spider is able to mix the silk into many recipes for what the web strand is to do. They are able to make a variety of sizes and strengths of web material. It can vary the mix, whether it is for catching, for walking on, for parachuting to travel through air, or even vary the webs elasticity.

Interestingly, a man recently designed a process that enabled him to weave hundreds of web strands together to make violin string. It is strong enough to handle the screeching rub of the bow during usage, but also, it created a sound uniquely different than normal wire.

So, what does it all mean? Not only was the exercise in web design, manufacturing and product usage educational, it taught me once again how God has an infinite imagination!

Ecclesiastes 4:12 – "*...a threefold cord is not quickly broken.*"

Our God is an awesome God!

A Fire that Can't be Quenched

Truth for Today – Galatians 6:3

It was 9:00 P.M. in Chicago when neighborhood residents heard the sirens. Sirens were not necessarily unusual at that time of night. Stepping out to their porches or looking out the windows they could see an orange glow. The factory fire was lighting up the sky so dramatically the fire could be spotted from miles away. Thick black smoke choked a nearby highway.

Hydrants in the area were lacking, so six fire department pumpers performed an "inline" operation. Connected by hoses, they were spaced out over a mile to pump water to the fire. Unfortunately the large factory was totally destroyed. The irony? The factory made fire extinguishers.

We live in a world where the unexpected happens. Dynamic, outspoken, world renowned Christian believers fail. We would expect the great Christian leaders of the world to be above failure and collapse. But again and again we see them fall.

Obviously each case is different, but there are lessons to be learned. It is not only the wealthy and famous who fall, but being renowned can be a difficult pedestal upon which to stand. Could it be that fame and wealth create a target for satan and our own desires?

- Proverbs 11:2 - *When pride cometh, then cometh shame: but with the lowly is wisdom.*
- Proverbs 16:5 - *Every one that is proud in heart is an abomination to the* L*ORD*: *though hand join in hand, he shall not be unpunished.*
- Proverbs 29:23 - *A man's pride shall bring him low: but honour shall uphold the humble in spirit.*
- Galatians 6:3 - *For if a man think himself to be something, when he is nothing, he deceiveth himself.*
- Matthew 6:24 - *No man can serve two masters: for either he will hate the one, and love the other; or else he will hold to the one, and despise the other. Ye cannot serve God and (money).*
- 1 Timothy 6:10 - *For the love of money is the root of all evil: which while some coveted after, they have erred from the faith, and pierced themselves through with many sorrows.*

A Fishy Rumor

***Truth for Today** –* Psalm 141:3

Every year for over a hundred years, our town of 10,000 has enjoyed a street-fair. Several blocks of the city are closed down for parades, carnival rides and ample amounts of great fair food.

Everyone has their favorites when it comes to the wide varieties of the food. My personal favorite is fried walleye fish provided by a local vendor who is well known in our community. The fish is moist, tender, salted and full of deep-fat-fried calories.

This past year the normal spot for the food stand was filled by another vendor. In vain my son and I searched for our walleye. Finally, we asked someone and he said, "Oh, I know who you mean. The man who had the walleye stand is pretty sick. It looks like he won't make it."

So, we moved on. A few minutes later we met another friend who asked about the walleye. I said, "We just found out that the vendor is very ill and probably won't live long." My son, said, "No, we were told that he's simply not going to be able to make it to the fair this year. He didn't mean that he was going to die."

As it turned out, my son was correct. How can two people hearing the same thing process it so differently? Communications are an essential part of our daily lives. Many times we wonder how and why rumors start. If my son had not been with me to correct me, I'm sure that soon others would hear the vendor was on his death bed.

Even with pure motives, we sometimes contribute to rumor generation. Those rumors can create great hurt, especially when motives are not pure. The Bible shares a number of verses on how to handle communications.

- Psalm 141:3 - *Set a watch, O LORD, before my mouth; keep the door of my lips.*
- Proverbs 15:2 - *The tongue of the wise useth knowledge aright: but the mouth of fools poureth out foolishness.*
- Proverbs 16:23 - *The heart of the wise teacheth his mouth, and addeth learning to his lips.*

Help me Lord to be a better fact-checker.

A Forked Tongue

Truth for Today – James 3

In middle school, our bus would always pass a particular farm house. Nearly every day, rain or shine, the family's dog would run to the road and chase his tail. It was entertaining, but I always wondered what a dog would do if they actually caught their tail? It all seemed a bit masochistic to me.

Sand Tiger sharks, prairie dogs, some snakes, frogs and spiders will cannibalize their young, their friends or peers. I recently saw a photo of a snake swallowing itself. It had succeeded in swallowing about 1/4 of its tail, though I'm not sure where a snake's tail starts or stops. The concept was bizarre, strange and shocking.

Galatians 5:14-15 – *Thou shalt love thy neighbour as thyself. But if ye bite and devour one another, take heed that ye be not consumed one of another.*

Over the years, I have done damage to others by what I have said, not said, or how I have said it. I witnessed the damage and tried to spend the time necessary to repair it. I likewise know what it is like to be on the receiving end of gossip, tale-bearing or false accusations.

A significant number of verses in the Bible are devoted to commandments, cautions or admonitions related to how one person can cut apart and consume another with words.

- Proverbs 18:8 - *The words of a talebearer are as wounds, and they go down into the innermost parts of the belly.*
- Proverbs 11:13 - *A talebearer revealeth secrets: but he that is of a faithful spirit concealeth the matter.*
- James 3:6 - *And the tongue is a fire, a world of iniquity: so is the tongue among our members, that it defileth the whole body, and setteth on fire the course of nature; and it is set on fire of hell.*
- Ephesians 4:15 - *But speaking the truth in love.*

Psalm 141:3 - *Set a watch, O Lord, before my mouth;*
keep the door of my lips.

A Great View

Truth for Today – 1 Corinthians 2:9

I was excited! While in Florida a woman shared something with me that stirred my interest. She said there was a Manatee Park in Fort Myers, Florida where you could watch manatees in their natural habitat. A large power plant along the Caloosahatchee River spilled warm water into a canal where manatees congregated on chilly days.

Since it was going to be a chilly 65°, Jeni and I decided to visit the park. We weren't alone as we joined hundreds of others wanting to see a wild manatee. Florida manatees measure 10 – 12 feet long, weigh approximately 1500 – 1800 pounds and live 50 – 60 years. Now considered an endangered species with only 5,000 in Florida waters, it seemed exciting to be able to see one.

On the day we arrived, three manatees were being released into a canal. Previously injured and now ready for the wild, a small group of specialists were taking care of the task. As we got close to the canal, the 100' fence was  lined by approximately 200 spectators packed about four deep. By standing on my tiptoes I was able to barely glimpse a manatee on a tarp about 150' away.

Later we stared in the dark water for a glimpse of a released manatee or others. Nothing. We watched and waited. Nothing. Then we heard a park guide say, "Most people come hoping to see a manatee. Actually, you'll stand for 20 minutes or so and get a three second glimpse of a snout sticking out of the water." We left without a sighting along with sad and unrealized expectations.

It seems life has its unfulfilled expectations: Rain on a picnic; snarled traffic on the way to a vacation; a dirty hotel room; cold water in a swimming pool; a too-done steak; a sour orange. The list goes on. But God reassures us that this earth is not Heaven and we won't be disappointed in what He has waiting for us there!

1 Corinthians 2:9 - *Eye hath not seen, nor ear heard,*
neither have entered into the heart of man, the
things which God hath prepared for them that love him.

A Herd of Horses

***Truth for Today** –* Isaiah 55:8-9

Driving on Highway 24 in central Illinois, I noticed something  "unusual" in a soybean field. Why would a hobby horse be placed in a field? Not just one hobby horse, but thirty hobby horses?

We could use the term "unusual", but possibly words like odd, strange, peculiar and weird would be more applicable.

We have tendencies to label things such as this as strange, and people who do strange things are likewise strange. But are there unexplained reasons that could provide logical, non-strange reasons for such things?

Possibly this farmer has a great sense of humor? Maybe he simply likes to get people's attention? Or, possibly it's in memory of a child who passed away in his youth? Perchance the hobby horses merely mark a ditch in his field to prevent his implements from dropping in?

How quickly do we pass judgment on people or things we don't understand? Do we assume we have enough facts to figure things out? The older I get, the more I realize there will always be things I don't know everything about. I am learning to simply take some things for what they are, without needing to "figure it out." Life is now simpler.

Seeing thirty hobby horses in a soybean field is simply entertaining and even funny. It helped make my day. God's Kingdom is full of unexplained things and situations. Can I let those things lay and trust Him? He provides the answers to the unanswerable.

Isaiah 55:8-9 - *For my thoughts are not your thoughts, neither are your ways my ways, saith the Lord. For as the heavens are higher than the earth, so are my ways higher than your ways, and my thoughts than your thoughts.*

A Little Bang and a Big Problem

Truth for Today – Ephesians 5:15-17

I have always enjoyed creating and building things. I'll never forget one project 40 years ago, when I built a 45 caliber black powder Philadelphia Derringer pistol. I had never owned or shot a black powder gun prior to that, so I was looking forward to the finished product.

Finally, it was now in my hands. A small gun with a big bore. My biggest concern was how much powder to pour in the barrel. I decided to load it lightly to make sure I didn't blow up the barrel and stock. So, I poured in the black powder, placed an oiled cloth patch over the barrel end and put a 45 caliber lead ball in the middle of it and pushed it to the back of the barrel. Then I placed the cap on the nipple and was ready for the test firing.

Fearful of an explosion, I put on a heavy glove and aimed the gun around the corner of my garage to protect my face from an accident and pulled the trigger. Nothing but a small pop. I put on a new cap and again the same thing. The caps popped but the small amount of powder in the barrel didn't blow the ball out.

So now I had a ball stuck in the barrel. I went to my shop, pumped up my air compressor, took out the nipple and blew air into the back of the barrel. The lead ball came out like a shot and slammed into the side of my pickup truck. The dent remained as a reminder that I'm not great at common sense or details.

The project became a reminder that there are always consequences to every action. I simply had not thought through all the details of what might happen. The dent was proof of that.

How many times do we say something too quickly and regret those hasty and harsh words? How often do we go somewhere that created an offense to others? Have we ever done something that caused others to question our spiritual integrity? Life is full of choices that create impressions, perceptions and consequences.

Lord, help me to take my time before rushing to action or judgment.

A Little Rest

Truth for Today – Proverbs 24: 30-34

It had been a long and difficult time in his Chinese prison. He was so looking forward to getting out of confinement and experiencing freedom.

Finally the day arrived. He walked out of prison, paused and smelled the fresh air. He knew he had a new life ahead of him.

As he walked away it wasn't long before he became hungry. With no cash in his pockets, he stopped at a home and knocked on the door. A 48 year old woman answered the door and found the ex-convict on her step demanding money. He barged into her home.

As the ex-con became more demanding, she told him, "You look so tired. Why don't you lie down and rest and then I will give you the money you need." He complied and promptly fell asleep. She called the police and he is serving another six years in prison.

The Bible is full of principles and commands that speak about hard work, as well as commandments against stealing and laziness.

- Proverbs 13:4 - *The soul of the sluggard desireth, and hath nothing: but the soul of the diligent shall be made fat.*
- 2 Thessalonians 3:10 - *For even when we were with you, this we commanded you, that if any would not work, neither should he eat.*
- Proverbs 15:19 - *The way of the slothful man is as an hedge of thorns: but the way of the righteous is made plain.*
- Proverbs 24:30-34 - *I went by the field of the slothful, and by the vineyard of the man void of understanding; And, lo, it was all grown over with thorns, and nettles had covered the face thereof, and the stone wall thereof was broken down. Then I saw, and considered it well: I looked upon it, and received instruction. Yet a little sleep, a little slumber, a little folding of the hands to sleep: So shall thy poverty come as one that travelleth; and thy want as an armed man.*
- Proverbs 21:25-26 - *The desire of the slothful killeth him; for his hands refuse to labor. He coveteth greedily all the day long.*

A Mistake?

Truth for Today – 1 Corinthians 12

I was looking forward to a quiet flight home. However, my seatmate was a lady who loved to talk.

We covered a variety of topics and I have no idea how we got to the subject of dogs. She shared that she had a Chinese Crested dog. Having never heard of it, she explained that it was hairless and very small. I am not a dog lover by any means, and I assure you that a small hairless dog would be at the very bottom of my list of preferred pets.

The next day I searched for a photo and was shocked at the images of the ugliest dog I had ever seen. Surely God made a mistake on this little piece of creation? Research tells me they tend to win first place in "Ugly Dog" contests.

The Bible in Genesis 1 tells us that at the end of every day, including the day He created dogs, God said "it was good." So, if that is the case, what is the value of a Chinese Crested Hairless dog?

Further research indicates they make absolutely excellent companion dogs for individuals who are invalid. The dogs are small, obviously not hair-shedders, and are incredibly social. They are content to lie quietly for hours without moving a muscle. Though athletic and agile, they are silently content. They attach quickly to their owner and are extremely loyal.

All that God has created, has purpose and value. Isaiah 55:8 says, *"For my thoughts are not your thoughts."* We simply cannot comprehend all that He has done, is doing and will do.

Genesis 1:26 tells us, *"and God said, Let us make man in our image, after our likeness."* When we fail or sin, it is difficult to understand God would still love us, or to believe we have value. But we are made in the image and likeness of God, and His love is perfect and complete. His love towards us is everlasting.

Romans 8:38,39 - *For I am persuaded, that neither death, nor life, nor angels, nor principalities, nor powers, nor things present, nor things to come, nor height, nor depth, nor any other creature, shall be able to separate us from the love of God, which is in Christ Jesus our Lord.* – Lord, help me remember that you have never created junk!

A Modest Shack

Truth for Today – John 14:1-3

At 58 years of age, Mukesh Ambani has the distinction of being the wealthiest individual in India. He is listed as #39 on the Forbes list of the wealthiest people in the world. His work in the petroleum refining and marketing world has been enormously successful.

With approximately $20 billion in assets, he reportedly spent $1 billion to build a mansion in Mumbai, India. It is a skyscraper that is 568 feet tall, and the height of a 40 story building.

Supposedly it is the second most expensive residence in the world, with Buckingham Palace taking the number one spot. What does the mansion consist of for Mukesh, his wife and their three children?

Six floors are devoted to parking, with enough space for up to 168 cars. There are three helipads for those arriving by air. The lobby has nine elevators. There is a spa, terraced gardens, a temple and a two story recreation center. A large ballroom is on one floor. There are guest suites and a large theatre that seats 50. Crystal, marble and mother of pearl are the design materials of choice.

Reportedly there are 600 servants who care for the family and home. At 400,000 square feet, it is a huge and lavish mansion. How can we get a perspective on its cost or extravagance? I know it is far beyond my comprehension.

The Bible says in John 14:1-3 - *Let not your heart be troubled: ye believe in God, believe also in me. In my Father's house are many mansions: if it were not so, I would have told you. I go to prepare a place for you. And if I go and prepare a place for you, I will come again, and receive you unto myself; that where I am, there ye may be also.*

Also, in 1 Corinthians 2:9 we read - *Eye hath not seen, nor ear heard, neither have entered into the heart of man, the things which God hath prepared for them that love him.*

I'm excited to read about Mukesh's mansion because I know it's nothing compared to what God has prepared for us in Heaven. Whatever He has prepared is far beyond our earthly comprehension. What awaits us in glory is better than anything on earth!

A Needle in a Haystack

***Truth for Today** – Proverbs 3*

While in Addis Ababa, Ethiopia, my friend and I wanted to spend time with a missionary couple, Gary and Peggy, whom I had known for years. They lived two hours south of Addis and were driving north to meet us. I called them late in the afternoon to arrange a meeting place in Addis.

Peggy answered her phone and asked me where in Addis we were, as they had just arrived in the city. We were staying at a guest house and I had no idea where it was located, nor did they.

As a side-note, it's important to understand the situation. Addis Ababa is a city the physical size of Chicago, with twice as many people. There are very few street signs and not much organization to the street layout. So, trying to find our friends in a city the size of Chicago seemed like a formidable task. Now, back to the story…

I am on the phone with Peggy, with no idea how to get her even remotely close to where we were staying. It was then I saw the English speaking Ethiopian administrator of the guest house in which we were staying, so I asked, "Can you tell my friends how to get here? They are somewhere in Addis."

When I told Peggy what I was doing, she told her husband Gary to pull off the road and park so he could talk to the administrator. Gary parked along the street, took the phone and was told which street the guest house was located on. Gary said – "That's the street I'm on!" The administrator told him to drive until he saw a sign, "Embassy of Togo – Residency". Gary said – "I'm parked and I see the sign outside my window." The administrator said – "Is there a white building close by with green doors at the entrance?" Gary said, "I'm parked right in front of it!"

The administrator handed me the phone and said, *"They are here!"* At that point I emerged from the guest house with the phone still to my ear, to see Gary and Peggy at our front door.

How do you explain that? It is impossible, except to quote Proverbs 3:5,6 - *Trust in the Lord with all thine heart; and lean not unto thine own understanding. In all thy ways acknowledge him, and he shall direct thy paths.*

A Purse for a Gun

Truth for Today – Genesis 2

As a seven year old, I learned principles related to trade, compromise, concession and negotiation. My cousins and I loved playing Cowboys and Indians. Those were the days prior to video games and anything electronic to capture our attention. So, we invented our own games and they filled our time together.

However, it wasn't often I had my male cousins around to play Cowboys and Indians, thus the need to learn about fair trade.

In the absence of my cousins, I would beg, plead and cajole my sisters to play Cowboys and Indians. Granted, they were not very good at it and certainly not willing participants, but that did not stop me from trying.

Invariably, the negotiations began for concessions in a compromised trade deal. My older sister would say, "Okay, we'll play Cowboys and Indians with you if you play church with us." Now that may sound equitable for the bystander, but it meant I needed to wear a dress, carry a purse and a doll.

I find it amazing at the compromises I would make to get something I wanted. I was willing to suffer humiliation and embarrassment to find fulfillment.

Satan certainly knows the defaults and tendencies of men and women. He exploited it in the Garden of Eden with Adam and Eve. In Genesis 3:6 we read – *"And when the woman saw that the tree was good for food, and that it was pleasant to the eyes, and a tree to be desired to make one wise, she took of the fruit thereof, and did eat, and gave also unto her husband with her; and he did eat."*

Today, compromises become temptations nearly every day. We sacrifice one thing to gain another. We take on a second job to provide additional income, but sacrifice time with our wives and families. We sacrifice family and friends for a relationship with another woman, man, drugs or alcohol. We may sacrifice eternal peace in Heaven for a lifetime of short-lived pleasure. Compromise...

A Really Soft Pillow

Truth for Today – Hebrews 4

The menu included lobster, prime beef filet, duck, Dom Perignon champagne and caviar. It's free for the eating 'after' you pay the $18,400 round-trip airline ticket cost between Singapore and New York. We'd all agree that the above isn't normal airline food.

Along with that great menu is a full double bed, a staff waiting to take care of you, and a personal toilet seat that reportedly is much more comfortable than the economy passenger seats further back in the plane.

All of this, and more, is available when purchasing tickets in the 'Suites Class' aboard a particular airline.

My dad used to say when visiting a pretty swanky place, "I've always wondered how the other half lives." In this case, I doubt that it is the other half.

When I read the news article regarding what is available in the Suites Class, I thought about something Jesus said about Himself in Matthew 8:20 – *"The foxes have holes, and the birds of the air have nests; but the Son of man hath not where to lay his head."*

He is known as the King of all kings and the Lord of all lords. Never has a king or lord willingly humbled themselves to the level of commoner, servant or slave to his followers. Never has someone cheerfully put himself into the sandals or shoes of the lowest of the low. Never has someone of His stature taken on the total debt payment of all of his subjects in his kingdom. Our Jesus did.

In every country around the world, there are those who believe they are entitled to extravagance and luxury afforded to a select few. We likewise also know how to treat ourselves well. But Jesus had nowhere to lay His sacred, holy and Deified head.

Hebrews 4:15 describes who Jesus was – *"For we have not an high priest which cannot be touched with the feeling of our infirmities; but was in all points tempted like as we are, yet without sin."*

1 John 3:16 - *Hereby perceive we the love*
of God, because he laid down his life for us.

A Scared Rabbit

Truth for Today – 1 John 2:1-2

She was a tiny and fragile eight year old sitting in a chilly and dark office. The small office was in the corner of the Addis Ababa, Ethiopia main bus station. She had been trafficked from her remote village and her eyes and demeanor gave her the look of a rabbit facing a pack of wolves.

Fresh off the bus, she had been waiting for her "trafficker" to take her to whatever unknown horror was awaiting her. It was then an alert man saw her and brought her to the office where two people spent their days and nights working with exploited girls. When we arrived, the office worker was interviewing her and trying to find out where she had come from. Her answers to how old she was, where her village was, what she was going to do, phone numbers of relatives all had the same answer. "I don't know." She was an uneducated and simple village girl snatched from her family.

The office worker told us they would spend whatever time necessary to determine her accent and dialect and determine the region she had come from. Then they would try to put the pieces together to eventually get her back to her village.

Scared, lonely, lost and one step away from horrible abuses, she was the fortunate one. She had advocates. Untold amounts of girls around the world have no advocates as they are trafficked and exploited for things unimaginable to most of us.

We as believers also have an advocate. Jesus Christ stepped into the gap and readily, willingly and effectively saved us from destruction.

1 John 2:1-2 - *My little children, these things write I unto you, that ye sin not. And if any man sin, we have an advocate with the Father, Jesus Christ the righteous: And he is the propitiation for our sins: and not for ours only, but also for the sins of the whole world.*

Not only is Christ our advocate, He has also paid the bill to save us from horrific abuses, eternal damnation and from ourselves. No wonder we call Him our Savior and Lord!

A Speeding Bullet

Truth for Today – Galatians 6:7-8

The Ohio Amish boy saw the horse and buggy going around in circles in his yard. He recognized it as the rig his 15 year old sister had taken to a Christmas party. Grabbing the horse, he saw his sister was not in the buggy and it was then he saw her lying on the ground in the lane. Seeing a head injury, he assumed she had fallen from the buggy. It was soon determined she had been shot. She died the next day.

Following the blood trail, the authorities found where she had been shot three miles away. A man from the area came forward after hearing of the injury and stated that he had been cleaning his 50 caliber muzzleloader gun and had discharged it into the air. He was 1.5 miles away from the girl when it happened. Evidence proved it was his gunshot and bullet which had killed the young girl. The man served a sentence for negligent homicide.

Accidents? Negligence? God's sovereignty? Fate? Destiny? God's will? Law of averages? Coincidence? So many questions and too few answers. But one thing is certain, there are consequences to actions. There is a law of sowing and reaping.

If we fail to learn from the experiences of others, we will likely be teaching others through our wrong choices in life. I am sure many hunters in Ohio became much more cautious in their hunting and gun handling after learning of this tragedy.

God does want us to be spared of tragedy and hurt, and thus, the epistles are full of cautions. Wisdom added to knowledge will spare us from many struggles and problems.

- Ephesians 5:15 - *See then that ye walk circumspectly, not as fools, but as wise.*
- 1 John 4:1 - *Beloved, believe not every spirit, but try the spirits whether they are of God.*
- Ecclesiastes 2:14 - *The wise man's eyes are in his head; but the fool walketh in darkness.*
- Proverbs 21:23 - *Whoso keepeth his mouth and his tongue keepeth his soul from troubles.*

A Stellar Smeller

Truth for Today – Psalm 139

As my dad got older, I watched him add more and more pepper, catsup, barbecue sauce, jalapenos and salt to his food. Now I find myself doing the same. With my sense of smell and taste buds operating at about 40%, I find myself needing added spice to enhance my eating pleasure. As anyone with a stuffy nose and a cold will attest, smell and taste are intertwined.

One of the great gifts God has given His creation is the sense of smell. However, humans are way down the list on having stellar smellers.

- The male silk-moth can detect a female from as far as 6.5 miles.
- Black bears can detect a food source from a distance of 18 miles.
- Grizzly bears can find a deer carcass submerged under water.
- It's reported polar bears can detect a seal through 3' of ice.
- Elephants can detect water 12 miles away.
- It's been said dogs can smell 100,000 times better than a human.
- Though dogs in general have a great nose, a bloodhound can smell three times better than other dogs.

Generally the nose is used for searching. Looking for food, a mate, danger, curiosity or someone who is lost. Just recently I read of a nine year old boy with special needs who was lost in a Florida woods. With panthers and snakes in the area, finding him quickly was imperative. A bloodhound was put on his trail and found him unharmed.

As believers, we are never lost. God knows where we are every second of our lives. That gives me comfort to know that He knows. When we stray, when we feel lost, even when we are lost, God knows.

Psalm 139:7-12 - *Whither shall I go from thy spirit? Or whither shall I flee from thy presence? If I ascend up into heaven, thou art there: if I make my bed in hell, behold, thou art there. If I take the wings of the morning, and dwell in the uttermost parts of the sea; even there shall thy hand lead me, and thy right hand shall hold me.*

A Valuable Defect

Truth for Today – Isaiah 43:1

A Lincoln cent begins its life in a metal processing mill where zinc and copper are mixed to make a special alloy. The alloy is processed into a 6,000 lb. coil of metal and shipped to a blanking production plant. There, small blanks the size of a Lincoln cent are punched out so rapidly you cannot see the press in motion.

The blanks are then run through an annealing furnace to make them soft and pliable. Then they are washed to remove the tarnish from the furnace and go into a machine to clean and shine the blank. From there the rims are punched to become a planchet.

Then the planchet goes into a press where the head and tails of each coin are stamped. 750 planchets are struck per minute (12.5 per second) with a force of 35 tons (70,000 lbs.) which is the equivalent of the combined bite strength of 110 great white sharks.

Then the coins are inspected and the perfect ones go to a bank and into the U.S. economy. But… every once in a while, a planchet hits the stamping die too soon or too late and it is struck in error. Rarely do those offset coins make it to the market as they are sorted out and scrapped at the mint. If they make it to the public it is rare.

I keep one in my possession to illustrate a simple principle. Defective and imperfect items can sometimes be much more valuable than a perfect specimen. A mis-struck Lincoln cent can be worth 500 to 5000 times its face value.

There are 7.3 billion people on earth. Talents, personalities, gifts, skills, experiences, environments, backgrounds, sizes, colors and shapes make us unique. A common component is that we are all imperfect. Sometimes the most difficult, tragic, horrible and devastating experiences makes an individual highly valuable in their ability to relate to others or to bring change to a broken world. The next time we look in the mirror and assess what we see, let's not forget that the true value of man is not what we will see in the mirror.

A Wasted Gift

Truth for Today – Ephesians 2

Christmas, birthdays, anniversaries and graduations all have something in common. Gifts are given. There is joy in opening the envelope and seeing a gift card for electronics, a restaurant, coffee, or a department store.

We file them away or put them in a wallet or purse and look forward to utilizing them. But many of us know the frustration we experience after we leave a restaurant or department store and realize we had not used the gift card. Or, we get to year end and realize the card has expired.

We are in good company. The Wall Street Journal reported that $41 billion is "the total amount of money on gift cards that went, or is likely to go unspent from 2005 to 2011."

Billions of dollars are wasted each year. The statistics cause me to reflect on the subject of "wasted gifts." A gift not accepted, redeemed or used is a waste.

The greatest gift that has ever been given is identified in John 3:16 - *For God so loved the world that he gave his only begotten Son, that whosoever believeth in him should not perish, but have everlasting life.*

The gift of salvation is free. Jesus willingly became a sacrifice for us on the cross. He was willing to give His life for just one person, but it is His desire that all would be saved. Tragically, every day, thousands die without receiving the greatest gift of all.

- Ephesians 2:8 - *For by grace are ye saved through faith; and that not of yourselves: it is the gift of God.*
- Romans 6:23 - *For the wages of sin is death; but the gift of God is eternal life through Jesus Christ our Lord.*
- John 15:13 - *Greater love hath no man than this, that a man lay down his life for his friends.*
- Revelation 3:20 - *Behold, I stand at the door, and knock: if any man hear my voice, and open the door, I will come in to him, and will sup with him, and he with me.*

A Window of Opportunity

Truth for Today – Proverbs 3:5-6

It was 1954 and my dad needed parts for a project. So, he grabbed me and we piled into the 1949 Chevrolet and headed to town. Things were different in 1954 than today. Towns were smaller, most everyone knew everybody else, it was safer and thus, leaving a child in a car alone for five or ten minutes wasn't illegal or unheard of.

I was five years old at the time and have no memory of the trip, but a few years ago, an older man who knew my dad and I, told me the story of that day.

He said, "I was downtown and saw you walking by yourself. I stopped you and asked if you needed any help. You said, 'No, I'm looking for my dad, and I know where I'm going', so I watched from a ways off to make sure you would be okay."

I had been too small to open the door of the car, so I had crawled out of the window in search of my dad. All ended well but the experience did prompt a few thoughts.

My desire to find my dad was apparently pretty important to me. I love the bond which I see in five year old children clinging to their mom or dad. The child has needs and they know where to go for unconditional love and security. That word picture challenges me in my desire to remain close to my Father.

Just as a five year old knows where to go for their love and security, that same child is developing an independence as well. My statement as a little boy of, "I know where I'm going and I don't need help", challenges me as well.

How often do I do my own thing, seek my own way, trust in my own judgment or determine my own path? Jesus made the statement, *"Except ye be converted, and become as little children, ye shall not enter into the kingdom of heaven."*

There are aspects of a little child that are certainly worth mimicking. There are traits that are not worthy of imitation. Proverbs 3:5-6 helps us to discern what is good and what is not – *"Trust in the LORD with all thine heart; and lean not unto thine own understanding. In all thy ways acknowledge him, and he shall direct thy paths."*

Abject Poverty

Synonyms for "abject" are words like – hopeless, miserable, wretched, horrible, dismal and utter. Add the defining word of "abject" to a word like poverty and we have a word picture. That word picture has many faces around the world.

The World Bank and the United Nations published the statistics for what the face of poverty looks like. The World Bank has found that 1.22 billion people live on less than $1.25 per day. The United Nations has stated that 2.8 billion live on less than $2.00 per day.

The good news is that the number of people living on less than those poverty levels is decreasing. The bad news is that there are still 2.8 billion living on less than $2.00 per day. That low level has consequences for those 2.8 billion people. Opportunities are minimal for education or health care. There are few opportunities for income generating employment.

Another deeper form of abject poverty is not having a personal relationship with Jesus Christ. The lack of sufficient food, education, health care and clean water are situations many endure in the timeframe called life. But the absence of Jesus Christ is a situation defined by infinity and eternity.

We have empathy for those living in abject poverty in their situations. We do provide funds and resources when and where we can. But the implications of not having Jesus or His saving grace are eternally more abject, miserable, horrible, wretched and hopeless.

We know God cares deeply about the suffering His creation endures and never does it become more apparent than in knowing His heart about those who do not know His Son.

Ezekiel 33:11 – *I have no pleasure in the death of the wicked.*

1 Timothy 2:4 – *(God) who will have all men to be saved, and to come to the knowledge of the truth.*

John 3:16 – *For God so loved the world that He gave His only begotten Son; that whosoever believeth in Him should not perish but have everlasting life.*

Acceptance

***Truth for Today* – John 3:16**

We would soon be opening a new Home of Hope for a Haitian family. A mom and dad would become parents to 12 former orphaned and highly vulnerable boys. Eight boys had already been selected for the family and we were searching for four more. The word had gone out in southwest Haiti for four male applicants, and the search began.

We began the hike up the mountain to the home to interview the four boys. But when we arrived we were met by 43 boys and girls, all orphaned and vulnerable. Desperation, hunger, a desire for family and a quest for a future and hope, brought the 43 to our door. We learned that some had walked for eight hours to have an opportunity.

The interviews took place and four boys were selected. Sadly, the rest left discouraged for their long journey home. It had been a very difficult day for everyone, but seeing the rejection on the faces of the children leaving is not one I'll soon forget.

Rejection. What a hopeless and desolate word. It smacks of loneliness, despair and discouragement. I wish there was a happy ending for the remaining 39 children, but the harsh reality is that there are not many happy endings for orphans in Haiti.

The experience reminded me of God's plan for His creation. Fortunately, the Word says in John 3:16 - *For God so loved the world, that he gave his only begotten Son, that whosoever believeth in him should not perish, but have everlasting life.*

I love the "whosoever" in that verse. No restriction and no rejection. I have a choice about being selected and accepted.

Thank you Lord for not being a respecter of persons!

Accused and Excused

Truth for Today – Isaiah 33:22

Nian was a 30 year old merchant selling grocery items at his small stall on a fishing island off the coast of China. One day, Nian's neighbor and family became violently ill after eating soup and squid. The two youngest children of Nian's neighbor, ages eight and ten, soon died.

The neighbor was a competing grocer and suspicion quickly turned towards Nian as having potentially poisoned the family. The Washington Post reports that 99.9% of suspects are found guilty in China, so there seemed to be little hope for Nian.

Reportedly, he was horribly tortured with beatings, slivers of bamboo were jammed between his ribs, and he was beaten with a hammer. He withstood the torture until they told him they would soon start the torture on his wife. Nian admitted guilt, was tried and sentenced to prison. Being on death row, it was mandatory that his hands and feet would be shackled the entire time. He had to rely upon other prisoners to dress him, brush his teeth and clean him. He had to lower his head into a bowl to eat.

Always professing innocence, his sister took up his cause. After the course of eight years of gathering evidence, doing forensic work, interviews, and seeking justice, Nian was declared innocent and finally freed in 2014. His case is being used to create an environment of reform within the justice system of China.

It is difficult to imagine the terror, horror and shame that goes along with being unjustly accused, wrongly incarcerated, and losing years of your life. But, unfortunately it happens in China, the U.S., as well as most countries.

Hearing of injustices can create a fear of legal and judicial systems. But as believers we need not fear the eternal judgment of God. He is described as having perfect love; He is fair and just; He is not guilty of being a respecter of persons; nothing can separate us from His love; and He takes no joy in the death of sinners or evil men. He is not biased, prejudicial, nor can He be bought or swayed. He is the perfect judge! I'm thankful to be in His balances and hands.

Advocacy

My son Rick and I were sitting beside a lake. We were watching birds and the occasional fish snatching a bug from the surface. It was a peaceful morning. That is, all was at peace except for our troubled minds.

I had received a phone call from the principal's office at Rick's school that morning, saying that Rick was being expelled for vandalism of property, and I needed to pick him up. The trip from the school to the lake was quiet except for Rick's explanation of the situation and his adamant statement of, "I'm not guilty."

As we sat by the lake, he told me the story. "I was walking down the hall at school and a boy told me that I'm in trouble. Then I was called out of my class to the principal's office. The principal told me that three boys had said that I had done a lot of damage to the contents of one of their lockers and they all had witnessed it."

Rick told me he had not done it but the principal had no option other than to expel him from school. Rick of course was frustrated, as was I.

Later that morning, my phone rang. It was the assistant principal at the school. He said, "I've known Rick for a long time and this doesn't sound like Rick. There's something else going on. Give me a few hours to work on this."

Two hours later he called back and said, "I've spent time individually with the three boys. One of them changed his story and then the other boys admitted their guilt."

The boys had concocted the story, did the damage themselves and decided to see if they could implicate an innocent person and get him expelled. Rick was the victim. Rick and I were very thankful for an advocate who went above and beyond to find truth and act upon it.

The story reminds me of my Jesus. He certainly went above and beyond to take care of us. We were guilty in our sin and still proclaimed innocent.

Which innocent victims are we advocating for today? Those without the Gospel and a Bible? Child soldiers in Africa? Trafficked and exploited children around the world? May God open our eyes to truth.

All it Takes is a Tap

Truth for Today – Psalm 40

The lioness watched from 100' away. Lying low in the African veldt grass, she was waiting for her chance. The lives of her cubs depended on her success. The gazelle was eating savannah grass with a watchful eye. Then there was a blur out of the grass and the race was on. The lioness was able to reach speeds of 50 mph but for only short bursts. The gazelle was able to reach a maximum speed of 30 mph but had superior agility and sustained speed.

The gazelle had agility and endurance. The lioness had speed. Who would win? The lioness knew she wouldn't be able to overtake him and grab his neck so she concentrated on one small vulnerable point. The right rear hoof of the gazelle.

The lioness kept up with the gazelle for twelve seconds. Then in a very short and quick burst of speed she reached a paw forward and lightly touched the right rear hoof. The speed and momentum of the gazelle caused him to stumble and fall. Then it was over.

1 Peter 5:8 gives us a great spiritual analogy. *"Be sober, be vigilant; because your adversary the devil, as a roaring lion, walketh about, seeking whom he may devour."*

There is certainly no question we are in a spiritual battle with things beyond our strength. Ephesians 6:12 tells us - *For we wrestle not against flesh and blood, but against principalities, against powers, against the rulers of the darkness of this world, against spiritual wickedness in high places.*

There is also no question each of us have our vulnerable spots. The gazelle has his hind hoof. Jesus was taken into the wilderness right after his baptism to be tempted of satan for 40 days.

Are we any different? Are we vulnerable? Do we have our weak points? The Bible gives us powerful encouragement.

- 1 John 4:4 - *Ye are of God, little children, and have overcome them: because greater is he that is in you, than he that is in the world.*
- 1 Corinthians 10:13 - *There hath no temptation taken you but such as is common to man: but God is faithful, who will not suffer you to be tempted above that ye are able; but will with the temptation also make a way to escape, that ye may be able to bear it.*

Along for the Ride

Truth for Today – 1 John 4

I had just left the house and was walking to my car parked along the curb. As I was unlocking my car door, I heard a rumbling noise. Looking up I saw my neighbor Rick coming towards me on his motorcycle. Then I noticed something that looked odd. He stopped and introduced me to his dog named Sam.

Turns out the dog enjoys cycle trips as much as my neighbor, so Rick got him some leathers, harness and goggles. This dog gets to go places, see things and all the while enjoy what every dog loves – wind in his face! It happens only because his master chooses to love and bless him.

It made me think about my Father in Heaven. Does my God care about me in ways that will bless me? What are the things I have that come from Him? A Biblical truth provides the answer in James 1:17 - *Every good gift and every perfect gift is from above, and cometh down from the Father of lights, with whom is no variableness, neither shadow of turning.*

As a father and grandfather, I know how much my children and grandchildren enjoy surprises and I also know how much joy it gives me to share new things with them. Our Father is no different. In Jeremiah 29:11 we read - *For I know the thoughts that I think toward you, saith the LORD, thoughts of peace, and not of evil, to give you an expected end.*

- Matthew 6:33 - *But seek first the kingdom of God and his righteousness, and all these things will be added to you.*
- Psalm 37:4 - *Delight yourself in the Lord, and he will give you the desires of your heart.*
- Ephesians 3:20 – *(God) is able to do exceeding abundantly above all that we ask or think, according to the power that worketh in us.*

An Accident Waiting to Happen

Truth for Today – Genesis 1

After a long day at work, he sat down to his evening dinner. As he ate a biscuit, he noticed that the biscuit was sweeter than normal. Asking his wife about it, she said she had not changed her recipe. Curious, he licked a finger and was amazed that the sweet taste was on his hand. As a chemist, he had been working all day with a coal tar concoction and had failed to wash his hands before dinner. That was the moment the product saccharin was born.

George as a chef in New York became agitated that an annoying customer was continually complaining about soggy French-fried potatoes. He decided to teach the customer a lesson. He cut a potato into thin, flat slabs, fried them to a crisp and dumped a large amount of salt on the slices. The customer loved them and the potato chip was created.

Frank was 11 years old in 1905 and loved soda pop. It was costly so he tried making it at home. He was satisfied with the product and happy to be saving money. One night he absentmindedly left his unfinished drink on his outdoor porch with a stirring stick in it. In the morning he was amazed that the overnight cold spell had frozen his drink with the stick solidly stuck in the product. That was the morning popsicles were invented.

James, a General Electric engineer was participating in research during WW II to find different rubber types for tires and boots. Mixing silicon oil with boric acid produced a rubber type that had no use. It was gooey and bouncy. Then a very non-military use evolved and today we have silly-putty.

Accidental inventions and creations are interesting to research. Inventions such as the micro-wave oven; post-it notes; penicillin; cornflakes; and the pacemaker were all accidental discoveries.

In God's universe, there were no accidental creations. Systematically and purposefully, He created a universe for us to discover. We are astounded when new things are found, unearthed or invented. But, He is the Creator and Author of it all. There are no mistakes or surprises with God.

An Air Chair

***Truth for Today** – Isaiah 45:6-7*

Leaving home at 6:00am to drive the 45 minutes to work in the early morning had its benefits, among them the light traffic. But one morning on a two lane highway, there was traffic and it was difficult to pass slower vehicles. I came up behind a pickup truck loaded with "stuff".

Wanting to pass, I got closer and closer when suddenly a large recliner chair came off the top of the pile of "stuff", sailed through the air, hit the pavement in front of me and bounced up and over my car. It was over almost before it started.

Stunned I thought of what it might have been like if that 75 lb. chair had hit my windshield at 50 mph.

Do you ever wonder how close to death we are in our lives? On highways, approaching one another, we pass four feet apart with each traveling at 55 mph.

We stand at a canyon and peer over a rocky edge at a valley 2000' below. We are caught in thunderstorms and wonder where the next lightning bolt will hit. Terrorism attacks, school shootings, plane crashes, tornadoes, tsunamis and hurricanes. Is there any order to the turmoil in our lives? Is there someone managing the chaos?

- Isaiah 45:6,7 – *That they may know from the rising of the sun, and from the west, that there is none beside me. I am the LORD, and there is none else. I form the light, and create darkness: I make peace, and create evil: I the LORD do all these things.*
- Job 12:10 - *In whose hand is the soul of every living thing, and the breath of all mankind.*
- Isaiah 14:24 - *The LORD of hosts hath sworn, saying, Surely as I have thought, so shall it come to pass; and as I have purposed, so shall it stand.*
- Jeremiah 32:27 - *Behold, I am the LORD, the God of all flesh: is there anything too hard for me?*
- Psalm 37:23 - *The steps of a good man are ordered by the LORD: and he delighteth in his way.*
- Matthew 6:34 - *Take therefore no thought for the morrow.*

An Anchor

I spent time recently with a man who grew up in the Azores, a group of nine islands in the north Atlantic. As a young man he followed the family occupation of whaling. Though most of the 20th century whaling world progressed into powerboats, explosive operated harpoons, bulldozers and warehouses, the men of the Azores continued the traditions of their whaling forefathers up to 1987.

Though a powerboat pulled their rowboats to the located whales, the men were on their own with their oars and the hand thrown harpoons.

My friend was young and strong and was given the responsibility of throwing the harpoon when they were close. When the harpoon struck, the whale would submerge, embedding the harpoon barbs and uncoiling the long and hefty rope that attached the whale to the boat. The boat became a reverse type of anchor for the whale. Eventually the whale would surface again and again until he tired and would be finished. Laws have changed in the whaling industry, but in the 1960's the methodology was what it was.

The concept of whaling reminds me of how satan is devious, deceptive, manipulative and destructive in his desire to bring down God's children. Whalers take advantage of a natural weakness of the whale in its need to surface to breathe. They also exploit the whales trusting and curious nature. Harpooning would be impossible if the whales were wary creatures. From a spiritual viewpoint, what can we learn? The Bible shares instruction and cautions to us.

- 1 Peter 5:8 - *Be sober, be vigilant; because your adversary the devil, as a roaring lion, walketh about, seeking whom he may devour.*
- 1 Corinthians; 1 and 2 Timothy - *Flee fornication; flee the love of money; flee from idolatry; flee youthful lusts.*
- James 4:7 - *Submit yourselves therefore to God. Resist the devil, and he will flee from you.*

An Empty Cup

Truth for Today – Philippians 4:8

I purchased airline tickets for Phoenix but the plane landed in Dallas, Texas. *It was okay, because it wasn't a non-stop flight to Arizona and we needed to change planes in Dallas.*

We arrived in Arizona and had no luggage at the baggage claim area. *It was okay because we didn't have any checked luggage.*

We picked up our rental car and headed to Flagstaff. Within 15 minutes, our car stopped. *It was okay because we had purposely pulled into a restaurant for lunch.*

I ordered a Western Omelet. The waitress brought a Turkey Club Sandwich and set it in front of me. *It was okay because it was Jeni's lunch and I slid it over to her. My omelet arrived 30 seconds later.*

Optimism or pessimism? Cup half full or cup half empty? Positive or negative? Hopeful or hopeless? Expectant or suspicious? Looking forward or looking backward? What is our perspective on life?

Our view on life has much to do with our personality; our environment as children and young adults; and our experiences, both good and bad in life. God does however, want us to look forward to better days. His promises are spread throughout His Word.

God promises us that He will take care of us every day in every way. God promises us that His love for us is unconditional. God promises us that His mercy and compassion never fail and are new every morning. He promises that His grace is sufficient. He promises a way of escape when we are tempted. He promises a Heaven that we cannot comprehend.

- 2 Timothy 1:7 - *God hath not given us the spirit of fear; but of power, and of love, and of a sound mind.*
- Romans 15:13 - *Now the God of hope fill you with all joy and peace in believing, that ye may abound in hope, through the power of the Holy Ghost.*
- Ephesians 5:8 - *For ye were sometimes darkness, but now are ye light in the Lord: walk as children of light.*
- James 1:2 - *My brethren, count it all joy when ye fall into divers temptations.*

And the Beat Goes On

Truth for Today – Job 1:21

In their lifetime, the average person in America will wear out 176 pairs of jeans; walk in 310 pairs of shoes; drink 86,000 cups of coffee; eat 8,000 slices of pizza; eat over 1,000 lbs. of chocolate; use over 39,000 gallons of gasoline; use 2.9 million gallons of water; and walk 115,000 miles which is the equivalent of walking around the world four times.

But those numbers are nothing compared to the 2,500,000,000 times the average heart beats in a lifetime. At 70 beats a minute, that is 100,000 times a day and 35 million times in a year.

James 4:13-15 says, *Go to now, ye that say, Today or tomorrow we will go into such a city, and continue there a year, and buy and sell, and get gain: Whereas ye know not what shall be on the morrow. For what is your life? It is even a vapor, that appeareth for a little time, and then vanisheth away. For that ye ought to say, If the Lord will, we shall live, and do this, or that.*

One thing is certain, there is a mortal clock ticking for each of us, and we have come to understand the meaning of Psalm 71:16 - *I will go in the strength of the Lord God.*

Given that mortal clock and the 2.5 billion heartbeats, God does ask us to redeem, salvage or be conscious of our time. How is our day going to be spent today?

- Deuteronomy 32:39 – *See now that I, even I, am he, and there is no god with me: I kill, and I make alive; I wound, and I heal: neither is there any that can deliver out of my hand.*
- 1 Samuel 2:6-7 – *The Lord killeth, and maketh alive: he bringeth down to the grave, and bringeth up. The Lord maketh poor, and maketh rich: he bringeth low, and lifteth up.*
- Job 1:21 - *Naked came I out of my mother's womb, and naked shall I return thither: the Lord gave, and the Lord hath taken away; blessed be the name of the Lord.*
- Job 33:4 - *The spirit of God hath made me, and the breath of the Almighty hath given me life.*

And the Beat Goes On Again

***Truth for Today** – John 20*

The New York Post recently published an article about a 72 year old man in India. Deepak was tending his cattle when his grandson saw him fall to the ground. Rushing to his grandfather's side, he felt no pulse or sign of life.

Others from the family gathered around and likewise concluded that Deepak had passed away. Some of the family began preparation for his cremation on the wooden funeral pyre. Wood was gathered and the wailing began. Then, one of the grandsons thought he saw the body move. Suddenly, Deepak's eyes opened and he sat up. I can't imagine the shock that shook the family as they witnessed all of that!

It has been attributed to a deep fainting spell. After everything calmed down, Deepak thought that possibly his family was a little too eager to light the match.

The news article reminded me of another resurrection many years ago in another location. Jesus had been accused, sentenced and brutally executed in front of many witnesses. He was placed in a tomb, secured, guarded and suddenly His body was gone. Then the greatest miracle and surprise of all time occurred when He reappeared. A miraculous resurrection that has never been repeated by anyone, anywhere at any time. Then God followed it all up with another miracle we identify as the ascension of Jesus. What a finale!

God is certainly able to do unexplainable, miraculous and unbelievable things at His will and pleasure. Will resurrections from the dead ever happen again?

1 Thessalonians 4:14-17 - *For if we believe that Jesus died and rose again, even so them also which sleep in Jesus will God bring with him. For this we say unto you by the word of the Lord, that we which are alive and remain unto the coming of the Lord shall not prevent them which are asleep. For the Lord himself shall descend from heaven with a shout, with the voice of the archangel, and with the trump of God: and the dead in Christ shall rise first: Then we which are alive and remain shall be caught up together with them in the clouds, to meet the Lord in the air: and so shall we ever be with the Lord.*

And the Battle Continues

Truth for Today – Revelation 20:10

Luo spent his life raising ducks. He had made a good living for his family and in 2007 decided to retire and build a retirement home for he and his wife. A year later the home was complete and they moved in.

However, the government decided to build a highway in his province and his home was exactly in the middle of where the road would be. The government offered him $35,000 in compensation, but since he had just spent $95,000, he refused.

There were laws preventing the government from automatically taking the land, so the negotiations began. But, Luo was adamant that the government needed to reimburse him. Finally, the government began construction and soon Luo's home was straddled by the highway. The government offered him $41,000 and again he refused. Now, completely surrounded by asphalt, Luo became the object of international attention. Who would win this battle of the wills?

So, what's today's devotion about? Stubbornness doesn't pay? The big bully always wins? The little guy gets the short end of the stick? Desperation brings success?

Finally the negotiations died and Luo accepted the latest offer of $41,000 and the house was demolished. Who won? I'm not sure. Some would think the government got their way, but at what price? I doubt there was a clear winner in this case.

The story reminds me of the ongoing war between God and satan. Beginning in Genesis the battle in the Garden of Eden gives us insight to the spiritual war. All through the Bible we see many more battles that tell us that the war is ongoing. We could be discouraged, but a glimpse at the end of God's Word tells us how the war will end.

Revelation 20:10 - *And the devil that deceived*
them was cast into the lake of fire and brimstone...

And the Winner is...

Truth for Today – Romans 8:37

In June of 2010, Zach Bertsch was diagnosed with Stage 4 colon cancer that had spread to his liver and lungs. Told there was no cure, at age 28 with a wife and two children under five, his future was without hope.

Three months later in September, he and his wife Jenny decided not to let the cancer win in terms of the impact it would have on their lives. Zach was given clear direction from God "to not waste his cancer."

They decided to seek funding to make a difference in the lives of orphaned and vulnerable children in Haiti. They started a fund-raising endeavor called the Cancer Redemption Project.

Their funding over the next three years provided the capital to accomplish many things in southwest Haiti:

1. Purchase 10 acres on which to build a campus for orphans.
2. Build six homes for orphaned and vulnerable children. Each home has a Haitian mother and father and 12 boys or girls.
3. Build a church in a region without a church.
4. Build a large school for their 72 children and other children.
5. Provide the operational funding to operate the campus and homes.

Zach lived long enough to see four of the homes filled with former orphans. His selfless vision and passion became an inspiration to many before he passed away on June 6, 2013.

Though living with pain and complications, he never wavered from his vision. He and Jenny's decision to "not waste his cancer" had been fulfilled and the fruit of their passion will be eternal.

Personally, I've never considered a cold, sore throat or hangnail as an opportunity to bring glory to God. Possibly I need to change my way of looking at life.

Anticipation

He had on a cowboy hat and boots and was walking up the steps of our Indiana church in 1957. I was eight years old and asked my Dad who the cowboy was. He said, "He's a movie star. His name is Herman Hackenjos and they call him Hack." Dad took me to him and Hack shook my hand! He was in 400+ westerns from 1931 through the mid-1960's.

He came to visit several times over those years and I was always in awe. I couldn't wait until he showed up the next time. I was filled with anticipation for his next visit!

Anticipation is defined in the dictionary as: *A feeling of excitement about something that is going to happen; the act of looking forward; visualization of a future event.*

What is my level of anticipation for Jesus' return? Is there an excitement?

- 1 Corinthians 15:52 says - *In a moment, in the twinkling of an eye, at the last trump...*

- Revelation 19:16 - *And he hath on his vesture and on his thigh a name written, KING OF KINGS, AND LORD OF LORDS.*

- Philippians 2:10 - *That at the name of Jesus every knee should bow...*

- John in Rev. 22:20 shared his anticipation – *Even so, come, Lord Jesus!*

Are we anxiously looking forward to His return with anticipation?

A-OK

Dad had a few health issues, among them was blood pressure that was difficult to regulate. He would pass out periodically due to the problems. So, when I received a phone call from my mom saying that dad had passed out and fell, I wasn't overly surprised. Then she said that he had fallen face first on concrete and his nose would not quit bleeding. I headed to the hospital to meet them.

Dad was with a surgeon who was assessing him when I arrived. I went in and was amazed at the blood on the floor and on my dad's gown. The doctor said there was no apparent tissue bleed in his nose so he would have to take him to the operating room to check out the source. I went back to my mom and explained what was happening.

Shortly, a nurse came by with my dad in a wheelchair. As dad saw us, he raised his right hand and with his thumb and index finger making a circle, he let us know that everything was going to be okay.

Later the M.D. shared that my dad's fall had bruised an artery in his sinus cavity that had burst and Dad would need to be transported to another hospital to surgically correct the problem.

Dad survived the surgery but had many post-surgical complications which eventually took his life two weeks later. He was sedated during that two week period so his A-OK sign was the last communication we had with him. What is there in a believer's heart and life that makes trauma, pain and the unknown A-OK? There was no fear on my dad's face. He was safe and secure. Why?

- Isaiah 43:2 - *When thou passest through the waters, I will be with thee; and through the rivers, they shall not overflow thee: when thou walkest through the fire, thou shalt not be burned; neither shall the flame kindle upon thee.*
- Isaiah 41:10 - *Fear thou not; for I am with thee: be not dismayed; for I am thy God: I will strengthen thee; yea, I will help thee; yea, I will uphold thee with the right hand of my righteousness.*
- Isaiah 46:4 - *And even to your old age I am he; and even to hoar hairs will I carry you: I have made, and I will bear; even I will carry, and will deliver you.*

Are We Heroes?

Truth for Today – Hebrews 11

The five year old girl had been playing in her front yard when a car slowed in front of her house. An older man offered her ice cream and lured her into his car. When found missing, the police were called and neighbors were alerted.

Two 15 year old boys decided to look for her. They got on their bikes and started searching the area. After 45 minutes they noticed a car with a suspicious driver slowly entering several cul-de-sacs. It was then they noticed the little girl in the front seat. They gave chase.

After 15 minutes of casually following the car, the driver panicked and let the girl out. The boys returned her to the waiting police and family. One cannot imagine the horror the little girl was saved from.

Heroes. What do heroes do? Wikipedia defines a hero as, *"Someone who in the face of danger or from a position of weakness, displays courage and/or the will for self-sacrifice for some greater good or all humanity."*

Heroes never set out to be heroes. In fact, heroes can't imagine themselves as doing anything heroic. But, at the right time, in the right place and for right reasons, average men and women do heroic things. I love heroes.

Hebrews 11 is a historical naming of Biblical heroes. Each of the men and women identified are heroes of faith. Men and women who were weak but trusted God, then became heroes.

As men and women of faith, we can make a difference through Christ who strengthens us. Is there an area of your community or world where you can walk beside the last, least, lost and lonely? Are you uniquely able to help find clean water for those in drought; food for those in famine; a family for a vulnerable child; healthcare for someone in need? We need not wait for a burning building or an abducted child.

Luke 6:38 - *Give, and it shall be given unto you; good measure, pressed down, and shaken together, and running over, shall men give into your bosom. For with the same measure that ye mete withal it shall be measured to you again.*

Are You Lost?

Truth for Today – Luke 2:41-52

He was having a great time on vacation with his family. Being seven and enjoying the remote Colorado wilderness scenery was something he'd never forget. Then his family was gone. Separated. Lost. Darkness was coming and he was alone. Wrapping his bare feet in his jacket to keep them warm, he waited for morning to begin walking. Twelve hours after becoming lost, a state trooper found him four miles from where he had been separated.

It was dark outside, snow covered the Michigan landscape and it was cold. The mom needed to run a quick errand and told her seven year old daughter to "Stay inside and I'll be back soon." When the mother returned home, the daughter was gone. Hours later, a bus driver saw the small girl walking along a street by herself and stopped to inquire. He soon knew she was lost, alone and waiting for rescue.

The workers at the school went on strike. The mother of the five year old girl dropped her off as usual, unaware the school was closed. The little girl couldn't find her way inside so began walking. Hours later an elderly couple found her and got her to a police station.

The boy was 12 years old when He became separated from His parents when they headed home from Jerusalem, after celebrating the Passover. Three days later they found Jesus in the temple teaching.

The illustrations of the seven year old boy and girl, as well as the five year old girl are different than that of Jesus. Jesus wasn't lost. He wasn't frantic or feeling deserted or even lonely. His parents were frantic, but He was calm. He was about His Father's business.

It gives me comfort to know that even when He was a boy, Jesus was fully boy and fully God. As my Savior, He was and is omnipotent, omnipresent and omniscient. Always able, always present and always having perfect knowledge and understanding.

Lord, help me to remain calm when I am in the midst of a storm. When I am lost, feeling deserted or lonely, help me to remember You know exactly where I am.

Around The World

Starvation, poverty, lack of clean water, famine, war, diseases and epidemics such as AIDS, cholera, Ebola and tuberculosis have created record numbers of orphans in nearly every country on earth. It is estimated by the United Nations there are approximately 153,000,000 orphans in the world.

It is nearly impossible to comprehend a number of that magnitude. Let's try to get it into a perspective we can understand.

- 153,000,000 orphans standing shoulder to shoulder will go around the 10,913 mile perimeter of the United States nearly four times.
- 153,000,000 orphans would fill the University of Michigan's stadium not once, but 1,330 times.
- 153,000,000 orphans would be the equivalent of the populations of:
  o New York City, Los Angeles and Chicago...
  o Plus the next 47 largest cities of the United States...
  o Plus the entire populations of Ireland, Nicaragua, Norway, Denmark, Costa Rica and Greece...
  o And finally the 62,000,000 population of France.

The Bible has a reoccurring theme on the subject of God's heart for the fatherless and orphan. He uses the concept of adoption and orphans to help us understand our own relationship with Him as He brings us into His family.

- Psalm 68:5 - *A father of the fatherless, and a judge of the widows, is God in his holy habitation.*
- Psalm 82:3 - *Defend the poor and fatherless: do justice to the afflicted and needy.*
- Romans 8:15 - *For ye have not received the spirit of bondage again to fear; but ye have received the Spirit of adoption, whereby we cry, Abba, Father.*
- Ephesians 1:5 - *Having predestinated us unto the adoption of children by Jesus Christ to himself, according to the good pleasure of his will.*

Attitude Changer

Truth for Today – John 8:1-11

It was December of 1964, I was fourteen years old, 85 lbs. and 5' tall. My mom asked me if I would do something for her. She and friends were going to visit ladies in a neighboring city and needed my help. She said they were going to give a Christmas party to women who really needed a Christmas.

It sounded interesting until she told me they needed me to be Santa Claus. I reluctantly agreed, hoping none of my friends would ever hear about it.

We loaded up a couple of cars with a Santa Claus outfit, gifts and food. I remember riding with my mom, her friends and a couple of aunts to Fort Wayne and finally arriving at the destination. I read a sign that said something about a mental health facility.

We entered a large room with fifteen or so ladies who were fifty to sixty-five years old. They were all significantly mentally challenged. Before that afternoon was over, all of those ladies had giggled and laughed their way into my heart. I was their hero.

That special day all those years ago had a lasting impact on me. It helped me develop my compassionate side and taught me valuable lessons. On that day, I learned about simple child-like faith.

As I walked into that room on that Saturday, I experienced a variety of emotions. I was fearful, ashamed to be there, concerned what others might think, but in spite of all that, I was looking forward to what would happen next.

How often do I permit my fears, anxieties, concerns, doubts and suspicions to get in the way of opportunities? How many life changing lessons have I forfeited due to worrying what others may think?

As I read about the life of Jesus, I see Him overcoming anxiety, fears and even more importantly the ever-present temptation of wondering what others might think of Him. The Pharisees and religious rulers of the day had expectations of Him. They tried to trip Him up at every turn. In every circumstance, He obediently did what God wanted Him to do. No more, no less. He didn't pass up opportunities to love others and to share truth with them.

Back-up Plans

It was a Friday afternoon in 1987 and things were busy. There were production schedules frantically struggling to be met and time was running out. Materials needed to be ordered and designs were waiting to be completed.

It was a typical day in the world of manufacturing. It was then the thought came to my mind that I needed to share the Gospel with one of our employees (I'll call him Joe). I knew he did not have a personal relationship with Jesus and I knew many were praying for him.

The thought continued to press on my mind, but busyness of the day got in the way. Friday afternoon passed and he left work.

On Monday morning I arrived at work and noticed three employees talking with a pained expression on their faces. I asked them what was wrong and they told me of the fatal traffic accident that Joe had suffered the night before.

I was shocked, guilt-ridden and ashamed. God had given me an opportunity and I had miserably failed. The typical phrases of: I wish I would have… I should have… if only I had… were on my mind.

My guilt took me to a friend nearby. I confessed my failure to him. He said, "Friday afternoon I felt the need to talk to Joe about his life and I shared the Gospel with him."

Of course I felt great relief, but I was still ashamed of my failure to carry out what God had asked me to do. But, on that day I learned a lesson that I will never forget.

God cares so deeply about our eternal welfare that He has back up plans. He is working with humans who make choices, have impure motives or faulty priorities. He knows us in deep and perfect ways. He entrusts us with great opportunities and important work, but knows us well enough to know that we are human. Human's forget, get too busy, have other priorities and can be selfish.

I'm thankful for the opportunities which God gives us. I'm thankful He trusts us with important things. I'm thankful that God uses His Holy Spirit to correct and teach me when I fail Him. I'm incredibly thankful He has back-up plans in place.

Bait

***Truth for Today** – Luke 4:12*

One of the best places in the world for catching huge largemouth bass is Lake Okeechobee in south central Florida. Its 730 square miles of water is unique in that the maximum depth is 13' with an average depth of 9'. The edges of the lake are filled with large bulrushes, reeds and marsh grass where the bass feed in 3' to 4' of water.

Generally fishing is done from boats in the middle of the aquatic vegetation. However, some fishermen enjoy putting on their wader boots and wading into the 3' shallows. I met one of those men.

He had been successful in catching largemouth bass. To keep the fish alive while continuing to fish, he tied a stringer around his waist and permitted his captive fish to trail behind him in the water.

Before continuing his story, let's look at another component of fishing in this large freshwater lake. It is estimated there are over 28,100 alligators in Lake Okeechobee with almost 1,800 of them being over 9'.

Now, with your imagination rolling, let's get back to the man's story. While wading and fishing with his captive fish following along, he felt a bump and a pull. Turning around he was amazed to know that his multiple bass had just been eaten by a large 'gator. Needless to say, he was out of the water in record time.

It reminds me of how easily we place ourselves in harm's way with our casualness to sin, yielding to temptation or not living our lives in the fear of God. Satan has a wide variety of seemingly benign things that subtly and nonchalantly bring us into bondage.

The progressive steps that lead to alcoholism, drug addiction, pornography and sexual addiction are evidence of his tactics. All bring us to a place of bondage while wondering how we got there. Clearly, being aware of our surroundings, satan's tactics, seeking early counsel, being in His Word and prayer assist us in living an overcoming life.

Luke 4:12 - *Thou shalt not tempt the Lord thy God.*

Battle Tactics

Truth for Today – Matthew 7:15

Sun Tzu was a Chinese general who lived from 544 – 496 BC. He was a great warfare tactician and knew how to do battle. We can learn from him about our personal and spiritual warfare battles with satan.

- Warfare is based on deception. When we are able to attack, we must seem unable; when using our forces, we must appear inactive; when we are near, we must make the enemy believe we are far away; when far, we must make him believe we are near.
- If your enemy is secure at all points, be prepared for him. If he is in superior strength, evade him. If your opponent is temperamental, seek to irritate him. Pretend to be weak, that he may grow arrogant. If he is taking his ease, give him no rest. If his forces are united, separate them. If leadership and soldiers are in accord, put division between them. Attack him where he is unprepared and appear where you are not expected.
- Hold out baits to entice the enemy. Feign disorder, and crush him.
- Pretend inferiority and encourage his arrogance.
- It is said that if you know your enemies and know yourself, you will not be imperiled in a hundred battles; if you do not know your enemies but do know yourself, you will win one and lose one; if you do not know your enemies nor yourself, you will be imperiled in every single battle.
- It is the rule in war, if ten times the enemy's strength, surround them; if five times, attack them; if double, be able to divide them; if equal, engage them; if fewer, be able to evade them; if weaker, be able to avoid them.
- He who knows when he can fight and when he cannot will be victorious.
- One defends when his strength is inadequate, he attacks when it is abundant.
- The general who advances without coveting fame and retreats without fearing disgrace, whose only thought is to protect his country and do good service for his sovereign, is the jewel of the kingdom.

Bearing the Cross

Truth for Today – Mark 8:34

In her 90's, life had become much more difficult and painful for her. With her eyesight failing, her hearing impaired, and weakness necessitating the use of a walker, she was discouraged. She said to me, *"I guess this is my cross to bear."*

It wasn't the first time I had heard the phrase, in fact, I had used it myself years ago when a situation had discouraged me. But what does the Bible say about "the cross"?

Of course, our knowledge of the cross begins with the wooden structure upon which Jesus was crucified. As was the custom, Jesus, on His way to Golgotha carried the cross towards His impending death. The torture, blood loss, scourging and beatings had taken their toll. Jesus stumbled and fell. He carried the cross as far as He could.

Jesus had a choice. In the Garden He had asked God to take away the responsibility of the cross and the torture of dying for the sins of the world. It was in the Garden where Jesus mentally picked up His cross and submitted to God's will. At that point, He willingly took His cross. It wasn't forced upon Him, it was His choice to receive it.

In Mark 8:34 we read the words of Jesus - *"Whosoever will come after me, let him deny himself, and take up his cross, and follow me."* As believers we are asked to "take up our cross."

However, the cross isn't discouragement, pain, old age, grief, loss or cancer. That's simply life. Our cross is a personal choice and a willingness to do God's will, obediently follow Him, while learning how to deny ourselves. Our cross isn't something that intrudes and forces its way into our lives, but rather it is something we willingly take on for God's greater Kingdom purposes.

Lord, help me to willingly submit to the work you have for me.

Being Born (again)

- A new born hippopotamus weighs from 60 – 100 pounds.
- A baby elephant weighs 250 pounds.
- A beluga baby whale is 180 pounds.
- A baby blue whale weighs in at 6000 pounds at birth.
- About the size of a chicken, the Kiwi bird lays an egg half her own weight.

According to Guinness, the largest human baby ever born was 23 pounds 12 ounces, was 34 inches long with six inch feet. The concept of very large babies causes us to think about a conversation that occurred 2,000 years ago.

John 3:1-4 – *There was a man of the Pharisees, named Nicodemus, a ruler of the Jews: The same came to Jesus by night, and said unto him, Rabbi, we know that thou art a teacher come from God: for no man can do these miracles that thou doest, except God be with him. Jesus answered and said unto him, Verily, verily, I say unto thee, except a man be born again, he cannot see the kingdom of God. Nicodemus saith unto him, how can a man be born when he is old? Can he enter the second time into his mother's womb, and be born?*

A 23 pound baby in a birth canal seems impossible. No less plausible, Nicodemus was having a difficult time grasping the concept of being born again. But, when Jesus stated, *"except a man be born again, he cannot see the kingdom of God"*, it seems imperative that we understand the concept.

- 2 Corinthians 5:17 - *Therefore if any man be in Christ, he is a new creature: old things are passed away; behold, all things are become new.*
- Matthew 18:3 - *And said, Verily I say unto you, Except ye be converted, and become as little children, ye shall not enter into the kingdom of heaven.*
- Acts 3:19 - *Repent ye therefore, and be converted, that your sins may be blotted out, when the times of refreshing shall come from the presence of the Lord.*

Being Good isn't Good Enough

Truth for Today – Ephesians 2:8-9

The Colorado school day in the winter of 1931 began decently enough for the children. But while in school, the temperature dropped and the snow began. The children were dismissed early and piled into school buses for their ride home.

Twenty of them, ages seven to fourteen got on one bus and began their trip home. Soon, the driver lost his way in the white-out and landed in the ditch. That began a 33 hour nightmare for the twenty children.

One of the children, a twelve year old boy, became a hero that day. Starting a fire for the other children and sharing his clothing to keep them warm, he sacrificially showed his leadership. Sadly, five of his classmates lost their lives during the ordeal, but Bryan was credited with saving the lives of the other fourteen.

He was invited to the White House to meet President Herbert Hoover. He told the news reporters he hoped to go to West Point.

But life was hard for Bryan. Just seven years after being declared a hero, he made a choice, broke a law and went to jail. He admitted he had made a bad decision and had done wrong. He went on to share the thought that just because he had been a hero, didn't excuse him from being punished.

Sometimes we may think "being good is good enough". In our culture and society, doing "good" may bring us accolades, money, prestige and fame. But in God's eyes, being good isn't good enough.

In Ephesians 2:8-9 we read - *For by grace are ye saved through faith; and that not of yourselves: it is the gift of God: Not of works, lest any man should boast.*

If we could be "good enough", there would have been no need for the Son of God to sacrifice Himself for mankind. How much money needs to be given by us to help the poor, provide food for the hungry, and perform rescues of the orphans to right the wrongs of a man? Ephesians answers the question. No amount of good is enough. It is only by faith in the death, burial and resurrection of Jesus, and the grace of God Himself that provides salvation.

Believing Without Seeing

Truth for Today – Proverbs 28:26

During WWII, many soldiers parachuted from airplanes having no idea where they would land. Would they land behind enemy lines, in water or in a tree?

In 2014, David and his uncle decided to burglarize a supermarket in England. Someone called police and the two burglars got onto the roof to escape. With police closing in, David decided to jump from the roof of the supermarket onto the roof of a car below. The car turned out to be a police car and David broke a leg in four places. He was taken into custody and will never walk normally again.

The eland antelope in east and southern Africa can run about 43 miles per hour. Males weighing approximately 2000 pounds can jump 8' high from a standing start. It's been said however, that the eland will not jump over an obstacle unless they clearly see where they will land. Thus, they are easily kept captive inside short fences they cannot see over or through.

Clearly, to minimize risk, we should look twice before we leap, as the old saying goes. But, as Christians we are taught to walk by faith and not by sight. Where does common sense, logic and due diligence end, and where does faith begin?

- Proverbs 9:10 - *The fear of the Lord is the beginning of wisdom: and the knowledge of the holy is understanding.*
- Proverbs 2:6 - *For the Lord giveth wisdom: out of his mouth cometh knowledge and understanding.*
- Proverbs 3:21 - *My son, let not them depart from thine eyes: keep sound wisdom and discretion.*
- Proverbs 28:26 - *He that trusteth in his own heart is a fool: but whoso walketh wisely, he shall be delivered.*
- 2 Corinthians 5:7 - *For we walk by faith, not by sight.*
- Hebrews 11:6 - *But without faith it is impossible to please Him: for he that cometh to God must believe that He is, and that He is a rewarder of them that diligently seek Him.*

Beneath our Feet

Truth for Today – Revelation 21

The trails, roads and highways of this world are saturated with the blood, sweat and tears of countless generations. The Roman road system stretched from Rome to the ends of the Roman Empire. Those roads were covered with hewn volcanic stones and rocks.

Trails in New Guinea, Haiti, Cambodia, Kenya, Australia and a hundred other places have countless trails used for centuries. They are covered with dirt, sand, mud and gravel.

Interstate highway systems and roads are worldwide and covered in asphalt and concrete. The dirt, stones, sand, rocks, asphalt and concrete beneath our feet pave our paths.

I've often wondered about the verse in Revelation 4:10 - *The four and twenty elders fall down before him that sat on the throne, and worship him that liveth for ever and ever, and cast their (golden, vs.4) crowns before the throne.*

What makes gold valuable? Surely it is its beauty and rich color, but more importantly is its rarity. Why is it that in Heaven, golden crowns are cast down? The beauty is certainly not diminished, but gold is no longer a rarity.

Revelation 21:21 - *...and the street of the city was pure gold, as it were transparent glass.* There are miles and miles of beautifully rich golden streets in Heaven. The gold is so abundant, that a gold crown is as nothing! Trails and roads on earth have nothing over the streets of Heaven.

Better Together

Truth for Today – Ecclesiastes 4:9-12

It has been said that there are only three species of God's creation that fight battles in formation.

Of course there are other species such as lions that work together to capture food. In working together, one may drive an antelope, buffalo or zebra toward other waiting lions. Other species may attack in swarms, like bees or hornets, but they are not in formation, but rather independent fighters.

Ants, crows and humans are reportedly the only species that specifically form together to strategically engage the enemy in formation. The Bible lays out clear principles to us as humans on why we should band together.

- Hebrews 10:24-25 - *And let us consider one another to provoke unto love and to good works: Not forsaking the assembling of ourselves together, as the manner of some is; but exhorting one another: and so much the more, as ye see the day approaching.*
- Colossians 3:16 - *Let the word of Christ dwell in you richly in all wisdom; teaching and admonishing one another in psalms and hymns and spiritual songs, singing with grace in your hearts to the Lord.*
- Matthew 18:20 - *For where two or three are gathered together in my name, there am I in the midst of them.*
- Matthew 12:30 - *He that is not with me is against me; and he that gathereth not with me scattereth abroad.*
- Ecclesiastes 4:9-12 - *Two are better than one; because they have a good reward for their labor. For if they fall, the one will lift up his fellow: but woe to him that is alone when he falleth; for he hath not another to help him up. Again, if two lie together, then they have heat: but how can one be warm alone? And if one prevail against him, two shall withstand him; and a threefold cord is not quickly broken.*

Alone we can do so little, together we can do so much.
Helen Keller

Blessed Guilt and Shame

Truth for Today – Deuteronomy 28

We live in a world that's full of poverty, chaos, oppression, persecution, wickedness, starvation, exploitation, trafficking, slavery and corruption. There are those of us who "have", while living in a world where the vast majority are "have-nots".

We hear the statistics and the inevitable guilt comes. Then the shame arrives. How can we live with ourselves? We may tend to shut our eyes or close our ears to reality and truth. Or, we may find ways to fill our lives with "stuff" so we don't have time to learn of the plight of the majority.

What does God expect of us? What does He want? My heart gets heavy as I think of the wretched environments the rest of the world lives in. My prayers seem self-serving. I pray for the have-not's and then with guilt thank Him for blessing me? Lord, provide for their needs... and thank you for blessing me?

Who am I that He would bless me? What am I to do with the blessings that I didn't ask for, but that He freely gives? Then of course I think of His Word, as it has the answers.

- 2 Corinthians 9:10 - *Now he that ministereth seed to the sower both minister bread for your food, and multiply your seed sown, and increase the fruits of your righteousness.*
- Ecclesiastes 5:19 - *Every man also to whom God hath given riches and wealth, and hath given him power to eat thereof, and to take his portion, and to rejoice in his labour; this is the gift of God.*
- Nahum 2:9 - *Take ye the spoil of silver, take the spoil of gold: for there is none end of the store...*

God as a sovereign and omnipotent Creator provides the blessings to those whom He chooses. It does come with strings attached however, as we read Luke 12:48 - *For unto whomsoever much is given, of him shall be much required.*

The question is not "Why am I so blessed?" but rather "How can I use these gifts for His honor, glory, praise and pleasure?"

That is the question.

Blind Love

I was talking to a friend of mine and asked him how his family was doing. He suddenly became animated and reached in his pocket to retrieve his smart phone. He had a huge grin on his face as he punched a few buttons and brought up a photo of his two day old grand-daughter. At that moment, his grand-daughter was 5040 miles away in Germany. But, the love that this grandfather had for this baby was intense and easy to see. This child had done nothing as yet, was a typical, wrinkled, pink-faced baby, had already created lots of pain to her mother, but was still incredibly loved.

How can we explain love? It is an emotion that defies explanation. Recently I read the accounts of three couples who had been married for over 65 years. In all three cases, one spouse had died and within 24 hours the other passed away as well. Can a person die of a broken heart? It seems that love has ties that are impossible to understand.

I take great comfort in knowing that Jesus didn't come to earth as a baby, to suffer torture, desertion, humiliation, pain or die on the cross as my Savior, simply to earn His Father's love. He already had that incredible love.

I take great comfort in accepting that principle as a simple truth. The Bible lays out the concept:

- John 3:16 - *For God so loved the world, that he gave his only begotten Son, that whosoever believeth in him should not perish, but have everlasting life.*
- Romans 5:8 – *God commendeth his love toward us, in that, while we were yet sinners, Christ (came and) died for us!*
- 1 John 4:8 - *...God is love.*
- Romans 8:38-39 – *For I am persuaded, that neither death, nor life, nor angels, nor principalities, nor powers, nor things present, nor things to come, nor height, nor depth, nor any other creature, shall be able to separate us from the love of God, which is in Christ Jesus our Lord.*

To be loved with unconditional love is a beautiful thing!

Blinded by Appetites

Truth for Today – Luke 15:3-7

The black Labrador dog had been someone's pet. His ability to shake hands and his gentle spirit indicated a good home sometime in his past.

But now his body was gradually becoming emaciated. He was dying. He was resisting contact with humans and would-be rescuers. Three weeks ago he had pushed his head into a gallon plastic container. Possibly there were remnants of food, or maybe it was mere curiosity that caused him to insert his head. In any case, his large ears didn't permit him to extricate himself from his prison.

He couldn't eat nor could he see. For three weeks he eluded rescuers. Finally, he fell asleep in a thicket and two dog-lovers captured him. The jar was removed and he was given care and nutrition. Now nicknamed "Jughead", he is awaiting a new home.

As it went with Jughead, we as humans sometimes insert ourselves into situations that ultimately do immense damage and even hasten death. Drugs, alcohol, gluttony, sexual addictions, as well as many other activities deprive us of clear vision and even of life itself.

It may be curiosity that creates the temptation to "try" something. Possibly we have appetites that are out of control that fuel addictions. In most cases, people regret that first puff, huff, taste, touch or look that took them to a dark, lonely and dangerous place.

Jughead ultimately was thankful for his rescuers, though he initially resisted them. I thank God today for individuals and organizations zealous in rescuing men, women and children caught in the mire and chains of addiction.

As individuals we are usually on the sidelines watching lives falling deeper and deeper into the addictive pits of lifestyles going awry. Jesus didn't give up in rescuing us from our past. He was committed to getting it done, whatever the cost. We can learn from his passion and commitment. Is there someone today who we can reach out to?

Lord, open my eyes, ears and heart to those waiting to be noticed.

Born to Sail

Truth for Today – Matthew 6:27-29

It began with boiling water in the middle of the south Pacific. The water bubbled and days later began hissing. Then smoke and sulfur fumes began to escape the water. Slowly the volcanic lava solidified and began creating a mass under the water's surface.

The mass grew and grew until it emerged from the water and created an island. The volcanic eruption began to subside until it was safe for men to explore.

Imagine their surprise to find spiders. How did they get there when the nearest land was hundreds of miles away?

It has now been verified that spiders can use their silky webs to travel those hundreds of miles. Spinning their silk, the substance creates a ballooning effect which permits the spiders to catch a breeze and sail over the sea. If they perchance land on the water, the tips of their feet can lightly keep the spider out of the water.

During testing, spiders didn't even need to use their silky webs to sail. They merely used their eight legs to elevate their wide abdomens high in the air. The breeze would catch their abdomen like a sail and carry them aloft.

I'm always amazed at the intricacies of God's creation. His imagination is awesome and never-ending. Scientists are still learning about God's diversity and ability to care for His creation.

Learning about how God creates such inspirational creatures and then provides for them in ingenious ways increases my faith. Is there anything in my life that God is unable to take care of? I think not.

Matthew 6:28-29 - *And why take ye thought for raiment? Consider the lilies of the field, how they grow; they toil not, neither do they spin: And yet I say unto you, That even Solomon in all his glory was not arrayed like one of these.*

Bread Fixer

Truth for Today - Genesis 2:8-15

Eating dinner one evening, one of my very young grand-daughters brought me a slice of bread, butter and grape jelly. She said, "Grandpa, can you fix my bread?"

I said, "Of course, but why do you want me to do it?" Her innocent and manipulative answer was simple, "Because I know how much you like butter and jelly and I know you'll fix mine like yours."

I am known as one who loves extras when it comes to topping off bread, muffins, ice cream, ribs or whatever. My motto is simple - If a lot is good, then more is better.

I think that Ephesians 3:20 says it very well – *(God) is able to do exceeding abundantly above all that we ask or think...*

When we have a need, do we trust God to take care of it with excellence? He promises that He is able to do that. We don't have to look too far in His creation to know that to be true. Under the microscope, through a telescope or merely with our human vision, we see the imagination of our God.

He didn't settle for mediocrity when He created the universe and everything in it. It could have been a black and white world, but He chose color. Not just one color but an infinite amount of colors.

He could have chosen to make one fish, but He never tired of creating 32,000 species.

He could have settled for flat land, but instead, He created hills, valleys, mountains, gullies, ridges, crests, canyons and mesas.

He is an infinite and eternal God who has nothing but time, unlimited energy, unconditional love and an insatiable desire to do exceeding abundantly above all we ask or think. Let Him surprise you with His imagination!

Building a Tower

Truth for Today – Psalm 77:14

Dan is a farmer from Indiana and a minister. He had the opportunity to go on a mission trip to build small homes in Mexico. The team arrived at the work site. They had their tools and material to do the construction, however, the Spanish interpreter was missing.

The team was anxious to get started but without the interpreter it was impossible to determine the particulars of the new home. Dan approached the soon to be owner of the home. The man began speaking in Spanish to Dan about the details. Dan listened.

Then, Dan turned around and gave the details and instructions to the team. One of the men said, "Dan, I didn't know you could speak Spanish." Dan replied, "I can't." The man then said, "But the home owner was speaking in Spanish." Dan said, "I didn't know, I'm just repeating what I heard him say."

What's the explanation? It can only be explained as a God thing. God takes care of His business.

Genesis 11 tells us about the Tower of Babel. It was a story about ungodly men with impure motives desiring something that didn't belong to them. God confounded their efforts by taking away their common language and replacing it with many languages. The resulting confusion stopped the construction of the tower.

Place the Mexico story next to the Tower of Babel story. In Mexico, you have Godly men with pure motives desiring something that God wanted. The result? God blessed their efforts with a common language. The outcome was a home for a family and a story to share with everyone. Again, God takes care of His business.

- Psalm 77:14 - *Thou art the God that doest wonders (miracles): thou hast declared thy strength among the people.*
- Mark 16:17 - *And these signs shall follow them that believe; In my name shall they cast out devils; they shall speak with new tongues.*
- Matthew 17:20 - *And Jesus said unto them, Because of your unbelief: for verily I say unto you, If ye have faith as a grain of mustard seed, ye shall say unto this mountain, Remove hence to yonder place; and it shall remove; and nothing shall be impossible unto you.*

Buried Alive

Truth for Today – John 3:16

It was just another day at the mine. Every day, men descended 2,300 feet underground via spiral service ramps to mine the gold and copper ore. They received 20% more in wages than other Chilean miners due to the safety record and issues at their mine in northwest Chile.

Suddenly they heard the dreaded sound of falling rocks and their fears began to grow. Thirty-three men were now trapped far below the earth's surface. They were able to get into a small shelter that had two to three days' worth of food supplies.

They immediately began rationing supplies and waited. Their careful regulation of three days of supplies stretched it to 14 days and then ran out. Above, families were desperately waiting for a rescue. The Chilean government actively became involved. Several bored test holes were drilled and finally on day 17, a drill broke into their shaft. The trapped miners attached a small note saying they were doing okay.

Over the course of the next weeks, supplies made their way to the men as more shafts were bored and rescue attempts proceeded. Finally after 70 days trapped underground, all 33 men were saved, one at a time, by being winched upward in a rescue capsule. The trip up and out took almost 18 minutes.

Can we imagine the 33 miners maintaining their composure and sanity by being buried alive? What about their families waiting anxiously for them?

After a $20 million rescue, all men were safe and sound. That equates to $606,060.61 per man. Is that the value of a man?

The Lord said in Matthew 16:26 - *For what is a man profited, if he shall gain the whole world, and lose his own soul?* Essentially we are told that the value of the world is less than a man's soul. The wealth of all the people in the world is estimated at $241 trillion. That's a lot of wealth! Is one soul worth all of that? Jesus says it is.

John 3:16 reminds us, *For God so loved the world, that he gave his only begotten Son, that whosoever believeth in him should not perish, but have everlasting life.*

But it was so Small

Truth for Today – Romans 12

Several states in the Midwest and Northeast experienced a massive snowstorm in January of 1978. The effect was several days of snow resulting in 36" of depth, which 50 mph gusting winds whipped into twenty foot drifts in some places.

The consequences were massive. There were many days without electricity, and 0° temperatures compounded the difficulties. The states affected, soon ground to a halt, as businesses and schools closed for days upon days.

Having a 10,000 layer chicken operation at the time, I saw additional consequences. We lost electricity on day one and were without grid generated electricity for many days. Though we had a generator, we needed to get the trailer mounted unit through six foot snow drifts to hook it up. Finally after 24 hours without electricity we got it operational.

The chickens continued to lay eggs and needed more feed. The roads were blocked and we needed to hire heavy equipment several times to clear the roads for the egg and feed trucks. Then gradually things began to change. The snow ended and began to melt. It was then I found a six foot wide by two foot tall x 200' long snow drift in the attic of our chicken house. The whipping wind had pushed the snow through small louvers under the eaves of the chicken house. There was nothing to do but let the drift melt which of course created ongoing huge problems for me and the chickens below.

It all started with one very small and incredibly fragile snowflake. It was tiny, minute, petite and insignificant. By itself it could accomplish nothing. But together, many insignificant fragile snowflakes seemingly stopped the world, or so it seemed to me.

Romans 12 and 1 Corinthians 12 describe the concept of our body being made up of many members. By themselves, those members of our body can be weak, but together they can do mighty and marvelous things. God's family is that way. Together great things can be done when unity for God's purpose is the goal.

Imagine what can be done when all God's people say Amen.

Camels have Gnats

Truth for Today – Matthew 23

It had been a very busy week in India and I was ready for down time. There's no better relaxing time for me when traveling, than looking for unusual items to purchase and re-sell in the U.S. So, my friends and I crossed the line from the modern city of New Delhi to Old Delhi. In the tight streets of traditional India we went into a variety of dark shops, until finally I found what I was looking for.

I purchased several expensive, old daggers and was very pleased. It was our last day prior to heading home, so my co-traveler room-mate and I returned to the hotel to pack. Finally with packing completed, he asked, "Did you get those daggers packed so that you're comfortable that they'll not get damaged?"

I said, "I had them packed, but I was still concerned that they would get damaged so I wrapped them in bubble-wrap and put them in my briefcase for carry-on." He looked incredulously at me and said, "You can't carry knives on the plane!"

Have you ever strained at a gnat and swallowed a camel? I had taken great care to get my nail-clipper out of my carry-on bag and packed it carefully in my checked-on luggage. But I had absent-mindedly forgot the fact that I would be taking multiple daggers on the plane with me!

With profuse thanksgiving to my room-mate I realized that he had just saved me from being arrested; having my expensive daggers confiscated; and spending quality time in an Old Delhi prison with new friends.

The experience made me remember some of Jesus' wise counsel.

Matthew 23:23-25 - *Woe unto you, scribes and Pharisees, hypocrites! for ye pay tithe of mint and anise and cummin, and have omitted the weightier matters of the law, judgment, mercy, and faith: these ought ye to have done, and not to leave the other undone. Ye blind guides, which strain at a gnat, and swallow a camel. Woe unto you, scribes and Pharisees, hypocrites! for ye make clean the outside of the cup and of the platter, but within they are full of extortion and excess.*

Cannibalism

Truth for Today – Galatians 5:15-16

Civil War Facts

- 3 million men fought in the U.S. Civil War from 1861 – 1865.
- 620,000 men died, equaling 2% of the U.S. population
- 23,000 men died at the battle of Shiloh which was more than all Americans killed in wars prior to the Civil War.
- At the battle of Antietam, 23,000 men were killed, missing or wounded making it the bloodiest day of the Civil War.
- At Cold Harbor, Virginia, 7,000 Americans fell in twenty minutes.
- Disease during the Civil War killed twice as many men as combat wounds.
- The 2nd day of fighting at Gettysburg involved 100,000 men of which 20,000 were killed, wounded or missing.

Though suspected and rumored, there are no reputable facts suggesting that cannibalism occurred during the Civil War era. However... the Apostle Paul symbolically suggested that cannibalism may be a temptation among people. In Galatians 5:15-16, he said - *For all the law is fulfilled in one word, even in this; Thou shalt love thy neighbor as thyself. But if ye bite and devour one another, take heed that ye be not consumed one of another.*

The strife, hatred and conflict experienced in the U.S. Civil War nearly destroyed the very country the armies were fighting for. Brothers against brothers, families against families and neighbors against neighbors was common. Certainly the war destroyed many lives as well as families. The grief, heartache and hatred continued for generations. Even after the war ended, the conflict remained and small groups continued the war with murder, mayhem and ransacking.

Though no one ate the flesh of another, destroying the spirit and soul of another could be considered horrendously worse. Paul's concern as He voiced God's heart is that those things have happened and could continue to happen in God's family and church.

One can only imagine what our country could have been, without the Civil War. Likewise, one wonders what could happen if God's family and church got along like He designed it to.

Can't Be!

As I approached a country intersection, I noticed the traffic was controlled by an overhead four-way blinking stop-light. I waited for the small vehicle coming from the right to take its turn to enter the intersection.

I looked at the driver and saw that it was a large dog. Incredulous, I watched as the vehicle slowly made the corner. The dog looked at me as he passed within six feet of my car. It was a surreal moment until my brain caught up with what my eyes were seeing. Sitting in the passenger seat was a man with a steering wheel. It was a U.S. Postal Service vehicle equipped for mail box deliveries.

Not everything is always just as it appears. Often I find myself judging a situation, or possibly something I see or hear, prematurely. It is usually difficult to wait for facts. Many times we rush to judgment or jump to conclusions. Just as with my driving dog illustration, as soon as I saw the passenger with a steering wheel, I saw the situation much more clearly.

Fortunately the Bible provides teachings and principles to help us navigate situations in our lives.

- 1 Corinthians 4:5 - *Therefore judge nothing before the time.*
- Proverbs 25:8 - *Go not forth hastily to strive, lest thou know not what to do in the end thereof, when thy neighbour hath put thee to shame.*
- James 1:19 - *Let every man be swift to hear, slow to speak, slow to wrath...*
- Proverbs 21:23 - *Whoso keepeth his mouth and his tongue keepeth his soul from troubles.*
- Proverbs 11:12 - *He that is void of wisdom despiseth his neighbour: but a man of understanding holdeth his peace.*

Can't Fill Those Boots

Truth for Today – Psalm 91

A family swimming party at Pine Lake meant a picnic and three hours of swimming with uncles, aunts, and cousins. It was a great summer day. I was twelve years old and my uncle asked me if I would be willing to go to his home after swimming and mow his yard. I told him that I didn't have any shoes with me, so he assured me that he had something I could wear.

When we arrived at his home he gave me a pair of his rubber gum boots. My feet swam in them but they at least covered my feet.

Fifty years ago, the riding mower was small and had three wheels. After about fifteen minutes of mowing I was trimming around a stump in his yard and the mower started to tip. I quickly put my right foot out to stop the mower from tipping over. I inadvertently stuck my foot under the mower deck. I heard and felt a thump.

Frantically I stopped the mower. I looked at the boot and the front two inches of the boot were gone. I pulled off the boot and was ecstatic to see five intact toes. There was no blood or mangled flesh.

Periodically I am reminded of that memorable day. My life would have changed dramatically had I lost those five toes. I wonder how many times I am saved from harm, injury and hurt. We have a Guardian…

- 2 Thessalonians 3:3 - *But the Lord is faithful, who shall stablish you, and keep you from evil.*
- 2 Samuel 22:3-4 - *The God of my rock; in him will I trust: he is my shield, and the horn of my salvation, my high tower, and my refuge, my saviour; thou savest me from violence. I will call on the LORD, who is worthy to be praised: so shall I be saved from mine enemies.*
- Isaiah 41:10 - *Fear thou not; for I am with thee: be not dismayed; for I am thy God: I will strengthen thee; yea, I will help thee; yea, I will uphold thee with the right hand of my righteousness.*
- Psalm 138:7 - *Though I walk in the midst of trouble, thou wilt revive me: thou shalt stretch forth thine hand against the wrath of mine enemies, and thy right hand shall save me.*

Can't Happen

***Truth for Today* –** James 4:15

Walking around a pond I noticed a tiny snake swimming along the edge. It was about the length and size of a pencil but as I reached for it, he tried to strike at me. I caught him and put him in a jar to show the kids when they got home from school. A few punched holes in the jar lid gave him air.

He was fun to watch but Jeni wasn't overly pleased with another critter in the house. In spite of Jeni's pleas to "Get rid of it now," I told her that I'd let it go in the morning. I said, "Trust me, he can't possibly get out of those small holes!"

In the morning, the jar was empty and I knew trouble was brewing. I finally found him curled around the stainless kitchen sink filter. Snakes can get through incredibly tiny holes. Lesson learned.

Rick loved the outdoors and all that lived in it. How an eight year old boy was ever able to catch a chipmunk, I'll never know. But, he brought his new pet into the house. Our response was immediate, "No way, he'll get loose." Of course, Rick had a quick answer of, "I'll keep him caged. Trust me, he won't get out."

Next morning, the chipmunk was gone. Have you ever tried to catch a chipmunk in the house? He lived in our basements suspended ceiling until Rick finally caught him.

I was confident that the snake could not escape. Rick was confident that his chipmunk would never get out of its cage. How often do we trust our intuitions, instincts, abilities and skills, only to be proven wrong? The Bible helps us develop a trust in God and His abilities and strengths, rather than in ourselves.

- Matthew 5:37 - *But let your communication be, Yea, yea; nay, nay.*
- Proverbs 3:5 - *Trust in the LORD with all thine heart; and lean not unto thine own understanding.*
- James 4:15 - *For that ye ought to say, If the Lord will, we shall live, and do this, or that.*
- Hebrews 6:3 - *And this will we do, if God permit.*

Casting Stones

Truth for Today – Galatians 6

The three of us were 12 and 13 years old. Our parents had given us permission to spend the day at a local state park. The park was unique in that there were many animal pens with elk, buffalo and deer, as well as a confinement area with cages of raccoons, opossums, a bear, mountain lion and fox.

Finally tiring of looking at animals, we took a hike on the paved road which took us past the fire tower that was open to the public. Looking up, one of us had the idea of filling our pockets with stones and dropping them from the tower. Loaded with ammunition, we ran up the 105 steps to the top of the 100' tower. Dropping the walnut sized stones was interesting, but again we were always looking for the "more interesting" things to do.

So I waited until a car drove slowly past the tower on the adjacent paved road and dropped my stone. It hit the car with a solid clunk. The car stopped. It was then we realized our error in that there was no escape route from our perch on the tower. The car slowly moved on and we escaped to a trail. Thirty minutes later a park ranger stopped us and got our confession.

He said that the stone had left a large dent in the roof of the car. He went on to say that the occupants were not going to press charges, but wanted us to know that someone could have been killed with our careless actions.

Numbers 32:23 state – *"be sure your sin(s) will find you out."* Many times our careless actions bring unintended consequences. But always there are reactions to actions, consequences to sin and certainly the law of sowing and reaping.

Chatty Critters

Truth for Today – Job 12:7-10

He was hiding behind a small box on the floor. He was rubbing the top of one wing on the underside of the other wing. His wings were up and open which created an acoustical megaphone for the incessant chirping I was hearing. How do you find a cricket?

The Bible says in Psalm 139:*14 - I am fearfully and wonderfully made.* Our human body is extremely intricate. Our ability to hear sound is a phenomenal thing. In His creation, God shows us just how intricately and wonderfully we are made.

Sound waves arrive at our outer ear. As the eardrum transmits those sound waves into the middle ear via the hammer, anvil and stirrup bones, it reaches the cochlea. The cochlea in the inner ear has very tiny hair cells which bend and move creating nerve signals that are carried to the brain via the cochlear nerve.

An amazing thing occurs in this process we call hearing. Now back to the cricket. How do we locate them? Our head looks in a particular direction from where the general sound is coming from. The sound reaches both ears, but not at the same time. We rotate our head unknowingly until the sound reaches both ears at the same moment. We lock onto the position. Perfect radar and it is not man-made.

Science and physics tells us that we can pinpoint a sound within a 2° area via our intricate ears. That means we are able to locate a sound from ten feet away within a three inch location.

This small illustration is only one of thousands that are present in our human body. Can we possibly imagine the mechanisms, chemical reactions, things happening at the speed of light within the eye, within the ear at the speed of sound, the prismatic miracles happening in the eye and the fluid motions of joints and muscles?

As we slowly begin to uncover the intricacies of ourselves, we begin to understand His power, creativity and depth. If He is able to deal with the minutest components of His creation, what can He do with our emotional, physical, relational, financial, mental and spiritual issues?

He is God of it all. He is the great I AM.

Clean and Spotless

Truth for Today – Isaiah 64

I read recently about the scents that renowned department stores use to entice customers to purchase costly perfumes. Smells can tempt us to purchase things we otherwise would not have purchased. The smell of pizza and other food draws us in like bugs to a light or like a shiny, lurching lure in the water attracts trout and bass. However, not all smells are good.

That sets the tone for an experience I had years ago. We had 10,000 chickens in a caged layer operation. They each produced about an egg per day, but those 10,000 birds also produced 3000 lbs. of manure per day. Normally the manure would be dry and could be spread with conventional means, but sometimes due to waterline issues in the chicken house, the manure would become near liquid.

One fall day when it was time to clean out the liquid manure, I used a large tractor-pulled manure tank that sucked the liquid from my pit, and when pressurized could blow it on the field. It was my first experience with the equipment, and I unknowingly sucked up stones and gravel into the tank as well.

When I got to the field, I pressurized the tank to begin spreading the liquid. From the tractor, I opened the hydraulic valve at the back of the tank. Nothing happened. I re-checked the pressurized tank, saw it was okay, went behind the tank, looked into the pipe and noticed something blocking the flow. It was then I saw the stones and gravel blocking the manure. I got a broom and poked the blockage, forgetting that the tank was pressurized. Suddenly the blockage broke loose and the liquid manure knocked me off my feet as I was hit full force with the load. I finally got it shut off, but was covered in chicken manure. It took days to get the smell totally gone, but the memories remain.

The Bible speaks about God's abhorrence of sin and how it separated Jesus from His Father and that sin cannot enter Heaven. Sin is horribly dirty and filthy. How thankful I am for the cleansing power of the blood of Jesus so we can become spotless, pure and blameless.

Isaiah 64:6 - *But we are all as an unclean thing,*
and all our righteousnesses are as filthy rags.

Cleave or Cleaver

Truth for Today – Ephesians 5

The two women were arguing as to who the child belonged to. We know the story well from 1 Kings 3 where we are taught of Solomon's wisdom, his role as King of Israel and mediator of disputes.

Another story from 2008 gives additional insight into the subject of asset division. In Cambodia, the couple had been married forty years. He had become ill and supposedly his wife refused to give him the care he needed. He became angry. Things continued to deteriorate in their relationship. Finally the husband asked his friends to help him divide their assets. They moved his belongings to one side of the stilted house and brought the saws, hammers and chisels out of the tool box.

They then proceeded to cut the house in half. They moved his half of the house to another property and set the half-house in place. The stressful mission was accomplished as the division of assets was completed.

God and His Word provide ample direction as to what a marital relationship should have as principles. When those principles are followed, division of assets is rarely needed. However, when those principles are violated, things become complicated and troubles have just begun. What does God suggest as priority principles?

- Luke 6:31 - *And as ye would that men should do to you, do ye also to them likewise.*
- Ephesians 5:22 - *Wives, submit yourselves unto your own husbands, as unto the Lord.*
- Ephesians 5:25 - *Husbands, love your wives, even as Christ also loved the church, and gave himself for it.*
- Colossians 3:19 - *Husbands, love your wives, and be not bitter against them.*
- Genesis 2:24 - *Therefore shall a man leave his father and his mother, and shall cleave unto his wife: and they shall be one flesh.*

Close Encounter

***Truth for Today* –** 1 Kings 12:6-8

Lake Okeechobee in central Florida is half the size of Rhode Island. It is also the second largest lake (second only to Lake Michigan) in the lower 48 states.

The lake is home to many birds, fish and aquatic plants. It is an outdoorsman's paradise. Recently, a fishing guide told me the story of an acquaintance of his who was a kayaker. The guide told Joe that kayaking wasn't a good idea due to the presence of many alligators. The boater didn't listen.

Kayaking among the channels of vegetation near shore, he felt a bump. Thinking he may have hit a log, he looked around and didn't see anything. Then another bump. Turning around he looked into the eyes of a large alligator only three foot from his kayak. Suddenly his kayak seemed really small and he felt very vulnerable. In reality the alligator was longer than his kayak. Safely to shore, I'm sure he thought about the wise counsel that he unwisely had not heeded.

Counsel and advice from others tends to make us defensive. When we are given warnings or direction, we may feel demeaned. After all, how does someone else know what our abilities, experience and skills might be? Who are they to tell us what to do, when to do it and how to accomplish it? It takes humility to accept the counsel of others. What does the book of Proverbs say about counsel and advice?

- Proverbs 11:14 - *Where no counsel is, the people fall: but in the multitude of counsellors there is safety.*
- Proverbs 24:6 - *For by wise counsel thou shalt make thy war: and in multitude of counsellors there is safety.*
- Proverbs 19:20 - *Hear counsel, and receive instruction, that thou mayest be wise in thy latter end.*
- Proverbs 3:5 - *Trust in the LORD with all thine heart; and lean not unto thine own understanding.*
- Proverbs 12:15 - *The way of a fool is right in his own eyes: but he that hearkeneth unto counsel is wise.*
- Proverbs 1:7 - *The fear of the LORD is the beginning of knowledge: but fools despise wisdom and instruction.*

Coffee to Go

Truth for Today – 1 Timothy 2:4

Jeni and I had just enjoyed an attraction in Pigeon Forge, Tennessee when the rain began. Needing to get to our hotel in the mountains above Gatlinburg, we took the less traveled bypass to avoid downtown traffic.

There were many curves and the roads were slick from the rain. As we were going around a tight curve I noticed an oncoming car sliding on the road and coming directly towards us. I steered off the highway onto the guard-railed berm. As I got closer to the guard rail I could see the steep hill beyond the rail. The car kept sliding and hit us broadside on the driver's side.

No one was hurt but the young couple in the sliding car was obviously shaken. The police arrived, insurance information was traded and we both drove away an hour later with our dents and thankfulness for no injuries. On the way to the hotel I told Jeni that I had failed to talk to the other couple about Jesus. I woke up during the night, saddened for not having used the emotional opportunity to share about Him.

Next morning as we left the hotel I was thinking again about the failed opportunity, but was also thinking that a hot cup of coffee would be nice for the hours of driving ahead. As we passed through Pigeon Forge, I began looking for a coffee shop. There were many restaurants and lots of people, and then I saw a fast food restaurant with a drive-thru. Seeing a dozen cars in the drive-thru line and not wanting to wait, I decided to go inside. I quickly got my coffee and turned around and came face to face with the couple with whom we had an accident. God had given me a second chance!

I thank God for vacations, cars to ride in, guard rails to protect us from steep hills, coffee for the road and for a God who cares about people. He is always working in the background to promote Himself, His Son and His Spirit. He holds the key to eternal life and desires that for everyone.

1 Timothy 2:4 – (God) who will have all men to be
saved, and to come unto the knowledge of the truth.

Coming Home

Truth for Today – 1 Thessalonians 4:13-18

A friend of mine called and asked me to go for a ride with him. He picked me up without telling me where we were going. I asked and he told me to be patient and I would see.

In a rural area, he entered a driveway to a home I'd not seen before. He stopped in the driveway and explained. "This is a home and yard I take care of for a man and his wife. I wanted you to see it."

We drove up to the yard surrounding the home and I was amazed at the beauty and neatness of the place. He said that the couple was gone for a few months and it was his job to keep it up while they were gone.

I asked him when they were returning and I'll not forget his answer. "I don't know when they're coming back, but I want it to look really nice no matter when they return."

The experience reminded me of the words of Jesus in Mark 13:33-37 – *"Take ye heed, watch and pray: for ye know not when the time is. For the Son of Man is as a man taking a far journey, who left his house, and gave authority to his servants, and to every man his work, and commanded the porter to watch. Watch ye therefore: for ye know not when the master of the house cometh, at even, or at midnight, or at the cockcrowing, or in the morning: Lest coming suddenly he find you sleeping. And what I say unto you I say unto all, Watch."* Jesus promised that He will be returning to earth.

- 1 Peter 4:7 - *But the end of all things is at hand: be ye therefore sober, and watch unto prayer.*
- Matthew 24:27 - *For as the lightning cometh out of the east, and shineth even unto the west; so shall also the coming of the Son of man be.*
- John 14:3 - *And if I go and prepare a place for you, I will come again, and receive you unto myself; that where I am, there ye may be also.*
- 1 Corinthians 15:52 - *In a moment, in the twinkling of an eye, at the last trump: for the trumpet shall sound, and the dead shall be raised incorruptible, and we shall be changed.*

Communications

***Truth for Today** – Psalm 16:11*

Communication - Merriam-Webster defines it as, *"The act or process of using words, sounds, signs, or behaviors to express or exchange information or to express your ideas, thoughts, feelings, etc., to someone else."*

With elderly aunts and uncles, I see their normal patterns of communication changing. With their strength ebbing, their hearing diminishing, their eyesight growing dimmer and their mind slowing down, it becomes increasingly more difficult to convey their thoughts and feelings to others.

Recently, my aunt who is 95, visited her brother who is 98 at the health care facility where they both live. Neither could see one another very well, except for shadowy dim shapes. Neither could hear the other except for a muted and weak voice. So they held hands. Grasped tightly, they communicated in a deep and emotional way. Communication comes in many packages.

As I think of how we communicate with our Father, it is certainly unorthodox and unconventional. We never see Him or hear Him directly, yet we know that He hears us and sees us.

An old preacher once told me, "I've learned how to talk to my Father lying face down on the floor." Unorthodox and unconventional, yet effective to say the least.

- Exodus 33:14 - *And he said, My presence shall go with thee, and I will give thee rest.*
- Jeremiah 29:13 - *And ye shall seek me, and find me, when ye shall search for me with all your heart.*
- Matthew 18:20 - *For where two or three are gathered together in my name, there am I in the midst of them.*
- Psalm 73:28 - *But it is good for me to draw near to God: I have put my trust in the Lord God, that I may declare all thy works.*
- Psalm 16:11 - *Thou wilt shew me the path of life: in thy presence is fulness of joy; at thy right hand there are pleasures for evermore.*

Construct or Destruct

***Truth for Today** – 1 Corinthians 13*

It seemed like my dad could build something from almost anything. There was no such thing as "junk" in his world. As a tinkerer, he could get by with baling wire, duct tape and someone else's leftovers. I never grew tired of watching him at work in his shop. He was a builder and designer of "things" so we were not surprised at the various patents he was awarded.

One memory I have is of a small jig-saw he made from an old sewing machine. The sewing machine provided the mechanical motions and various pieces of metal and wood provided the machine structure and table. I was intrigued.

One day when he was away and I was exploring his workshop, my seven year old eyes saw the jig-saw. Opening up his large wooden toolbox, I found screwdrivers, wrenches, hammers and pliers. I went to work on his jig-saw and soon had it dismantled on his workbench. I was amazed at the number of parts it took to make a jig-saw operate. I soon was bewildered as to how to put it back together.

My dad came home to the mess I had made of his jig-saw. Kindly, he said, "You're a much better de-structor than you are a con-structor." Then he permitted me to help him put it back together.

The Bible cautions us in our relationships to be builders rather than destroyers. It seems that our human nature has a default to tear down, destroy, gossip, criticize, judge and thus hurt others. Fortunately the born again conversion experience gives us a Holy Spirit and a Christ-like mind that fights against the flesh of our old nature.

- Galatians 5:17 - *For the flesh lusteth against the Spirit, and the Spirit against the flesh: and these are contrary the one to the other: so that ye cannot do the things that ye would.*
- Romans 12:10 - *Be kindly affectioned one to another with brotherly love; in honour preferring one another.*
- John 13:34 - *A new commandment I give unto you, That ye love one another; as I have loved you, that ye also love one another.*
- 1 Thessalonians 3:12 - *And the Lord make you to increase and abound in love one toward another, and toward all men.*

Contentment with a Cost

Truth for Today – Philippians 4

The animal kingdom can reveal many truths to us if we pay attention. While driving in rural Indiana, I passed a farm with horses. Two adjoining pastures were enclosed with barbed wire fences with a horse in each. On the right side of the common fence, a horse was reaching through to eat grass on the left side. Six feet away on the left side was a second horse stretching his head through the fence and eating from the right hand pasture.

Immediately I thought of my jealous or envious nature which sometimes comes to the surface. How often is the grass greener on the other side of the fence?

Certainly, the Bible is clear on teaching about the subject. We are not unaware of God's principles regarding contentment.

- Philippians 4:11-12 - *Not that I speak in respect of want: for I have learned, in whatsoever state I am, therewith to be content. I know both how to be abased, and I know how to abound: everywhere and in all things I am instructed both to be full and to be hungry, both to abound and to suffer need.*
- Philippians 4:19 - *But my God shall supply all your need according to his riches in glory by Christ Jesus.*
- 1 Timothy 6:6-8 - *But godliness with contentment is great gain. For we brought nothing into this world, and it is certain we can carry nothing out. And having food and raiment let us be therewith content.*
- Matthew 6:33 - *But seek ye first the kingdom of God, and his righteousness; and all these things shall be added unto you.*

We tend to forget that happiness doesn't come as a result of getting something we don't have, but rather of recognizing and appreciating what we do have. – Frederick Koenig

The richest person is not the one who has the most, but the one who needs the least. – Anonymous

Contranym

Truth for Today – Isaiah 55

T-Ball, Little League, Middle and High School baseball all create opportunities for young boys and young men to learn about competition, physical fitness and other life lessons.

Boys respond differently to those lessons. For some, those competitive athletics are a positive experience, for others it may be negative. Coaches, fathers, mothers, team-mates all play a role in how those experiences play out.

A father told me about the experiences two of his sons had with baseball and competitive athletics. He said they were both gifted and loved the sport, however one son learned more than the other in the process.

One was continually on winning teams, the other son repeatedly on losing teams. In other words one became a loser while the other was a winner.

The dictionary defines "contranym" as *"a word that can mean the opposite of itself."* A word like "fast" can mean "moving rapidly" or "fixed in position". "Oversight" can mean "watchful" or "something not noticed".

The dad shared that the son on losing teams learned more about life situations than the son on the winning teams. In other words, the loser became a winner. A contranym.

The Bible seems to be full of contranyms. A kernel of corn must die to live and bring fruit (death brings life); to find our life we must first lose it (lost means found); sinners become pure and the sinless (Jesus) became sin.

God seems to have a way of getting His points across in unique and memorable ways. They initially do not make sense but those imaginative methods of communication encourage us to think like Him. That is not an easy thing.

Isaiah 55:8 - *For my thoughts are not your thoughts, neither are your ways my ways, saith the LORD.*

Win, lose; death, life; lost and found... whatever. God has a fabulous plan that works in wonderful ways if we know and learn His heart.

Cool Pool Party

The pool party in Mexico was in full swing. Lots of young men and women enjoying the party scene with plenty of liquor, flashing lights and loud music. As promised it would be a party to remember. Liquid nitrogen was poured into the large swimming pool, which held about 30 party-goers, to create a low hanging mist or fog over the pool area.

Those outside the pool could barely see the people in the pool. Then the coughing started. It was either the chemical reaction of the nitrogen with the pool chlorine, or the liquid nitrogen robbing the surrounding air of its oxygen. The result was chaos and it happened quickly. Eight young people ended up being treated at a nearby hospital and one young man was in a coma for two weeks.

How often do we let our self-serving desires outweigh good judgment? Physical and mental cravings such as narcotics, alcohol, nicotine, overeating and more can all create long term health issues. When we put our lusts and cravings ahead of good judgment or God's principles and commandments, we and others suffer. We might believe that we are the only victims when we satisfy ourselves, but there are second-hand victims walking alongside.

The Bible has many illustrations whereby we may learn. David had lusts, desires, envies, hungers and thirsts that led to abuses of power that did horrific damage to himself and others. All of Israel suffered from his choices. The list goes on as we read of Absalom, Judas, Peter, Jezebel and Balaam.

- Romans 6:12 - *Let not sin therefore reign in your mortal body, that ye should obey it in the lusts thereof.*
- Galatians 5:24 - *And they that are Christ's have crucified the flesh with the affections and lusts.*
- 1 Timothy 6:9 - *But they that will be rich fall into temptation and a snare, and into many foolish and hurtful lusts, which drown men in destruction and perdition.*

Psalm 37:4 - *Delight thyself also in the Lord:*
And he shall give thee the desires of thine heart.

Credentials

Truth for Today – Luke 4:18-19

We develop perceptions about people, don't we? Possibly it's based upon their appearance, where they live, what they drive or who their friends are. But many times we base it upon their vocation. Those perceptions can be negative or positive, but rarely neutral. And rarely are our perceptions completely accurate.

Recently, I met a man and developed a perception about him based upon his position within an organization. The perception was positive due to his professional manner, the size of the company, and his reputation within the business community.

He is Chief Financial Officer, Senior Vice President and Treasurer for a very large company which has $10 billion in assets. That type of position carries with it huge amounts of prestige, responsibility, authority and power. But, those things of themselves do not speak for his personal integrity, heart and spiritual condition. So, who is this guy and what is he truly like?

Then I learned the important things. He is a man of God with a testimony of faith. He loves his wife and family with a big heart. But additionally, every Sunday noon you find him in the parking lot of his church in a T shirt and jeans serving lunches to the homeless of his city. He, along with others are serving, talking and sharing the Gospel to those who are the last, least, lost and lonely. He is known among the homeless as a friend and confidante.

Positions of authority, prestige and power are one component, but they don't define who and what we are. Though Jesus Christ had all those things, He made it clear that He didn't come to earth for that. He came to sacrifice Himself, to serve others, to lift others up and to glorify His God. I am thankful to know men like my new CFO friend. His love for Jesus is making a difference for others.

Luke 4:18-19 - *The Spirit of the Lord is upon me, because he hath anointed me to preach the gospel to the poor; he hath sent me to heal the brokenhearted, to preach deliverance to the captives, and recovering of sight to the blind, to set at liberty them that are bruised, to preach the acceptable year of the Lord.*

Crooked as a Dogs Hind Leg

***Truth for Today* –** Matthew 18:21-35

My thirteenth birthday was soon and I had dropped hints about what I wanted more than anything else. I had a BB gun for the last few years, but I felt I was ready to graduate to a .22 rifle.

My birthday came and the rifle was in the wrapped gift. Dad did due diligence in teaching me about gun safety. Among other things he also said, "Never point a gun at something you don't want to shoot and always keep your safety on until you're ready to pull the trigger."

It was late fall and we headed to the back 40 acres of our farm where there were many fence rows. It was a cool day and spending time with my dad and our Rat Terrier dog Tippy hunting rabbits was perfect. The rabbits were somewhere else that day, so my mind wandered as I followed my dad. Looking to the left I saw our dog running in the neighbors field about 100' away.

I broke both of my dad's commands in the next five seconds. I pointed my rifle at our dog and thinking the safety was on, I pulled the trigger. I was stunned at the noise of the gun followed by Tippy's yelp. I shot her in the back leg and she was frantic. Tippy walked to us dragging her leg, and then ran off on three legs. The next two days were difficult as my dad was obviously disappointed with me, as well as concerned about our dog. Finally Tippy limped home from wherever wounded dogs go, and dad took her to the vet. The vet removed the bullet and Tippy came back home with a forever limp.

My dad forgave me quickly, as did Tippy. Forgiveness is a wonderful thing when it is granted. Had I disobeyed? Yes. Was I given mercy and grace? Yes. Did I deserve mercy and grace? No.

The forgiveness was special, but every time I saw Tippy limp from the bullet injury, I was reminded of my disobedience and the consequences of my actions.

Hebrews 4:16 - *Let us therefore come boldly unto the throne of grace, that we may obtain mercy, and find grace to help in time of need.*

Crossing the Finish Line

Truth for Today – 2 Timothy 4:6-8

Juan was determined to break a Guinness world record. He set out in November of 2010 to bicycle 155,350 miles in five continents in five years. Finally the end was near. Scheduled for completing his goal in November of 2015, he was hit and killed by a truck in Thailand in February 2015. He was nine months short of his goal.

He had biked on four continents, in 49 countries and had 793 flat tires. The tragedy left a wife and two year old son behind.

The tragedy reminds me of how often my objectives are not realized. I may have good intentions and passion, but for reasons beyond my control, I am unable to accomplish a goal.

The world we live in is less than perfect and certainly unpredictable. I'm reminded of the life of the apostle Paul as he shared a concern of his own in 1 Corinthians 9:27 - *But I keep under my body, and bring it into subjection: lest that by any means, when I have preached to others, I myself should be a castaway.*

Paul was concerned with the uncertainties of life and how they could affect his ultimate goal. But he likewise was aware of what God had told him in Philippians 4:13 - *I can do all things through Christ which strengtheneth me.*

In 2 Corinthians 11, Paul wrote of the beatings, stonings, whippings, shipwrecks and perils he had endured while living out his faith. Yet, he persevered through the trials and calamities of his life.

In Philippians 1:20-21, Paul shared his commitment to finish in faith. *According to my earnest expectation and my hope, that in nothing I shall be ashamed, but that with all boldness, as always, so now also Christ shall be magnified in my body, whether it be by life, or by death. For to me to live is Christ, and to die is gain.*

Finally at the end of his life, Paul was able to say in 2 Timothy 4:6-8 - *For I am now ready to be offered, and the time of my departure is at hand. I have fought a good fight, I have finished my course, I have kept the faith: Henceforth there is laid up for me a crown of righteousness, which the Lord, the righteous judge, shall give me at that day: and not to me only, but unto all them also that love his appearing.*

Damage to Others

***Truth for Today** – Ezekiel 18:20*

While admiring the mountains, valleys, wildlife and lakes of the Rocky Mountain National Park in Colorado, we were always on the lookout for something new.

On a family vacation we were making memories quickly. Then, up ahead, we noticed a long line of cars parked along the road. Grabbing my camera, we headed to see what the attraction was.

About 80' away, knee-deep in a marsh, was a moose. There were 50 or so people lining the guard rail snapping photos. With no clear vision, I stepped over the guard rail and took a few steps closer. The moose spooked and sloshed off into the distance. I heard muttering from the crowd and noticed some not-so-nice looks. My children still talk about my blunder.

A few days ago I noticed ten or so people snapping a photograph of an alligator about 25' away. I snapped my photo and decided to use my iPad for a photo as well. As I opened it, the magnetic lid fell off and hit a metal railing with a clang. The alligator was gone in a flash. Again, I received the not-so-nice looks as my presence wasn't appreciated.

How often do our actions ruin things for innocent people? Just as my two illustrations created consequences for those around me, there are other things we do that do damage to others. The Bible shares thoughts about the issue:

- 2 Samuel 12:14 – (Nathan to David after David's adultery, deception and murder) - *Because by this deed thou hast given great occasion to the enemies of the Lord to blaspheme, the child also that is born unto thee shall surely die.*
- Exodus 34:7 – (The Lord to Moses) - *Visiting the iniquity of the fathers upon the children, and upon the children's children, unto the third and to the fourth generation.*
- Ezekiel 18:2 - *The fathers have eaten sour grapes, and the children's teeth are set on edge?*

According to scripture we will each be eternally and ultimately responsible for our own choices and decisions in life. But there are choices we make that can have daily and lifetime consequences for others.

Danger is Lurking

Truth for Today – Psalm 34

During the summer of 1968 a small group of young men went hiking at a reservoir. The reservoir water spilled out of a dam into a river. The river had steep cliffs on one side. One of the young men had the bright idea to climb the cliffs to the top.

So, without ropes, we started the climb. I remember the fear I experienced half-way up when I knew there was no turning back. The cliff was steeper than I had anticipated; the earth easily crumbled; and there were few handholds. Fortunately the few roots and rocks we could grasp made it possible to reach the top without injury.

That evening I shared (with some degree of pride) our climbing adventure with another friend. He quoted Matthew 4:7 to me - *Thou shalt not tempt the Lord thy God;* and I was humbled.

How often are we surrounded by danger and have no idea? How regularly do we rely on God to deliver us from the problems and issues we heap upon ourselves? I recently saw a photo of a beautiful butterfly resting on the head of a butterfly eating lizard. The butterfly is oblivious to danger.

I am thankful for a God who has my back and takes great care in preserving me in spite of my carelessness. What an awesome God we serve.

- 2 Corinthians 1:10 – *(God) Who delivered us from so great a death, and doth deliver: in whom we trust that he will yet deliver us.*
- Psalm 34:17 - *The righteous cry, and the Lord heareth, and delivereth them out of all their troubles.*
- Psalm 34:19 - *Many are the afflictions of the righteous: but the Lord delivereth him out of them all.*
- Psalm 97:10 - *He preserveth the souls of his saints; he delivereth them out of the hand of the wicked.*
- Matthew 6:13 - *And lead us not into temptation, but deliver us from evil: For thine is the kingdom, and the power, and the glory, for ever. Amen.*

Degaje

Truth for Today – 1 Corinthians 12

I was in a mountain home in a remote village in southwest Haiti. It had been a long hike and I looked forward to washing my face with cool cistern water. The house owner turned on the water outlet and I cupped the cool water and splashed it on my face.

When I reached for the second handful of water, the faucet slipped off the pipe and landed in the bucket. Quickly the owner grabbed a piece of wire and adeptly fastened it around the faucet, looped it around the pipe and twisted. Good as new. Degaje.

I looked over the barbed wire fence on a ranch in Haiti at people who were using piped water for washing their clothing and watering their cows. I noticed one cow drinking from a half of a tractor tire. The farmer had found a worn out rear tractor tire, cut it in half and buried enough of the round part to create a water trough for his cattle. Degaje.

Punctures in rubber tubes for Haitian bicycle tires are intricately repaired with small pieces of wire. Some of the tubes have 20 or so punctures and are expertly wired and repaired. Degaje.

The term "degaje" is Haitian Creole for "making do with what you have." Haitian ingenuity is almost a form of art. It is fascinating to watch what people with very few resources can effectively do. Degaje is part of the Haitian culture and is a huge part of who Haitians are and defines much of their life.

Watching degaje in action reminds me of what God does with my meager gifts. He doesn't expect miracles from me, as He is willing to watch me "make do" with what He has equipped me with.

1 Corinthians 12 is a great study on the unique gifting and talents which God has given each of us. He doesn't expect the eye to smell or hear. Likewise the hand to walk or the feet to do sign language. We are created with uniqueness to perform particular duties for which we've been suited. We make do with what we have.

The question I have to ask myself is whether I am willing to use what I've been given, or do I complain about my lack of gifting or talents? Do I wish I had a different set of gifts?

Directionally Challenged

Truth for Today – Psalm 1:1-6

Have you ever walked into a hotel room, turned on a light and heard the echoing sound of the scampering of something across the floor? Maybe you got a fleeting glimpse of a cockroach? I've heard them and seen them and wondered why they are repelled by light?

Why are some bugs repelled by light while others are attracted? Let's contemplate on those attracted to light.

Did you ever wonder what is happening while sitting around a campfire and seeing bugs by the hundreds, kamikaze diving into the fire? Why are they attracted to light? Theories abound but we will concentrate on two.

First, there is the theory that bugs have an internal navigation system that helps them steer through dark nights. Their navigation is GPS'ed on the lights emitted by the moon and bright stars. If you introduce another bright light like a fire into their world, they are thoroughly confused and fly blindly in circles which usually culminates in their untimely demise in the fire.

A second theory is that seeing a bright light indicates a clear path. There are obviously no obstacles between the bug and light of the fire, so it's like a super highway, except that it ends in a fiery crash.

Thinking about the disasters that happen to the confused or lost bugs cause me to think about the spiritual analogy. When I focus and concentrate on something other than God, His Son, His Holy Spirit, His Word and His principles, potential confusion and lack of focus occurs. Crash and burn!

What does the Bible say about the principles of maintaining a Biblical focus, concentration, direction and purpose?

- Colossians 3:2 - *Set your affection on things above, not on things on the earth.*
- Matthew 6:33 - *But seek ye first the kingdom of God, and his righteousness; and all these things shall be added unto you.*
- Proverbs 4:25 - *Let thine eyes look right on, and let thine eyelids look straight before thee.*
- Romans 8:5 - *For they that are after the flesh do mind the things of the flesh; but they that are after the Spirit the things of the Spirit.*

Dirt Diggers

Truth for Today – Ephesians 4:29

The echidna is a spine covered mammal living in Australia. An adult can be as large as 20 inches. They are unique as dirt diggers since they use all four legs at once to burrow into the dirt. All strong claws and legs thrash the ground and within one minute, the large animal can be totally burrowed into the ground and unseen. Their body literally sinks into the earth beneath them. Their actions have been likened to how a sinking ship disappears in the sea.

The badger has been classified as the fastest dirt digger in the world. Their heavy muscular body make them a great digging machine. Their very strong claws give them advantages that other digging animals don't have. A badger was observed digging through an asphalt surface within two minutes to disappear in the dirt beneath.

Men had dreamed about cutting a canal between the Atlantic and Pacific Oceans to decrease the travel time of ships. In 1524, the concept was first proposed with plans drawn up in 1529. Due to politics, international issues and costs, the 46 mile Panama Canal didn't start until 1881 and was finished in 1914. It is estimated that 268 million cubic yards of dirt had been moved.

Have you ever been wrongfully accused of wrong doing? Has someone questioned your motives or even suggested that your motives were impure? A single statement, innuendo or suggestion can create questions in people's minds about our motives, decisions or activities. People who are backbiters, tale-bearers or gossip mongers have a unique gift in digging and slinging dirt at others.

Sadly, many good and pure people have been buried by a mountain of imagined dirt. Are we known as a dirt digger? Do we thrive on hearing or saying things about others that are negative?

Lord, help me find the good in others and refrain from
digging or throwing dirt on those whom You've created.

Discretionary Jesting

The view was spectacular. The mountains were on both sides of the boulder and rock strewn river. It had rained and the vegetation was brilliantly green. Streams of water were running here and there in the semi-dry river bottom causing us to carefully use rocks as stepping stones to keep from getting wet.

We had just visited a mountain home in southwest Haiti for 12 formerly orphaned boys. On the return to our vehicles, our team of twelve split up with half of our group on one side of the river with a missionary, and I was taking the other half on a trail on the other side.

Not being able to see each other through the vegetation, I called the missionary on the other side to check progress. When he answered I said, "Jan, I've broken my ankle on the mountain trail and need to be carried down." My intent was to follow it up quickly with a "just kidding", but the phone went dead. I tried again and again to reach him but could not get reception. I knew that we were making memories, but not good ones.

Upon arrival at the truck we found three of our group. They said that the missionary and two others had turned around to try to find me on the mountain. A long 30 minutes later they came back, hot and tired but thankfully full of mercy.

I was the oldest in the group, but apparently not the wisest. Other than the missionary, I was the most experienced on that trail but certainly not the most mature. Spontaneous decisions and jesting generally don't go well together. Good natured fun can have its place, but many times jesters and jokers are not known for discretion.

Though Ephesians 5:4 is more about crude humor, it is still a good reminder to me to be careful in my talking. - *Neither filthiness, nor foolish talking, nor jesting, which are not convenient: but rather giving of thanks.* – Lord, give me discretion and wisdom in my conversation as well as a spirit of thanksgiving.

Do I Have Value?

***Truth for Today* -** Genesis 1

In a world of 7.3 billion people, we can sometimes lose perspective on our uniqueness and value. Though we desire to be valued by our family, friends and neighbors, it is vital that we understand our value in God's eyes.

Matthew 10:29,31: *Are not two sparrows sold for a farthing? And one of them shall not fall on the ground without your Father. Fear ye not therefore, ye are of more value than many sparrows.*

There are an estimated 40 varieties of sparrows around the world. They number in the billions with some flocks having a million or more. Do they matter? There are so many, so how can He possibly care for each of them?

God's promise to care for every single one of those billions of sparrows is indicative of His caring heart.

However, we might say, "Of course, I know I have more value than a sparrow; that's a no-brainer. I have a soul." But do we really see the significance of what God is saying? If God places that much value and significance on a sparrow, how much more does He value us?"

"God sees us with the eyes of a Father. He sees our defects, errors, and blemishes. But He also sees our value. What did Jesus know that enabled Him to do what He did? Here's part of the answer: He knew the value of people. He knew that each human being is a treasure. And because He did, people were not a source of stress, but a source of joy." – Max Lucado

Do the Humble Stumble?

Truth for Today – 1 Corinthians 2:1-3

Having a popular, powerful and wealthy father had benefits for a favored son. A lavish lifestyle soon created expectations and entitlements for the boy. History teaches us that David's son Absalom was renowned for his beauty. From the top of his head to the soles of his feet, there were no blemishes.

He was popular, powerful and wealthy with great similarities to his father. But one thing was different. He had a head of hair like no one else. It seemed to be a great source of pride. It grew so thick and heavy that he had it shaved once per year and the crop weighed 6 lbs.

But often there's a price to pay for popularity, power and wealth. Absalom developed a rebellious spirit that desired his father's throne and paved the way for a rebellion. We know the story of the uprising and Absalom's death. Absalom rode a mule under a large oak tree and his hair was caught in the branches. The mule went on and Absalom hung there by his pride, until he was killed.

Proverbs 16:18 says, *"Pride goeth before destruction, and an haughty spirit before a fall."* Are there areas of our lives that create pride in our lives? Do we have gifts, talents or qualities that create a "holier than thou" or "better than you" attitude towards others?

Jesus had no pillow on which to lay his head. He had no beauty or anything about his appearance that would be envied by others. He had no possessions. Though popular among the last, least, lost and lonely, he was despised by royalty and the elite.

As we look in the mirror; when we write our résumé; as we develop our obituary or legacy; it is always good to keep our God given gifts, talents, experiences, appearance and successes in perspective.

The apostle Paul seemed to understand. It seems that he learned how to maintain a humble perspective of himself:

1 Corinthians 2:1-3 - *And I, brethren, when I came to you, came not with excellency of speech or of wisdom, declaring unto you the testimony of God. For I determined not to know anything among you, save Jesus Christ, and him crucified. And I was with you in weakness, and in fear, and in much trembling.*

Does God Know Everything About Me?

Truth for Today – Matthew 6:25 - 34

There are times I wonder if God cares enough about me to know all of my hurts, desires and troubles. Does He know and does He care?

The everyday disappointments, tragedies, traumas, losses, discouragements, unrealized expectations; issues related to finances, relationships, health, emotional stress and worries can bog us down. We can feel incredibly alone during those times and wonder if God is even aware.

Luke 12:7 reassures us: *"...even the very hairs of your head are all numbered."*

stimates help me understand just how many things God is actually taking care of:

- On average, each person has 150,000 hairs on their head
- We lose an average of 50 - 75 hairs per day
- Each follicle has the ability to replenish itself 20 times over a lifetime

Multiply that complexity and those numbers by the 7.3 billion population of the world and we see the enormity of what God is able to accomplish, control and keep track of.

Thank you Lord for taking care of the things
I cannot. Thank you for always having my back!

Does God Know Where We Are?

Truth for Today - Genesis 1

Recently I had my mind expanded:

- Our earth is rotating on its axis at 1000 miles per hour
- Our earth is traveling at 66,000 miles per hour around the sun
- Our sun and planets are orbiting around the Milky Way galaxy at 486,000 miles per hour
- Our galaxy is traveling at 370 miles per second thru the universe

Those numbers beg the question: Does God have any idea where we are?

Joshua 1:9 - *Have not I commanded thee? Be strong and of a good courage; be not afraid, neither be thou dismayed: for the LORD thy God is with thee whithersoever thou goest.*

Hebrews 13:5 - *...I will never leave thee nor forsake thee.*

Of course God knows where each of us are on our journey. He's the One who created it all: Matter, time, mass, speed, light, infinity, positioning and each person. When I feel alone, lost and uncared for, it helps to know that He is there with me, wherever I am.

Does it Really Mean That?

Truth for Today – Isaiah 1:19

Nine year old James was riding his bicycle around a lake in central Florida. It was another hot Florida day and the water beckoned to him. Though it was posted as a no-swimming area, James decided to take a quick dip.

While swimming he felt something grab him and reached down to feel a snout and teeth. Hitting, punching poking and prying, James finally was released from the alligators grip.

At the hospital he received treatment for the 30 teeth bites. Asked later if he ever intended to swim in the lake again, he responded with a quick "no".

Recently I was able to snap a quick illustrative photo of a reason to obey rules. "No Swimming" signs were posted, but there is nothing like an alligator to lend credibility to the rule.

In our Christian walk we read countless warnings, rules, commands, principles and guidelines to help us stay away from sin and failure. However, if we don't personally see the danger, it is difficult to adhere to hypothetical rules. If we've not seen others experience the danger, again, it is challenging to accept the guidelines others impose upon us. In fact, the rules may seem overbearing and restrictive.

But, from a Christian's perspective, the rules, guidelines and counsel is coming from the God of the Universe who has our best interests in mind.

- John 14:15 - *If ye love me, keep my commandments.*
- Luke 6:46 - *And why call ye me, Lord, Lord, and do not the things which I say?*
- Isaiah 1:19 - *If ye be willing and obedient, ye shall eat the good of the land.*

Don't Look Down

Truth for Today – Philippians 4:13

When I was ten years old I went to my first circus. Though intrigued by the animals, clowns and various acts, I was especially intrigued by the men and women performing a tight-wire walk high above the arena.

Walking tight-ropes wasn't something I desired to do or could do, so those performers became super-hero's to me. Since that time, over the years, I've watched men breaking tight-wire records for longest walks, highest walks, and walks over famous landmarks.

Recently, famous high-wire walks have occurred over waterfalls, canyons and between skyscrapers. The other day I watched a video of a young man climbing a 919' chimney. When he got to the top he walked on a 12" wide steel beam across the open top. Now, 12" may seem wide, but looking down 919' while standing on that beam seems a bit insane.

So, if we position a 12" wide beam one or two feet off the ground, we wouldn't think twice about walking on it, would we? In fact, we'd probably try it with a one or two inch wide piece. At what point do we become uncomfortable? At what point do we say, "no way?" When we are three feet off the ground? When we are eight feet off the ground?

The issue is risk. When risk is minimized, we can do outrageous things.

As believers, how do we minimize risk? How do we face uncertain futures, trauma and death? In talking to many people who have faced horrible things in their lives, there is one thing I've found consistent. Believers say, "It wasn't easy, but it was easier than I had imagined. God got me through it."

We know the clichés. *God makes a way... He has the whole world in His hands... God said it, I believe it and that settles it... If God brings you to it, He will bring you through it... Where God guides, He provides.*

In essence, the clichés are accurate, but in a real world it's easier said than done. Bottom line is that God is the one who took the risk, paid the price and equips us. The gain outweighs the risk.

Don't Mess with Mama

Truth for Today – James 1:27

As an eight year old walking in a field, I heard loud chattering and watched a male red winged blackbird fluttering on the ground. It held out a wing and thrashed the dirt with its feet and other wing. As I approached the injured bird, it kept moving further and further away. I kept following and finally it flew away. Confused, I asked my dad about it. He said, "It was protecting its babies in their nest. He acted injured to lure you away and he did his job well."

That same year my dad got into a pig pen and was attacked by a large sow protecting her little pigs. She knocked dad down and would have injured him severely if our dog had not chased the pig away giving dad a chance to escape.

We know the frightening and horrific stories of hikers getting between a bear and her cubs. It lends credibility to the saying, "You don't know anything about mama bear until you mess with one of her cubs." One of the instinctive characteristics of being part of a family is the security, safety and protection that goes along with it.

Around the world there are millions of orphaned and vulnerable children. Sadly, the number of those children is rising. War, AIDS, poverty, exploitation and trafficking all contribute to the horrible realities of how children are treated.

But, God has a principle. *All children deserve a family.* Family is what God created. When the Biblical Esther lost her mom and dad, God provided another family. Children deserve security, safety and protection. God encourages the concept in James 1:27 in asking us to visit the orphans. The original Greek for "visit" is "to look after, inspect and watch over."

Children are extremely vulnerable and highly likely to be hurt, damaged and devoured by an exploitive world. How can we be their advocates and caretakers? Possibly we can learn something from the world of animals?

Don't Waste My Time

Truth for Today – Hebrews 4:12

As the owner of a large manufacturing facility was giving me a tour of his factory, he shared his business philosophy with me.

He shared that making money was not the reason he was in business. His goal was to have a business that provided jobs to people and would also be a place where non-believers could be introduced to Jesus Christ.

Then he made a comment that sealed his philosophy. He said, "We place Bibles in our restrooms, in the hope that our employees will use them while there." Then with a smile, he said, "I consider that a wonderful waste of time!"

As I thought about his statement I recognized that normally, employees reading a book on the job is a waste of the employer's time. But I was impressed at the passion he had for his employees and the Gospel.

Reading the Word of God provides huge benefits, not only in this life, but eternally.

- 2 Timothy 3:16 - *All scripture is given by inspiration of God, and is profitable for doctrine, for reproof, for correction, for instruction in righteousness.*
- Romans 15:4 - *For whatsoever things were written aforetime were written for our learning, that we through patience and comfort of the scriptures might have hope.*
- Hebrews 4:12 - *For the word of God is quick, and powerful, and sharper than any two-edged sword, piercing even to the dividing asunder of soul and spirit, and of the joints and marrow, and is a discerner of the thoughts and intents of the heart.*
- Psalm 119:105 - *Thy word is a lamp unto my feet, and a light unto my path.*
- Mark 13:31 - *Heaven and earth shall pass away: but my words shall not pass away.*
- John 1:1 - *In the beginning was the Word, and the Word was with God, and the Word was God.*

Don't Worry About Me

Truth for Today – Romans 5:8

Life was good. She was eight months pregnant and was enjoying the beach in New South Wales, Australia with her husband and young son. Hearing a woman scream, she saw two young boys being swept out to sea. Their mother screamed that the boys didn't know how to swim.

In spite of being eight months pregnant she dove into the water and swam to the boys. She tried desperately to hold the boys up so they could breathe, but she couldn't swim to shore with them. Finally another man swam out to help and together the boys were rescued. Twenty-three days later she gave birth to a little girl.

Sacrifice. The willingness to give up something precious for something else. Why would someone be willing to give up their life for someone else? Why would this young mother put her own life and that of her unborn daughter at risk for strangers?

Merriam Webster defines sacrifice as, *"the act of giving up something you want to keep... to help someone."* It isn't in our human nature to sacrifice something we want to keep. It takes supernatural courage, strength or principles to make sacrifice possible.

Time is a diminishing resource and thus sacrificing our time for someone else takes effort. Likewise, our hard-earned money is precious. Therefore, giving either to others requires strong principles.

All of this reminds me yet again of the sacrifice of Jesus, the Son of God. What did He sacrifice? What did He gain? He sacrificed a perfect relationship with His Father as He took on the evil and sin of the entire human population. He sacrificed the golden streets and mansions of Heaven for an earth where He had no place to lay his head. He sacrificed the adoration of all the angels for a world that despised and abused Him.

But He had principles and purpose. He chose obedience, love, sacrifice, pain and death over Himself. That is counter-intuitive!

Romans 5:8 - *But God commendeth his love toward us,
in that, while we were yet sinners, Christ died for us.*

Duh...

***Truth for Today** – James 4*

It was a great day. We were spending time at a small zoo with our grandchildren. It was the kind of zoo where you can get up close and personal with animals and birds. It was also the kind of zoo you can get through in about 25 minutes, if you take your time.

As we moved past the goats and llamas, we came to the porcupines. As we watched them through the wire fence, I noticed a sign. *"DO NOT PET PORCUPINE."*

I am pretty sure that even children too young to read know that they should not pet a porcupine. Why state the obvious?

I am guessing that an insurance company stipulated that the sign must be posted to prevent potential litigation. Or possibly the owner of the zoo knew from a first-hand encounter the pain of a porcupine quill. He wanted to personally make sure that no one else had to endure the pain.

As I read the Bible, I am amazed at the many times the obvious is repetitively stated. Does God think we are unwise, thoughtless and ignorant? Why would God spend so much time telling us about the treachery, deceitfulness, fraud, lying, scheming and devious nature of satan? Why would He continually tell us to pray, understand wisdom and His Word? Why would He repeatedly caution us against sinning?

Is He doing it to avoid litigation? Isaiah 53:7 describes Jesus before his accusers - *He was oppressed, and he was afflicted, yet he opened not his mouth: he is brought as a lamb to the slaughter, and as a sheep before her shearers is dumb, so he openeth not his mouth.* There will be no explanations or excuses as we stand before the Creator of the universe. God does not have to explain Himself or be cautious about mistakes or litigation.

He provides clear and repetitive warnings to save us from pain, ourselves, our sin nature, our flesh and eternal destruction. He loves us!

Easily Swayed

Truth for Today – Genesis 3:6

The mail arrived. I sorted through the advertisements and the bills. Then I saw it. The envelope was unlike any I had seen before. It was brilliant in its elegant color. The envelope exuded richness and was addressed to me. My name was in a type-set that reminded me of something very official and important.

I opened the envelope and found the contents just as excessive and luxurious as the envelope that held it. It was an opportunity for a credit card. The solicitations for credit cards come often, but this was different.

I began reading the text. This advertisement had succeeded in being in my hands longer than the usual 3 seconds. I was already into this solicitation for 45 seconds. I read that I was among the 1% of the population that was getting this opportunity. I was feeling special!

Then I read that the credit card was made of a layered composite to guarantee that I would be noticed when I used it. That appealed to my pride.

Then I read the benefits for the card. Other than the composite slickness and being among the 1% selected beneficiaries, there were no additional miles, rebates or other things that would appeal to me.

Then came the final crushing blow. The annual cost of the card was a tad bit under $500. It hit the inside of my trash can with a whack, but the advertisement had been in my hands for at least three minutes. That is a record for me. The card was marketing genius, but it was simply too slick.

It caused me to think about another slick promotion from long ago. Satan has had several thousand years of passing off his products. It started in the Garden of Eden.

Genesis 3:6 – *And when the woman saw that the tree was good for food, and that it was pleasant to the eyes, and a tree to be desired to make one wise, she took of the fruit thereof, and did eat, and gave also unto her husband with her; and he did eat.*

Our human nature is still prone to temptations. John 2:16 – *For all that is in the world, the lust of the flesh, and the lust of the eyes, and the pride of life, is not of the Father, but is of the world.*

Enslaved

Truth for Today – Galatians 5:1

Life in southwest Haiti for the family was very difficult. With only a small garden and mango tree, their ability to find enough food for a dad, mom and eight children was challenging. Each month, the parents were seeing their children become more fragile. Finally, the dad gave away his oldest daughter to a family in a nearby large city.

The agreement was that the new family would provide education, food and loving care to the ten year old girl. One less mouth to feed in his family made complete sense and the promise that his girl would thrive meant everything to him.

The reality was that the girl became a restavek child slave for the new family. Working from dawn to dusk, with no education, little scraps of food, and a never ending list of chores which turned her life into a literal hell. Abused, forgotten and lonely, she wept herself to sleep on the meager straw mat placed on the hard ground.

Slavery. A word that creates a mental image of horrific abuse and human tragedy. It is almost a general term we might forget, until you put the word next to the face of a sad and frightened ten year old girl. Then, it is impossible to forget.

There are an estimated 300,000 restavek children in Haiti. Many are abused and treated like slaves. 80% are girls under the age of 13. Fortunately, it is now an issue that is getting international attention. We pray that someday the practice will diminish and ultimately stop.

Slavery. Merriam-Webster dictionary defines it as, *"submission to a dominating influence; the state of a person who is chattel (property) to another."*

Satan has incredible amounts of resources, tools and deception to bring God's creation into enslavement. God created Man to live in a state of freedom, never bondage. Sadly, the choices of men and women, beginning in the Garden makes each of us vulnerable to a life of captivity and slavery.

I've seen the joy on the face of children rescued from slavery in Haiti and Ethiopia. Likewise I've seen the joy on the face of men and women released from satan's bondage. One is an earthly joy lasting a lifetime. The other is lifelong plus eternity.

Even the Little Critters?

Springtime brings a welcome end to the cold and bluster of a long and harsh winter. Likewise, spring brings new life, color and activity to our lives and environment. We only need to take a short walk in May to see the green leaves, butterflies and colors that God faithfully brings us every year.

Every year I think of the cycle of life as well as the built-in food chain that runs so efficiently. It brings new insight into the Lord's teachings in Matthew 6 where He speaks about the fowls of the air and the lilies of the field. God takes care of His creation.

Just when I think I understand how big God's job is in caring for His creation, I read something new that expands the concept to new levels. As an illustration, I read recently in David Blatner's book, *Spectrums: Our Mind-boggling Universe from Infinitesimal to Infinity,* the following quote: *"There are more insects in a single square mile of good fertile soil than there are human beings on earth."*

Imagine 7.3 billion insects in a square mile! Larvae, eggs, creepers, burrowers and crawlers. All feeding off one another. The earth under our feet is alive! God tells us that it is all under His control. It brings new meaning to the omnipotence of God.

There are times I become overwhelmed by responsibility. The heaviness can bring feelings of burnout. I feel like throwing my hands up in despair and saying, "what's the use." But God keeps going and going and going. He is the great provider even when I get to the end of my rope. When I get to the end, He is just beginning. James 4:6 tells us that it is then that *"he giveth more grace."*

Matthew 6:31-34 - *Therefore take no thought, saying, What shall we eat? or, What shall we drink? Or, Wherewithal shall we be clothed? (For after all these things do the Gentiles seek:) for your heavenly Father knoweth that ye have need of all these things. But seek ye first the kingdom of God, and his righteousness; and all these things shall be added unto you. Take therefore no thought for the morrow: for the morrow shall take thought for the things of itself. Sufficient unto the day is the evil thereof.*

Excuse my Excuse

Truth for Today – Romans 1:20

The diet was difficult. He loved his sweets and he loved his carbs, so fasting from those things took immense amounts of willpower. But, he had made headway and began losing a few pounds. Then, he crashed. Someone asked him how the diet was going and he said, "I was doing great until I accidentally ate a dozen cookies."

We've heard the excuses about non-completed homework assignments. "It wasn't my fault that the dog ate my homework." "It wasn't my fault that someone knocked my homework into a mud puddle."

We enjoy hearing the excuses which speeding drivers give to officers. "Oh, I thought that the I-95 sign was the speed limit." "I was speeding so the wind would push the snow off my windshield and I could see where I was going." "My car has a recall on it for unexplained acceleration and I'm taking it to the dealership." "I was hurrying to get to McDonald's before the breakfast menu ended."

I would assume God hears it all as we minimize sin in our lives. At the least, we tend to minimize it with words like, faults, failings, shortcomings and mistakes.

After eating the fruit of the tree, Eve explained her sin to God by saying, *"The serpent beguiled me, and I did eat."* Adam had his own excuse, *"The woman whom thou gavest to be with me, she gave me of the tree, and I did eat."*

When Moses challenged Aaron about the golden calf the Israelites were worshipping, Aaron said, *"And I said unto them, whosoever hath any gold, let them break it off. So they gave it me: then I cast it into the fire, and there came out this calf."*

The Bible explains that all have sinned and come short of God's glory. We are without excuse. But, the exciting part is that we are not without a Savior and Redeemer.

Romans 1:20 - *For the invisible things of him from the creation of the world are clearly seen, being understood by the things that are made, even his eternal power and Godhead; so that they are without excuse.*

Extremes

Jeni and I stood near the top of Niagara Falls and witnessed the massive amounts of Niagara River water relentlessly plummeting over the edge to the pools and rocks 167' below. An estimated 750,000 gallons of water flow over the edge of the American, Bridal and Horseshoe Falls every second.

That is a huge amount of water! We can try to absorb the magnitude of that number with our eyes, and seek to measure the massive volume and power of it with our ears. But, inevitably it is too massive to comprehend.

On another note, some of God's creation is so small that we will never see, hear or comprehend the magnitude of it. In their book, *Mathematics and the Imagination*, Edward Kasner and James Newman share this illustration. *"The number of electrons which pass through the filament of an ordinary fifty-watt electric lamp in a minute equals the number of drops of water that flow over Niagara Falls in a century."*

There is absolutely no way I can fathom the magnitude of either end of God's majestic spectrum. In reality, whether we are considering the electrons in a lightbulb, or the gallons of water in Niagara Falls, there are things much greater in magnitude on both ends of the spectrum that we still know so little about.

God's creation has much to teach us about His awesomeness. Our minute personal world is small compared to His Creation, yet He cares so deeply about us. In 1905 Civilla Martin wrote a song...

Why should I feel discouraged, why should the shadows come,
Why should my heart be lonely, and long for heaven and home,
When Jesus is my portion? My constant Friend is He:
His eye is on the sparrow, and I know He watches me;
His eye is on the sparrow, and I know He watches me.

Eyes Wide Open

Truth for Today – Ephesians 5:15

Two low pressure winter storms collided over Ohio on January 25, 1978. The resultant weather was known as a "bomb" in the terms of weather forecasters.

By the time the storm was finished, Indiana had received nearly 36" of snow, temperatures of 0° with wind chills of minus 50°, drifts as high as twenty feet, gusting winds as high as fifty mph, visibility of near zero and heavy loss of electricity.

On the 25th, Jeni and I along with our two young children were evacuated from our farm home by snowmobile. We were taken to a neighbor who unlike us, still had electricity.

The next day, in spite of the cold weather, drifting snow, near zero visibility and ongoing snowstorm, my neighbor Gene and I took two snowmobiles to answer another neighbor's call of distress. It was a two mile trip on a road with a left hand turn onto another road. When we reached the end of our road, we turned left. We followed the telephone poles at the side of the road to keep our bearings, as visibility beyond that was impossible.

Suddenly there were no poles. The blowing snow had covered the road, fields and ditches so it was a flat plane. We stopped to collect our bearings in the white-out, only to realize that we had absolutely no idea which direction was north. There were no visible things to see other than blowing snow. We knew that running into a farmstead was minimal. Staying out in the storm wasn't an option. We were lost.

Then we realized that the wind didn't seem as strong as it had been elsewhere. We wondered if we weren't on the lee side of a building that was diverting the wind. We gradually moved towards the diminished wind and nearly bumped into an old deserted barn that we recognized. Now we knew where we were and found our way to the road and finished our mission.

Ephesians 5:15 - *See then that ye walk circumspectly, not as fools, but as wise.* The word "circumspectly" in the original Greek means to observe with great carefulness everything around you, for the purpose of making right decisions. It's a great lesson to me as I ponder my world, its direction and try to make wise decisions.

Eyes

Jeni and I were eating breakfast at a family restaurant in Sedona, Arizona. Across the aisle was a man, his wife and family. We all received our food about the same time and finished at the same time.

We picked up our bill and went to the front desk cashier. The other family, with bill in hand, followed right behind us, slipped past us and left without paying their bill. We watched as the family got in their car and left.

I would imagine their vacation was more economical than mine. It prompted me to think of the eyes watching us every day and the reminder was good for me.

First and most important is remembering that God is able to see it all. Proverbs 15:3 - *The eyes of the LORD are in every place, beholding the evil and the good.*

Secondly relates to our children as they watch and learn from our choices and actions. Matthew 18:6 - *But whoso shall offend one of these little ones which believe in me, it were better for him that a millstone were hanged about his neck, and that he were drowned in the depth of the sea.* As we look on the innocence, love and admiration in our children's eyes, we understand how quickly that can be damaged.

And then of course are the many other eyes watching and drawing conclusions about our lives. Those reflections prompt me to try to live out Ephesians 5:15 - *See then that ye walk circumspectly, not as fools, but as wise...*

Lord, help me today to remember that You are watching and to remember that countless others are watching. I pray that I can be a good example to others as they see Jesus in me.

Face to Face with the Gospel

Truth for Today – Acts 11

I had just purchased items at the local hardware store and was exiting the building. As the large sliding doors opened in front of me, I noticed an Asian woman standing next to a car.

She was saying something very loudly to a couple who was about 50' ahead of me. As I got closer, I heard the words "church" and "God".

The couple walked on, or rather, I should say they hurried on! Then, she saw me. With eyes locked on mine, she pivoted, walked up to me and said, "You go church", and "You find God!"

Intrigued, I tried to engage in conversation with her. Unfortunately, her limited vocabulary had only a few words and phrases. I learned enough to know she was passionate about Jesus, passionate about sharing the Gospel, and only recently arrived from South Korea.

Some research after that encounter revealed that the believers in South Korea are passionate about outreach and evangelism. In 1945 only 1% of their country's population was Protestant. Today Protestants number over 18%.

In 1980 South Korea had only 93 missionaries abroad. By 2009 it was over 20,000. South Korea provides the second largest number of missionaries to the rest of the world, which is second only to the U.S.

I was face to face that day with a believer who wanted to make sure I believed. I was "witnessed" to. I was "outreached". I was her mission project. I didn't mind, other than the lingering and challenging questions that this encounter spawned. I was absolutely captivated by her passion, emotion and conviction.

How am I doing with my zeal and passion for the un-churched, unsaved and lost of the world?

Romans 1:16 - *For I am not ashamed of the gospel of Christ: for it is the power of God unto salvation to every one that believeth; to the Jew first, and also to the Greek.*

Fear and Shame

Having been bitten by a dog when I was 10 years old, the experience placed me on a path of not trusting or appreciating dogs. I get sweaty palms and my heart rate increases when I'm in a situation with a dog. The threat can be real or it can be imagined, but fear takes the upper hand.

Hearing people say, "He's never bitten anyone", or "She really likes people", or "His tail is wagging which means he likes you", doesn't make any difference. Something happened in my brain when I was 10 years old. Memories were permanently etched.

FEAR - Jeni and I went to pick up a part from a man who lived on a farm and had his office in his barn. As I drove in the driveway, my first thought was wondering if this man had a dog (heart rate increase #1). I looked in his yard and saw a dog house (heart rate increase #2). I didn't see a dog tied or in the dog house, which meant he was loose (heart rate increase #3). I looked at Jeni and she smiled at me.

SHAME - She understood and kindly asked, "Do you want me to go in the office and ask if they have a dog?" Shamefully, I said "Yes, if you would?" She got out without hesitation and found out there was no dog, which of course paved the way for my grateful but ashamed entrance to the office.

Isn't it amazing how fear can paralyze us? Why is it that it can turn to shame so quickly? When we don't have control of our fears, we are ashamed of our weakness and lack of courage.

All of it prompts me to think of my Jesus in the Garden of Gethsemane. Luke 22:42 shares a conversation Jesus had with His Father. He said *"Father, if thou be willing, remove this cup from me: nevertheless not my will, but thine, be done."* What a great example of love and obedience overcoming fear. Are we willing to trust and do God's will in spite of our fears?

Fear in High Gear

Truth for Today – Romans 8:38-39

Pine Lake. Several acres of summer-time swimming recreation. A beach, slides, hot dogs, water tag, diving boards and the tower. Ah, the tower. Forty feet of opportunity.

I remember sitting on the narrow path leading to the deep part of Pine Lake where the tower was located and watching those who jumped from the tower. There were four platforms. One at ten feet, at twenty, thirty and forty feet.

Finally gathering enough courage, I went to the edge of the lowest platform and jumped. Then up the ladder to the twenty foot edge. With my heart racing I jumped. Then up again to the third platform. Shivering with fear more than the cool air, I leaped.

Then up the narrow ladder to the top. The top platform was very small. Mustering the courage to stand up, I immediately dropped to my knees. I couldn't jump. I backed down the ladder in shame. Over the next two or three years I went to the top again and again, but was never able to make the leap.

Today, fifty years later, not jumping from the forty foot level is a regret I have. A missed opportunity. An opportunity that fear had victory over.

How many times in life do we let fear have victory over opportunity? I think often of our Jesus in the Garden of Gethsemane asking His Father to remove the opportunity of the cross. Did Jesus experience fear? I believe He did. Fear is not a sin, but letting fear succeed over God's commands or opportunities can become sin. Jesus overcame the fear He was experiencing. The Bible tells us...

- Isaiah 43:2-3 - *When thou passest through the waters, I will be with thee; and through the rivers, they shall not overflow thee: when thou walkest through the fire, thou shalt not be burned; neither shall the flame kindle upon thee. ³ For I am the LORD thy God, the Holy One of Israel, thy Saviour...*
- Isaiah 46:4 - *And even to your old age I am he; and even to hoar hairs will I carry you: I have made, and I will bear; even I will carry, and will deliver you.*

Feasting

Truth for Today – Isaiah 25:6

At the Big Texan Steak Restaurant in Amarillo, Texas, customers can order the 72 ounce (4.5 pound) steak with shrimp cocktail, baked potato, salad and roll. If the patron is able to finish the entire meal in one hour, the meal is free.

Molly Schuyler set a new record by eating one meal in a little under five minutes and then ate a second meal in ten minutes. For a 120 pound lady, nine pounds of steak and all the accompaniments was quite the accomplishment. Reading about Molly intrigued me, so I began reading of other feasters:

- Jamie who ate 60 Krispy Kreme donuts in 9.2 minutes
- Jonathan consumed 40 Chicken McNuggets in 2.3 minutes
- Takeru ingested 25 yellow marshmallow Peeps in 30 seconds
- Oleg ate four 32 ounce bowls of mayonnaise in eight minutes
- Dick swallowed six pounds of Spam in 12 minutes
- A record-holder for eating 46 ears of sweet corn in 12 minutes
- Patrick gorged himself on 266 jalapeño peppers in 15 minutes
- Tim ate 11.81 pounds of burritos in 10 minutes

Interestingly, most records are followed by the disclaimer that *"Speed eating should only be tried by professionals."* I think that gives new meaning to the word professional.

On another note, elephants eat up to 600 pounds of food per day and consume about 50 gallons of water. That's volume!

The Bible speaks about feeding on the Word of God. Other verses speak about God preparing a feast for us. Vivid imagery...

- Isaiah 25:6 - *And in this mountain shall the LORD of hosts make unto all people a feast of fat things, a feast of wines on the lees, of fat things full of marrow, of wines on the lees well refined.*
- John 6:51 - *I am the living bread which came down from heaven: if any man eat of this bread, he shall live forever: and the bread that I will give is my flesh, which I will give for the life of the world.*
- Jeremiah 3:15 - *And I will give you pastors according to mine heart, which shall feed you with knowledge and understanding.*

Fickle Followers

Eggs, sandwiches and tomatoes flew through the air and pelted the head of state. It wasn't the Middle Ages, but rather, the 21st century.

The president of a European country was standing on the podium with several other neighboring country presidents to commemorate an important anniversary for his regime.

The security forces brought out large umbrellas to protect the heads of state from the thrown objects. For one, it was too late, as an egg hit one of the visiting presidents on the head. One would imagine that the visiting presidents would think twice about accepting another invitation to this particular neighboring country.

The news article caused me to reflect on how it went for our Lord Jesus 2000 years ago. There was no leader more perfect, righteous, pure, holy, servant-minded, loving and sacrificial than our Savior.

Yet, there has probably been no other leader treated as horribly as Jesus. He was tortured, rejected, deserted, forsaken, derided, ridiculed, scorned, unjustly accused and finally murdered. He had no advocate, in fact His own Father rejected Him.

It is impossible to comprehend the love, obedience, passion, vision and principles that gave Jesus the courage and resolve to carry out His unique mission. How do we describe it? One song by the *Cathedrals* and written by *Lillenas/Goss*, helps me grasp it:

Wonderful grace of Jesus, greater than all my sin; How shall my tongue describe it? Where shall its praise begin? Taking away my burden, setting my spirit free, for the wonderful grace of Jesus reaches me.

Wonderful the matchless grace of Jesus. Deeper than the mighty rolling sea. Higher than the mountains, sparkling like a fountain; all sufficient grace for even me. Broader than the scope of my transgressions. Greater far than all my sin and shame... O magnify the precious name of Jesus - Praise His name!

Finally there is Freedom

Truth for Today – 1 John 4:10

Joe had been serving a four year sentence for larceny. At an opportune time in September of 1976, he escaped from his prisons work-farm. A day later a mother and daughter in the area were stabbed to death and an informant identified Joe as the killer.

Joe was convicted on two counts of second-degree murder and was sentenced to life in prison. Though he pleaded innocence throughout the years, there was no advocate. Then a lawyer decided to pursue his case. In 2012, a small packet of hair from the crime scene was found by court clerks on a high shelf in an evidence vault. The hair had been found on the victim's body and purportedly belonged to Joe.

DNA testing for evidence did not begin until 1986, ten years after his arrest. DNA testing of the newly found hair proved it was not Joe's. His fingerprints, DNA and hair had not been present at the crime site. The informant recanted his trial testimony.

Joe was freed from prison in January, 2015, after serving 39 years for a crime he had not committed. If it had not been for a lawyer who believed in Joe; the newly found hair; the technology of DNA testing; and a recanted testimony, Joe would have served out the rest of his life in prison.

The story reminds me once again of how much God cares about our soul, our life on earth and our eternal life with Him in Heaven. He goes above and beyond to take care of His family.

- Jeremiah 29:11 - *For I know the thoughts that I think toward you, saith the Lord; thoughts of peace, and not of evil, to give you an expected end.*
- Romans 5:8 - *But God commendeth his love toward us, in that, while we were yet sinners, Christ died for us.*
- John 3:16 - *For God so loved the world, that he gave his only begotten Son, that whosoever believeth in him should not perish, but have everlasting life.*
- 1 John 4:10 - *Herein is love, not that we loved God, but that he loved us, and sent his Son to be the propitiation for our sins.*

Fire Breathing Hornets

Truth for Today – Romans 8:28

It was a cold winter Sunday morning and the heat coming from the furnace duct in our kitchen floor felt great, until I stepped on it with my bare foot. It was very hot. Getting down on hands and knees, I felt it with my hand and it was almost too hot to touch.

I went to the basement to check my electric furnace and again, the ducts were incredibly hot. Then I smelled a whiff of smoke and the Sunday morning turned into a nightmare. In a panic, I called the fire department knowing that the high heat could trigger a fire at any moment. They arrived and determined that a furnace element had failed to turn off and was continuing to produce heat.

A tragedy had been diverted. A furnace repairman arrived to correct the problem. Then I noticed him swat at something, then again, and again. We noticed that there were several hornets harassing him.

Finally we opened a small door in the furnace room that led to an adjacent crawl space. There we noticed a huge hornets nest just five feet away. The crawl space was filled with angry hornets. The smoke from the furnace problem had stirred the hornets just as if we had poked a stick in their nest.

We dealt with the hornets, but I've often wondered what would have happened if the furnace had not malfunctioned? Having a hornets nest in our home along with nine active and vulnerable grandkids didn't seem like a good combination. Though the furnace problem had been a huge annoyance on that winter morning, I believe it was a blessing in learning about the hornets' nest.

Again, it was a lesson to me, to not be overly exasperated at situations in life. Often there are lessons to be learned from even the most tragic and trauma filled situations. It was a reminder that God is always able to bring good from bad.

Lord, help me to see the good in bad situations and to remember that you are the God of the universe.

First Impression

Truth for Today – Ephesians 4:29-32

Exiting the airport terminal in a large city, I was waiting for a shuttle to take me to my rental car. Standing in the median near me was a man who was incredibly angry. He was yelling at a taxi driver about having to wait too long for a ride. Dozens of onlookers were watching and simultaneously gathering impressions about the man.

After a few minutes of the tirade, a stranger standing beside me said, "That's so sad and I am so disappointed in him." I asked him if he knew him and he said, "Yes, most of us know who he is." He then gave me the man's name and I recognized it as well.

The angry man was a famous NFL football player who had played in the Pro Bowl more than once. The stranger beside me said, "It's disappointing to see a national celebrity act like that."

Many people that day shook their heads in disgust as a meek taxi driver took an incredible amount of verbal abuse from what appeared to be a bully.

There could have been a thousand reasons that day as to why he acted the way he did. But, there was only one first impression and I carry the memory yet today.

How many first impressions have I made over the years? How many were favorable and how many were not? Are there some I'd like to do over? We have our good days and we have our bad, but God does give us principles by which to live. Following those principles will certainly give us opportunities to make, develop and maintain good relationships with others.

- Ephesians 4:29-32 - *Let no corrupt communication proceed out of your mouth, but that which is good to the use of edifying, that it may minister grace unto the hearers. And grieve not the Holy Spirit of God, whereby ye are sealed unto the day of redemption. Let all bitterness, and wrath, and anger, and clamor, and evil speaking, be put away from you, with all malice: And be ye kind one to another, tenderhearted, forgiving one another, even as God for Christ's sake hath forgiven you.*

- Luke 6:31 - *And as ye would that men should do to you, do ye also to them likewise.*

First Impressions (again)

Truth for Today – Colossians 3

While in Gatlinburg, Tennessee we visited the Ripley's Believe It Or Not Odditorium. We viewed many exhibits of odd and unusual people, places and things. I learned later that I had unknowingly been one of those odd exhibits.

At one of the displays were photos of a woman who could do very unusual things with her tongue such as rolling it in a circle, bending it, flattening it, and other shapes. There was a large mirror at the display with the encouragement for viewers to try out their tongue acrobatics. I tried and tried, but failed in achieving anything spectacular.

Continuing on through the displays we arrived at a window. Looking through the window we were face to face with people trying to do the tongue shapes. Then we realized that what we had thought was a mirror earlier, was in fact a one-way window for others to discreetly observe those at the tongue display. My tongue distortions were obviously observed by many. I can't imagine their first impression of me.

As people we rarely have the opportunity to undo a first impression. We are measured by what people see us do, our appearance and by what we say. The Bible gives us direction on how to conduct ourselves.

- Ephesians 4:29 - *Let no corrupt communication proceed out of your mouth, but that which is good to the use of edifying, that it may minister grace unto the hearers.*
- Colossians 3:17 - *And whatsoever ye do in word or deed, do all in the name of the Lord Jesus, giving thanks to God and the Father by him.*
- Ephesians 4:26 - *Be ye angry, and sin not: let not the sun go down upon your wrath.*
- Colossians 3:8 - *But now ye also put off all these; anger, wrath, malice, blasphemy, filthy communication out of your mouth.*

Lord, help me to look, act and speak in a
manner that mirrors the life of Jesus.

Fixing the Problem

***Truth for Today** – Matthew 27

It was a cold and rainy night. Needing to go to a meeting, I didn't relish the thought of leaving my new bride and a warm home. We had a 1964 Chevrolet Corvair at the time so I climbed in and cranked the heat on high. With a rear engine that was air cooled, getting warm air took a long time and it was minimal.

After a mile of driving in the cold rain, with a fogged up windshield and cold feet, I thought that there must be a heater vent closed. So, while driving, I reached under the dash and searched for a vent.

Suddenly, my finger was pulled under the dash. I pulled my hand out and noticed that my middle finger was bleeding and the fingernail was damaged. I had stuck my finger into the rotating linkage of the windshield wiper motor.

The fingernail was still attached at the end of my finger, but the rear of the nail had been ripped up and out of my cuticle and skin. So I headed to the emergency room. In pain, I was finally taken to an examination room. The doctor inspected it and asked the nurse to get a surgical kit. Laying out ugly looking scalpels, I knew that he was going to slice under the nail to remove it from the finger. At that point, I decided to grab the nail and pull it off. Of course it hurt, but using a scalpel seemed incredibly more painful.

The accident reminds me of the realities of life. Many times we create problems, pain or trauma in our lives due to poor choices. Sadly, the consequences to our choices create more pain. Often the cures to our mistakes are even more painful. Yet, if we do not deal with the original issue, the pain will be never ending and more damaging. We cannot ignore problems. Injuries escalate to infections. Infections not treated can progress to gangrene and often to amputations.

Whether our injury is emotional, physical, relational, financial or spiritual, steps need to be taken to rectify the problem.

Jesus underwent immense pain to take care of a universal problem called sin. He faced it and fixed it. No one would ever accuse Him of merely treating a symptom! He fixed the problem.

Floods on Dry Ground

Truth for Today – John 4

The ten year old Haitian girl was small, tired and busy. Several times a day she would carry two plastic jugs of water from a small stream to her home. There are rivers and creeks but little infrastructure to get the water from its source to a home. So, she does what thousands of other children do. She carries water.

One of the dreams of all villagers and their kids is to have their own community well and pump. When it happens, it is difficult to describe their joy and happiness as the lives of villagers are changed in a huge way.

At Torbeck, in southwest Haiti, in 2008 we had a water well drilled. When the drillers hit water, 500 gallons per minute started gushing from the artesian water supply underground. It flooded the area.

300 gallons per minute gushed out of the 6" diameter casing while another 200 gallons per minute forced itself up the outside of the casing. A total of 500 gallons per minute. Water? We had plenty of water! No more trips to the river for the kids!

Finally after days of hard work, it was capped and controlled, but not before flooding a field and a few homes. When I see the well I think of *Isaiah 44:3 - For I will pour water upon him that is thirsty, and floods upon the dry ground...* isn't it just like our God to take care of our needs in exceedingly abundant ways?

Focus on Me

Truth for Today – Hebrews 12:2

The Merriam Webster Dictionary defines "focus" as – *The subject on which people's attention is focused.*

I remember vividly the time when Rick and I had an encounter with a grizzly bear and her two cubs in the Wyoming Teton's. Full of fear, I didn't move my eyes from her. I was intently focused.

Kindergarten and elementary school teachers have their work cut out for them when children return from summer vacation. Helping kids develop and maintain their focus, is the focus of the teachers.

The Alpine Swift is a small bird that lives in Europe in the summer, and then winters in Africa. Their migration is over thousands of miles. In 2011, small electronic sensors were attached to several Swifts. The scientists learned something astounding. For over 200 days, the birds stayed in the air! Never landing, always eating what God provided in the sky, and obviously sleeping while flying.

The Bar-Tailed Godwit is another record setting bird. A plump shorebird with a curved beak has been known to fly as many as 7,242 miles non-stop in their annual migration from Alaska to New Zealand.

Focus. The birds are focused on one thing – their destination. If they lost that focus and explored islands, they would arrive late and alone, if at all.

The Bible shares thoughts about our need as believers to focus. We are taught many times to "keep the main thing, the main thing."

- Matthew 6:19-21 - *Lay not up for yourselves treasures upon earth, where moth and rust doth corrupt, and where thieves break through and steal: But lay up for yourselves treasures in heaven, where neither moth nor rust doth corrupt, and where thieves do not break through nor steal: For where your treasure is, there will your heart be also.*

- Hebrews 12:2 - *Looking unto Jesus the author and finisher of our faith; who for the joy that was set before him endured the cross, despising the shame, and is set down at the right hand of the throne of God.*

Follow the Leader

***Truth for Today** – 1 Peter 1:18-19

He loved his pets. His two pet goats brought him relaxation and joy as he watched them frolic, run and jump in his front yard. However, they became a bit of a nuisance as he let them eat the flowers from his wife's garden. But it got worse when he let them wonder through his house. At times they would chew on the furniture which created conflict between Abe and his wife.

When he passed away, Mrs. Lincoln gave Abe's goats away and the White House returned to normal.

Warren G. Harding was an avid poker player and it is reputed that he gambled away the entire White House china set in a poker game.

Andrew Jackson faced a dilemma. A man accused him of cheating on a bet for a horse race and then insulted his wife Rachel. In 1806, the duel was fought and Andrew killed the insulter.

As Vice President, Andrew Johnson became 17th president of the United States when President Lincoln was killed in office. However, when he was sworn in as Vice President in Lincoln's second term, Andrew was drunk. Hungover from a night of drinking, his acceptance speech was slurred and incoherent, but the swearing in was completed.

The list could go on and on of important people doing strange, bizarre, inappropriate things which were unbecoming to their role as a leader. But, as Christians we have a perfect, spotless and blameless man to follow, whose name was Jesus.

- 2 Corinthians 5:21 - *For he hath made him to be sin for us, who knew no sin; that we might be made the righteousness of God in him.*
- 1 Peter 1:18-19 - *Forasmuch as ye know that ye were not redeemed with corruptible things, as silver and gold, from your vain conversation received by tradition from your fathers; But with the precious blood of Christ, as of a lamb without blemish and without spot.*

Foolish Move

Truth for Today – Romans 12:1-2

Walking along a lake I noticed a 14" turtle on a round concrete culvert. All four legs were up and extended and I wondered if it was stuck. It looked at me as if searching for a rescue.

Watching the turtle, it made me think about my human nature and my relationship with God. How many times do I get into a circumstance or predicament that creates problems for myself?

There is a Biblical principle called "Sowing and Reaping". Other variations would speak about actions and consequences; the pebble and ripple effect; actions and reactions; and cause and effect.

The principle is that our actions create consequences. If those actions create positive and good change, we consider it a wise action. If, however the actions produce negativity, hurt, damage or evil, we consider the action sinful or foolish.

With a free-thinking mind we must take responsibility for our actions, reactions or lack thereof. The Bible lays out the principle in a variety of verses:

- Galatians 6:7-8 - *Be not deceived; God is not mocked: for whatsoever a man soweth, that shall he also reap. For he that soweth to his flesh shall of the flesh reap corruption; but he that soweth to the Spirit shall of the Spirit reap life everlasting.*
- Hosea 10:13 - *Ye have plowed wickedness, ye have reaped iniquity; ye have eaten the fruit of lies.*
- Proverbs 22:6 - *Train up a child in the way he should go: and when he is old, he will not depart from it.*
- Romans 12:1-2 - *I beseech you therefore, brethren, by the mercies of God, that ye present your bodies a living sacrifice, holy, acceptable unto God, which is your reasonable service. And be not conformed to this world: but be ye transformed by the renewing of your mind, that ye may prove what is that good, and acceptable, and perfect, will of God.*

Fool's Gold

Truth for Today – 2 Chronicles 9

Solomon seemingly had it all. Wisdom, adoration of men and women, power, prestige, horses, armies and wealth. People would visit his kingdom to simply view the extravagance, wealth and beauty.

In 2 Chronicles 3 we read about the massive amounts of gold that lavishly decorated Solomon's temple. In chapter 9, we read about the 666 talents of gold that annually came to Solomon's kingdom and was used to make drinking cups, shields, a throne, footstool and more.

I am amazed trying to visualize 666 talents of gold coming to him. Imagine… 60,000 lbs. of gold equating to 30 tons every year!

On another note, I've thought about how the twenty-four elders in Revelation 4 threw their golden crowns on the ground when they found themselves in the presence of God. Of course, the elders were in the company of God Himself. But, additionally imagine a 20 lb. golden crown on your head as you tried to bow before the King. I think I would remove my crown as well.

Beyond that, the elders were kneeling on gold! Streets were paved with it. The extravagant abundance of the gold would certainly make gold less valuable, wouldn't it?

I believe there will be trillions of surprises when we arrive in Heaven. But the two that I cannot wait to comprehend are the high value that God places on earthly things we consider mundane and common; and the low value He will place on things we consider valuable on earth.

On earth, the people who are considered the least may have the highest seats in Heaven. Consider the story of the rich man and the beggar Lazarus in Luke 16.

On the other hand, consider a cubic inch of earthly gold being worth $13,650 while in Heaven we scuff it up with our sandals!

Isaiah 55:9 sums it up well - *For as the heavens are higher than the earth, so are my ways higher than your ways, and my thoughts than your thoughts.*

Forces of Evil

Truth for Today – Isaiah 46:9-10

I'm not a computer geek nor do I even remotely resemble a techie expert. However, I sincerely appreciate the technology associated with computers and various software programs. In many cases my relationship with computers is a Love/Hate relationship.

For instance, I recently sent an email to a co-worker asking her to "review my attached document." When I hit the send button, a pop-up appeared saying, "Did you forget to attach your document?" My computer was right, I had forgotten. How in the world did my computer know that? That's part of the "love" relationship.

Another component of my software program is the auto-correct feature. It is able to correct spelling errors as well as grammatical problems. I love it! Well, at least most of the time. But the auto-correct feature is now the subject of the "hate" part of today's topic.

Why is it, when I type "God" my computer program tries to correct it to "good"? Is there some sort of satanic over-ride in my computer? Why does my computer have the right to downgrade God to a mere "good"? I resent it when my computer does that. God is good, but the term good is only 1 gadzillionith of who God is. He is God!

Why is it, when I type the word "satan", my computer insists on capitalizing it? I hate it when that happens. satan is not worthy of a capital S. Again, is there a dark force incorporated into my software program? I think not, but I resent it when my computer tries to minimize God and maximize satan!

The world we live in is certainly trying to turn good into bad and bad into good. I'm thankful for the Holy Spirit who is cautioning me along the way to be wary and skeptical of turning black and white into grey.

Isaiah 46:9-10 - *Remember the former things of old: for I am God, and there is none else; I am God, and there is none like me. Declaring the end from the beginning, and from ancient times the things that are not yet done, saying, My counsel shall stand, and I will do all my pleasure.*

Fortuitous

***Truth for Today** – Psalm 23*

The dictionary definition for "fortuitous" is, *"happening by chance; having good luck; synonymous with unexpected, unanticipated, unpredictable, unforeseen, coincidental, random, accidental, etc."*

As followers of Jesus Christ, we see miracles and Gods providence, instead of seeing them as merely good luck and coincidence. I never tire of hearing the stories of how God is working in someone's life. I will share a personal illustration.

I was in need of a particular part for a repair. I went to a Walmart without success in finding what I needed. On my way home I drove past a mega sized hardware store and felt the urge to check there, though I knew it wasn't their specialty.

As I parked my car, I sensed an urge that I needed to move and park in a different spot, so I moved. As I got out, I noticed that I had now parked almost beside another car with a couple, whom I knew, in it. I waved at them and went in the store.

Fifteen minutes later, I walked out and the couple was still there. They got out of the car and approached me. They said, "This may sound weird, but we had been praying in our car that if we saw you here, we would take that as an indication that God wanted us to talk to you. Then you drove in, parked and then re-parked. We are having marriage difficulties and would like help to escape the rut we're in."

I had not prayed that day for them, nor had I prayed that I would be in the right place at the right time to meet someone's desperate needs. I was unaware of their difficulties. But there was an urge to drive into that parking lot and an impulse to re-park.

Fortuitous? Coincidental? Accidental? Or, is there a Creator who cares about His creation enough to have their backs? That day increased my faith, their faith and it is easy to say that God takes personal interest in all of our lives.

Matthew 6:33 - *But seek ye first the kingdom of God, and his righteousness; and all these things shall be added unto you.*

Foxholes

Dad was 24 years old and 8000 miles from home, which was 120 acres of farm ground that had pigs, cows, chickens, corn and beans. But on this day in January of 1945, his home was a foxhole with volcanic rock in the Luzon, Philippines.

The foxhole was necessary as the American forces were seeking to take Luzon back from the Japanese army. The volcanic dirt and rock foxhole was hard and rough, but it was his new, temporary home and at least out of the way from the bullets flying over the G.I.'s heads.

Night-time came, along with the blackness, fear and sounds. The warning had been issued. "Stay in the foxholes, no matter what, as the Japanese are trying to infiltrate the area."

Then, dad heard a noise and felt something brush his body. He knew that he would be spending this particular night with a large rat that had landed in his tiny foxhole.

Fear is an emotion that grips the heart, stomach and minds. It can come and go quickly as the threat leaves, or it can stay for hours. I cannot imagine the fear that gripped our American young heroes during their many wars for our country, over the course of the last century. They were and are in strange and lonely places, far from family, in imminent danger, facing life and death. How do they cope?

I know that my dad was a strong and faithful believer. I know where his strength came from and he was my hero.

Isaiah is my favorite encourager. The chapters from Isaiah 40 to 49 are full of encouragement which God shares with us. I keep many verses close at hand and in my head and heart. Here are two...

Isaiah 41:10 - *Fear thou not; for I am with thee: be not dismayed; for I am thy God: I will strengthen thee; yea, I will help thee; yea, I will uphold thee with the right hand of my righteousness.*

Isaiah 43:2-3 - *When thou passest through the waters, I will be with thee; and through the rivers, they shall not overflow thee: when thou walkest through the fire, thou shalt not be burned; neither shall the flame kindle upon thee. For I am the LORD thy God, the Holy One of Israel, thy Saviour...*

Free but Not Cheap

Truth for Today – John 3

There is something in our human nature about getting something for free. It can create barbaric actions in the best of men. We have seen the demolition of stores during rioting as men, women and children carry off products through the haze and smoke. I have been guilty of desperately trying to guess the number of jelly beans in a jar to win something I didn't even want to eat. In fact, I was in line with children trying to do the same thing. I am embarrassed.

I have seen mobs of women trying to get to the front of the line in a grocery store to win free kitchen products. It was ugly!

In 1889, two million acres of government property (formerly Indian land) were opened up for western expansion and settlement.

It was stipulated that at 12:00 noon on April 22, 1889, settlers would line up to race to the territory to claim it as their own. They could claim up to 160 acres and could retain it, if they improved it.

One can only imagine what it looked like as 50,000 people lined up to race when the gun went off. Men and women were on horses, in buckboards and Conestoga wagons, and on foot.

The bugle sounded. Men on fast horses were soon to the horizon only to arrive at their spot to see a wagon pulled by slow oxen already staking out their 160 acres. Fighting began as people realized many people had hid in the adjoining woods the night before to arrive early. The lawsuits and court cases went on and on.

This historical example makes me thankful that God says His salvation is free, but not cheap, to anyone who wants to follow Him.

- 1 Timothy 2:4 – *(God) who will have all men to be saved, and to come unto the knowledge of the truth.*
- John 3:16 - *For God so loved the world, that he gave his only begotten Son, that whosoever believeth in him should not perish, but have everlasting life.*
- Ephesians 2:8 - *For by grace are ye saved through faith; and that not of yourselves: it is the gift of God.*

Freedom or Bondage

Truth for Today – John 8:36

Clarence had a full life ahead of him in 1967 when he stole $200 at age 18. Apprehended and sentenced to eight years in prison, he knew he couldn't do the time. So, he escaped prison two times over the next several years with additional time being added every time he was captured.

Then in 1976 he escaped for the third time and was never found. He disappeared into a mass of humanity. Without a social security number or driver's license, he was an unknown.

Then, in 2015 at the age of 66 and having experienced 39 years of so-called freedom, his health deteriorated. Unable to receive any health care, he decided to surrender. He desperately wanted to go back to prison to receive medical care, so he made the call. When the sheriff arrived, Clarence wept with joy and relief.

Freedom is not freedom if we are still tied to our bondage. The story of Clarence reminds me of the freedom we can have in Christ. Unfortunately, when we are bound to our past with guilt, unconfessed sin, or a legalistic mindset, freedom is lost.

True freedom in Christ is the *abundant life* we read about in John 10:10. God wants us to experience peace, joy, happiness and freedom. Are we still tied to our past? Are we carrying the baggage of guilt and sin?

Jesus said in John 8:36 - *If the Son therefore shall make you free, ye shall be free indeed!*

Friend or Foe

Truth for Today – Numbers 22

Haiti has two rainy seasons per year and I was in the middle of one of them. Normally I'm at a place where I can stay moderately dry and comfortable, but on this trip four of us were on mule-back in the mountains.

The rain came and went, then came again and each time left more water and mud on the mountain trail. We were trying to make our way to a mountain top to visit eight orphans in need of a home.

Under the mud were the never-ending slabs of unseen rock. The mules at times would lose their footing and mule and rider would hit the mud. Finally reaching our destination at nightfall, we wearily climbed off the mules. In the morning, we resumed our travel down the mountain. After two days on the mule, I didn't know which was worse. The torturous time on the back of the mule doing damage to my back-side, or the walking and sloshing in the mud when I got off. So, it was a continuous time of riding and walking, riding and walking.

Finally we reached the valley and a rock trail. I knew that I had to get off the mule. My backside simply couldn't take it anymore. I took my foot out of the saddle stirrup and jumped off. Unfortunately in my haste to exit my mule, I failed to take my other foot out of the stirrup. I hit the rock trail with the full free-fall force of 200 lbs.

With my hands and a knee bleeding, I ungracefully with help, got unhitched from my mule and stirrup. Needless to say, I walked the rest of the way. I was pure entertainment that day to my Haitian friends.

The experience caused me to reflect on my life. How many times do I seek out things that will bring me comfort and ease, when later I find out that the option had its downsides as well?

How many times do I try to get out of a painful situation only to find that in my haste I made matters worse?

How often do I get tangled in things that I need help in getting untangled?

My life has plenty of illustrations of mistakes I've made that I wish I could undo. Balaam had his donkey as a teacher and I had my mule.

From the Frying Pan into the Fire

Truth for Today – 1 Corinthians 15:19

The southwest coast and tip of England is ruggedly beautiful. Towering cliffs drop to a rough Celtic Sea bordering the North Atlantic Ocean. Brock at 14 years old loved the outdoors and was enjoying the view atop the 100' cliff, along with his 16 year old brother.

Then, suddenly Brock's foot slipped on moss and he tumbled over the edge. He hit outcroppings and rocks in his descent to the bottom. When he finally landed on a ledge close to the water, he was severely bruised and had a fractured pelvis.

But he knew that those were his least worries as the tide was coming in and he would soon be covered by the cold sea if he remained where he was. He began his difficult climb to safety while his 16 year old brother started the dangerous descent to reach his injured sibling.

As Brock, tired and injured, grasped rocks and crags to pull himself slowly upward, he felt a sharp pain in his hand. He realized that he'd been bitten by England's only poisonous snake, an adder!

Brock's brother went for help while Brock's arm swelled to three times its normal size. He was rescued from the cliff and airlifted to a hospital where he received the anti-venom needed to save him.

As I thought of his ordeal I thought of the old adage, "He jumped from the frying pan into the fire." Brock had survived the 100' fall, escaped the incoming tide and potential drowning, and then was ultimately bitten by England's only poisonous snake. That's a lot of story-telling Brock will be able to tell his grand-children.

As I think of what God saved me from through the death, burial and resurrection of His Son Jesus, I am humbled. Without Christ as our Savior, we would be in really difficult, dangerous and eternally condemning tight spots. The Apostle Paul recognized it as well, as he states in 1 Corinthians 15:19 - *If in this life only we have hope in Christ, we are of all men most miserable.*

From the Inside Out

Truth for Today – Genesis 3

The nose-horned viper is a venomous snake which lives in Europe. Growing to a length of approximately 36", they eat rodents and insects. In the past, they've been known to cause human deaths on a regular basis, though that is waning due to anti-venoms now available.

Biologists found an 8" dead viper in Macedonia. The snake had attacked, bitten and swallowed a 6" centipede. The centipede immediately began eating the inside of the snake in its desperation to escape. When found, the snake was dead from being eaten internally. The centipede died with his head outside the tail end of the snake, having eaten his way through the viper and then died from the venom.

We sometimes consider the bizarreness of how the animal kingdom operates. It is almost unbelievable to hear of circumstances where one animal eats another causing its own death. Yet, as another illustration, a 13' Burmese python was found dead with a 6' alligator sticking out of its stomach. How can it be that an animal would ingest something that could actually kill it?

Then I think of the spiritual analogy. Are we as human beings immune from those animal kingdom traits? Are there products we put inside our body that cause damage? Are there things we look at or listen to that can do damage to our physical, emotional, mental, relational and spiritual beings?

The types of food we eat and the volumes of it can do great damage to our physiology. Pornography has a huge effect on the emotional, spiritual, relational and physical components which God has created within us. Alcohol, narcotics, nicotine and caffeine all have their effects. We are warned that certain products can affect our blood pressure, our cholesterol levels, create heart or liver disease, yet we continue because it tastes good, looks good and we cannot resist the temptation. Are we any different than the animals?

Genesis 3:6 - *And when the woman saw that the tree was good for food, and that it was pleasant to the eyes, and a tree to be desired to make one wise, she took of the fruit thereof, and did eat, and gave also unto her husband with her; and he did eat.*

Front of the Line

Truth for Today – Matthew 27:1-50

Jeni and I were enjoying the beauty of Niagara Falls and Horseshoe Falls. It is difficult to find the words to describe the phenomenal power and magnificence of the Niagara River rushing over the cliffs to the depths below. The thunder of the water, the mist, and the rainbows swirling in the spray are beautiful.

We decided that if seeing it at ground level was great, what would it be like from the top of the 775' Skylon Tower? So, we purchased our tickets for the 52 second ride in the Yellow Bug Elevator.

As we were standing in line for the elevator, I thought about two things. First, this is a large group getting on the elevator. Second, based on past experience at other tower observation decks, you probably enter in the front side of the elevator and exit out the back.

So, if you're the first one on the elevator, you're the first one off. I mentioned it to Jeni who reluctantly but submissively gave in to my self-serving logic. So casually I wormed my way to the front of the large group and we were the first ones on.

A quick 52 seconds later the elevator stopped and I quickly saw that the entrance door would also be the exit door. We were the first ones in and the last ones out. Jeni just looked at me and smiled. She didn't need to say anything, I knew what that smile was about.

Sadly, there is a human default and nature in me that is selfish. Unfortunately, though I know it to be sin, sometimes it rises above logic, reason, the Bible and has its own way. The symptoms are obvious: A desire to be first; a craving to get the best; a passion to treat myself better than others. Sad but true.

The Bible speaks about it in several places. Philippians 2:3-5 – *Let nothing be done through strife or vain glory; but in lowliness of mind let each esteem other better than themselves. Look not every man on his own things, but every man also on the things of others. Let this mind be in you, which was also in Christ Jesus.*

James 2:8 – *If ye fulfill the royal law according to the scripture, thou shalt love thy neighbor as thyself, ye do well.*

Clearly, putting myself first and getting the best is contrary to scripture and certainly not the example of Jesus.

Front Row Seat for a Battle

Truth for Today – Revelation 21:10-21

I got to the pond and sat on the pier. The water was clear and so still there was barely a ripple. I looked over the edge of the pier and noticed a small glistening speck about the size of pencil lead, on top of the water. Then I saw several more.

Suddenly a water-bug about the size of a fly, hydro foiled towards the speck! As the bug approached and bumped into the spot, the spot jumped an inch into the air away from the water-bug. I was astonished that the spot was alive and that it could actually jump!

The world around me stopped momentarily as I observed the marvel taking place in front of me, as life and death was unfolding! The chase continued within a square foot arena until the living speck disappeared into what it must have perceived as the cavernous jaws of that tiny water bug. I watched enthralled as more and more spots jumped evasively until they became breakfast.

It was then I heard a splash and saw the flash of a bluegill as the water bug became his breakfast. I sat enthralled about the cycle of life, and was in awe as to how God takes care of all His creation.

The ripples of that splashing bluegill started to spread over the pond. The ripples just kept going and going and going...

It takes effort to slow down enough to watch God at work. The busyness of life or the entertainment it invents is certainly second rate, compared to the grandeurs that God provides.

How often do we take time to meditate, watch, listen or relax? Can we leave our cellphones and other gadgets behind and see what God has as a surprise for us?

Psalm 46:10 - *Be still, and know that I am God...*

Get the Roots

***Truth for Today** – Luke 6:22-49*

When I was twelve years old, I worked for my uncle during the summer months. My job was to hoe the weeds and thistles out of his acres and acres of soybeans and corn. One day, he took me to a remote field and gave me a hoe and the instructions for the day. "Make sure when you hoe the Canadian Thistles you get the roots. Otherwise they'll grow right back."

It was a hot, hot day and an invitation to go swimming seemed like a really good thing to accept. I hurried through the field, not paying much attention to thistle roots. It soon became easier to cut those ugly brutes off at ground level than it was to get the roots. After all, from the road, who would know whether the roots were gone or not? My work was finished so I went swimming.

A week later, my uncle picked me up to hoe another field. On the way, he took me to that earlier field and pointed to a thriving batch of Canadian Thistles. I received another lesson that day about "roots"! Those thistles had grown back in all their glory! My lack of dedication and motivation had found me out and I had an opportunity to do it all over again. Life lesson - *Get the roots.*

That lesson applies to many of life's experiences. Sometimes it's easier to gloss over a hurt than it is to deal with it. We can learn "denial" as an unhealthy coping mechanism. Often "denials" come back to haunt us later.

A hurt left uncared for can easily turn to resentment, bitterness and hatred. Though not easy, it is best to acknowledge a hurt and deal with it Biblically. Anger is one of those thistles. How do we deal with the results of our anger? The Bible has great instruction.

Ephesians 4:15 - *But speaking the truth in love...*
Ephesians 4:26 - *...let not the sun go down upon your wrath.*

Give Me a Minute

Truth for Today – Matthew 25

The Bible asks us to be wise in how we use the 1,440 minutes God gives us in each 24 hour day. Ephesians 5:16 and Colossians 4:5 instruct us to *"redeem our time."* Barnes in his commentary clarifies the term "redeem" - *to rescue or recover our time from waste; to improve it for great and important purposes.*

Each of us fill our days with activities, whether productive, non-productive, active or leisure. Some sources indicate that we in the USA, over the course of a lifetime, fill it this way:

- 115 days laughing
- 26 years sleeping
- 7 years lying awake, trying to sleep
- 2.5 years on our smart-phone
- 3.7 years eating
- 4.4 years driving
- 10.4 years working
- 3.3 years surfing the internet
- 9 years watching television and movies
- Women will spend 1.5 years of their lives cleaning
- 2.6 years washing clothes
- 6 months waiting in lines
- 20 weeks spent "on hold" while on our phones
- 4.2 months shaving
- 1 year being sick
- 5 months complaining

So, reflecting on God's encouragement for us to become productive and good stewards of our minutes, what are we doing with our time? Where do we line up with reading the Bible, being in prayer, helping the poor, last, least, lost and lonely?

Time is what we want most, but what we use worst. - William Penn

Give Me the Needle

His left arm was covered with tattoos which appeared to be koi, a Japanese fish. I was intrigued by someone going through the pain of tattooing and of course the permanence of that decision.

My thoughts took me to an uncle of mine. He had an eagle tattooed on his arm back in the 1930's and of course, still had it when he passed away at 93 years old. I remember the times he expressed his regrets about having received it, but he always ended up sadly saying, "It is what it is."

The concept of a tattoo is a subject that merits discussion in Christian circles and there are certainly differing views. In 2003, the Pew Research Center indicated that 23% of Americans have a tattoo; 32% between the ages of 30-45 have at least one; and 72% of those with a tattoo keep it hidden from view. Another study indicates that of those with tattoos: 32% claim an addiction to ink; 29% did it to indicate rebellion; 31% to make them more attractive and sexy.

All that being said, Isaiah 49:16 states, *Behold, I have graven thee upon the palms of my hands; thy walls are continually before me.*

Scholars indicate there was a custom in Isaiah's day, of men tattooing things upon their hands they wanted to always remember. I found it interesting to know that God spoke of the concept. It points out to me that there are things which He loves so much, and that He never wants to forget. Could it be that we as His family are among those things?

Tattooing a palm is one of the most painful places to tattoo. It is always in remembrance and up front. It would take a lot of love to engrave in such a painful place. That, in an unusual way, speaks of His undying and unconditional love for His children.

God is certainly able to determine the theology of getting a tattoo, but I wonder what He thinks of the $1.65 billion spent each year in the U.S. for the practice?

Behold, I have graven thee upon the palms of my hands.

Give Us This Day Our Daily Bread...

Truth for Today – Matthew 6:26

What's for dinner this evening? Are we getting three meals a day? Why am I gaining weight? I stepped on the scale awhile back and saw that I had just hit 200 lbs. again. Ouch! How is the United States faring compared to the rest of the world in the food category?

In 2007, a study was made to determine the number of calories consumed per capita among 176 countries.

- America is #1 at the very top of the list showing consumption of 3770 calories per day.
- Haiti was #173 of the 176 at 1850 calories.

An elementary conclusion would be that we as U.S. residents consume twice as many calories as our Haitian neighbors.

How many refrigerators and freezers do we own? What's in them? If we bought nothing else, how long could we live on what we have available in our homes? How many food runs to the grocery store do we make per week? How many times to a restaurant?

As we hear the statistics of worldwide starvation, poverty, malnutrition, stunted and underweight children, we tend to feel guilty for the blessings we have. What should we do?

Another study identifies the obesity levels of countries:

- The U.S. is #18 with 33% of our citizens considered obese.
- Haiti is #137 with 8% of their citizens considered obese.

Of course, we all know there are genetic factors at play, as well as physical illnesses and conditions which can propagate obesity. But for some of us, it's good to hear the statistics and feel challenged to make a few changes.

Our culture enables us to over-eat, and at the same time, my self-control is weak. I enjoy smorgasbords, cafeterias, potlucks, all-you-can-eateries, super-sized party pizzas and fast food. We have many opportunities to indulge ourselves and inevitably do damage to our bodies.

Maybe my prayer needs to change to... "Give us this day our daily 2000 calories and the desire to share the abundance."

Go Fetch!

Truth for Today – Numbers 32:23

The rumors were circulating on the streets, evidence was mounting that there was cause for further action, so the police officers obtained their search warrant.

They approached the house to look for the drug paraphernalia they suspected would be inside. Knocking on the door, the suspect took off on foot and the officers lost him.

But fortunately, the suspect's dog was excited about this new game and ran after his master. Bo led the officers directly to the place in the tall grass where they found the suspect hiding.

The illustration from Alabama lends credibility to Numbers 32:23 - *...be sure your sin will find you out.*

God continually provides assurance that He is in charge. Though the battle wages between good and evil, purity and sin, we know who wins in the end. Evil and sin will not be a part of God's Kingdom.

- John 16:33 - *These things I have spoken unto you, that in me ye might have peace. In the world ye shall have tribulation: but be of good cheer; I have overcome the world.*
- 1 John 4:4 - *Ye are of God, little children, and have overcome them: because greater is he that is in you, than he that is in the world.*
- Acts 10:38 - *How God anointed Jesus of Nazareth with the Holy Ghost and with power: who went about doing good, and healing all that were oppressed of the devil; for God was with him.*
- Galatians 1:4 – *(Jesus) who gave himself for our sins, that he might deliver us from this present evil world.*
- 1 John 3:8 - *For this purpose the Son of God was manifested, that he might destroy the works of the devil.*
- Colossians 1:13 – *(God) who hath delivered us from the power of darkness, and hath translated us into the kingdom of his dear Son.*
- John 12:31 - *Now is the judgment of this world: now shall the prince of this world be cast out.*
- Luke 10:18 - *And he said unto them, I beheld Satan as lightning fall from heaven.*

God Has a Long Arm

Truth for Today – Proverbs 16:5

Our church was providing assistance to families in our community who were struggling. I was responsible for finding potential families and identifying projects that fit our skills.

The local Family Services organization gave me the name of a widow that was in need of a new roof and suggested I check it out. I parked in front of her home. My Christ-like nature was in charge until I stepped foot on the sidewalk leading to her front door. It was then that my flesh nature kicked in as I thought, "It would be nice if someone I knew saw me doing this good work."

As the thought entered my mind, I was walking between two 9' tall evergreen shrubs overhanging the sidewalk. Suddenly I heard a horrendous chatter and something hit me on my head. I crouched down and looked up to see a noisy Blue Jay in the branches ready to dive bomb me again. I ran in pain to avoid another attack.

I touched the top of my head and my fingers had blood on them. Later looking in the mirror I saw that some of my hair was also missing. That Blue Jay was a very effective nest protector. I skirted the large shrubs and made my way to the front door of the widow's home. This time, I approached with much more humility.

God teaches us often in His Word about pride and humility. They are difficult lessons to put into practice. A few failures, botches and disasters generally assist us in our learning.

- Proverbs 11:2 - *When pride cometh, then cometh shame.*
- Proverbs 16:18 - *Pride goeth before destruction, and an haughty spirit before a fall.*
- Galatians 6:3 - *For if a man think himself to be something, when he is nothing, he deceiveth himself.*
- Proverbs 27:2 - *Let another man praise thee, and not thine own mouth; a stranger, and not thine own lips.*
- James 4:6 - *...God resisteth the proud, but giveth grace unto the humble.*
- Luke 14:11 - *For whosoever exalteth himself shall be abased; and he that humbleth himself shall be exalted.*

God the Caretaker

***Truth for Today* – Job 39**

Most of us have noticed the spiral clay nests attached to walls, cliffs or other vertical structures. Long, narrow and about one quarter inch wide and one to two inches long, they house the larvae of the mud dauber wasp.

The mud dauber is a stinging wasp that has an interesting trait. After crafting a spiral clay nest, it leaves one end open. Then it goes in search of spiders. Sometimes it mimics death in a web, attracting the spider to it. The spider is quickly stung and a small amount of venom paralyzes it. Then the wasp carries the immobile spider to the nest and stuffs it into the tube.

Then it goes in search of another spider and another. Finally after several spiders, sometimes as many as a dozen, are stuffed into the tube, she lays an egg on the abdomen of the last and seals the nest.

About two or three days later, the egg hatches and the larvae dines on the paralyzed spiders. Finally large enough to fend for herself, the new wasp breaks free and begins the life cycle for her offspring.

As I think of God's promise to take care of the lilies and sparrows, I am amazed at the detail that goes into each of His creation. He truly cares for His own in extraordinary ways.

When troubles, trauma or discouragement come into our lives, it's good to remember the mud dauber wasp. God has placed immense amounts of resources and detail into His created beings. We have more reserve than we know. When our human reserve runs short, He provides yet more grace. He is watching and He has our back.

God's Creatures

I realize that a dog may be a man's best friend. I know that pets offer companionship for lonely people. I recognize that some people simply love having a cat, dog, goldfish, hamster or Vietnamese Potbelly pig around the house. I also recognize that some people have more money than they know what to do with.

That being said, here are a few gifts wealthy pet lovers can purchase for the pets they love:

- A dog collar with an 8.5 carat sapphire and 600 inset diamonds, all set in an ostrich leather band. Price - $899,000
- A mink hoodie to keep your dog warm. Price - $1,259
- A Louis Vuitton monogrammed dog carrier to transport your canine on planes, cruises or around the world trips. Price - $2,780
- A Christmas ball ornament with your pet's portrait hand painted on it. Price - $625 or a set of 12 ornaments for $7,500
- A treadmill for your dog - $1,399
- Weekly massages for your dog - $4,000 annually
- Wagyu Kobe American Strip Steaks for your dog - Steaks are aged 28 days - Price per steak - $44.99

This devotion could go in a dozen directions. How to be good stewards of our financial assets? Our need to share with the last, lost, least and lonely of the world? How many Bibles could be purchased instead of the above gifts?

Or, we simply recognize that God Himself has said that He cares for the lilies of the field and the sparrows in the air. Possibly these gifts are an extension of what He wants for the dogs of this world?

Possibly this devotion merely causes us to reflect on our judgement of other people's habits? Now that we've judged some pet lovers, what are we spending our money on? What extravagance do we permit in our lives that could be better spent on others?

Lord, help me consider how my
gifts, talents and assets belong to you.

Going Nowhere

Truth for Today – 2 Timothy 3

God gave me the ability to sleep nearly anywhere and anytime. It is a gift that is especially useful on airline flights, particularly long international flights.

On a recent leg from Addis Ababa, Ethiopia to home, I fell asleep before leaving the Addis airport. Sometime later I awoke. The cabin was relatively dark and many of my co-passengers were asleep as well.

I sat there thinking about the quiet peacefulness of the flight. As I looked across the cabin, and out a window, I saw darkness and realized that it was night-time. Settling back, I looked towards the front of the cabin and saw a few lights through another window. I got up to see the sights of the city we were flying over.

When I got to the window and peered out, I saw that we were parked at an airport terminal! I asked the stewardess where we were and she replied, "We are in Khartoum, Sudan to pick up passengers. The passengers have all been brought on and we have a mechanical malfunction that needs to be fixed."

I had slept through the take-off, flight, landing and boarding of our aircraft and I simply had no clue. My mind had been deceived. I thought I knew exactly what was going on, where we were, and yet had no idea that I was wrong on every count.

It caused me to reflect on other times in life where I had been deceived. Times when I had drawn hasty conclusions about someone because of their appearance, attitude, something they said or how they said it. Times when I based a decision on inaccurate information, too little information or listening to less than credible counsel.

One of the things I've learned in life is, "Nothing is exactly as it seems." There is always something going on that I don't see or know about, or I am in need of more information to make an appropriate analysis of a situation.

It's at those times I am thankful for my Bible. Knowing it is inerrant and infallible gives me comfort in believing all answers to life are within.

Guard Duty

My dad found himself 8500 miles from home in New Guinea for part of his tour of duty during WWII. Some of his time as a medic was spent in assisting a dentist and doctor.

When morphine was available, G.I.'s were given guard duty to safeguard it. Sadly, some soldiers had become addicted to it and would do almost anything to obtain it.

Dad was given guard duty one night. Though he had no gun, he was asked to make sure that no one broke in for the drugs.

A G.I. came in and told my dad that he should move aside. Dad said, "I can't do that. I have my duty to stand guard." The soldier pulled a .45 pistol and pointed it at my dad and screamed his demand again. Dad said, "I can't do that. I have my duty to stand guard."

The demand came again and again, with my dad's continued response. Finally, the .45 lowered and the man left.

I often think about my dad's experience. It isn't in our nature to give our life for something that is not ours. I believe my dad would have done his duty to the end because that is who and what he was.

What is our commitment level for duty? What are we willing to give?

I think of Jesus who gave His life for something that wasn't His. He gave His life for *our* sins. It was an unbelievable sacrifice. He took on the sins of humanity, though He was sinless Himself. He gave up Heaven for thirty-three years to develop relationships with people and to experience life on the ground. He took on the pain of torture and the agony of betrayal, in place of His perfect life in Heaven.

But, that is who Jesus was and is. He couldn't do otherwise.

2 Corinthians 8:9 - *For ye know the grace of our Lord Jesus Christ, that, though he was rich, yet for your sakes he became poor, that ye through his poverty might be rich.*

Philippians 2:7-8 - *But made himself of no reputation, and took upon him the form of a servant, and was made in the likeness of men: And being found in fashion as a man, he humbled himself, and became obedient unto death, even the death of the cross.*

Guilty Innocence

Truth for Today – 1 Peter 1:17

Jeni and I were looking forward to a traditional Japanese dinner at a beautiful restaurant in Tokyo. There were about eight of us crowded around a rectangular table sitting on floor cushions, with our legs stretched under the low table.

We had taken our shoes off in the traditional fashion and had placed them on the floor by the end of our table. The meal was phenomenal and we were finished. As someone exited the table they inadvertently bumped a bowl of soup that tipped over and spilled over the edge of the table. As I got out, I saw that the soup had neatly poured itself into one of my empty shoes.

It was decision time. What was I to do with a shoe full of Japanese soup? I did the logical thing, or so it seemed to me. I picked up my shoe and poured the soup into a bowl and started wiping my shoe. A nearby waiter had an immediate negative reaction. I have no idea how many Japanese customs I had broken, or how many cultural taboos I was guilty of, but I know I felt horribly guilty of something!

I was guilty beyond the shadow of a doubt, but ignorant. I was condemned but innocent. I was innocently guilty or possibly simply guilty of ignorance.

1 Peter 1:17 - *(God) who without respect of persons judgeth according to every man's work.*

God is the most righteous, unbiased, all knowing, purest Judge ever, who can see all and know all. Imagine the God of the universe with His Son by His side determining an individual's standing and relationship with Him. He alone is capable and able to determine judgment of sins of omission, commission, ignorance, mitigating and extenuating circumstances. All I know is I am thankful God is the judge and no man has that responsibility or authority. He is God!

Hands and Paws

Truth for Today – 1 Corinthians 13

I was observing three young girls in Haiti who were formerly orphaned and vulnerable. Now, living in a new home with a lifetime mom and dad and nine other girls is life changing for them. The girls, though not birth siblings, have a special bond together that we know as "family". As these  three girls sat together, I looked at their hands.

They were intertwined, connected, touching and full of meaning. Their hearts are just as connected as their hands. They are sisters and they have one another's backs.

Looking at the intertwined hands of the girls, I was reminded of a very unique trait inherent with sea otters. Though sea otters tend to be individualistic, they often sleep on their backs in the Pacific, in groups, with their paws intertwined. The entangled legs and paws help prevent them from drifting out to sea while sleeping. Groups from two to 2,000 sea otters have been viewed sleeping together at the same time, thus the appropriate term of "raft", identifying what a group of sea otters is called.

How important is unity? The Bible shares several thoughts:

- 1 Corinthians 1:10 - *...that ye be perfectly joined together in the same mind and in the same judgment.*
- Ecclesiastes 4:10-12 – *For if they fall, the one will lift up his fellow: but woe to him that is alone when he falleth; for he hath not another to help him up. Again, if two lie together, then they have heat: but how can one be warm alone? And if one prevail against him, two shall withstand him; and a threefold cord is not quickly broken.*
- Romans 12:10 - *Be kindly affectioned one to another with brotherly love; in honour preferring one another.*

He Cares for the Lilies

Truth for Today – Matthew 6:28

He was taking care of his tiny garden in a small village four miles outside of Les Cayes, Haiti. I walked up to him and complimented him on his good work. He smiled.

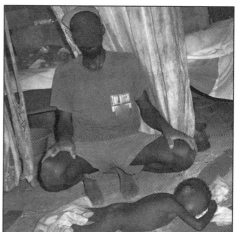

I noticed his three small children playing in his yard and asked him how his family was. He said that his wife and these three children were good. Something in his answer made me ask if there was something that wasn't good. Then he went on to say that he had a fourth child that was ill and motioned me into his one room hut.

On the dirt floor on a small matte was a tiny girl, whom I thought had died. I checked for a pulse and barely felt life. Her eyes were halfway open and her eyes were rolled back. I checked for breathing and couldn't feel a breath.

The father said that she'd been vomiting and had diarrhea for a few days. He and his wife didn't have anything more they could do for her and were waiting for her to die.

We gave him 500 Haitian goudes ($10.00) to get her to the clinic for IV fluids and meds. Two days later the little girl was playing in the yard.

I'm reminded of Matthew 6:28 – *Consider the lilies of the field, how they grow; they toil not, neither do they spin.* She was a little girl helpless, without hope, yet God cares enough about this remote place and these seemingly unknown people, to make a way. He is worthy of all honor, glory and praise. We, in our moment of need are no less worthy of His attention.

He is Able

Truth for Today – Ephesians 3:20

Genesis 1:3 - And God said, let there be light: and there was light.
Genesis 7 – Gathering of the animals and the flood
Genesis 11 – The introduction and confusion of languages
Genesis 21 – Isaac conceived by very elderly Abraham and Sarah
Exodus 3 – Burning bush not consumed
Exodus 7-12 – Water turned to blood and other plagues
Exodus 7 – Aaron's rod changed to a serpent
Exodus 14 – The parting of the Red Sea
Exodus 16 – Manna to feed the millions
Exodus 17 – Water from a rock
2 Kings 6 – The axe head floated
Joshua 6 – The walls of Jericho crumble and fall
Judges 6 – Gideon's fleece wet and dry
Isaiah 38 – The sun going backwards
Matthew 8 – Storm at sea calmed
Matthew 9 – Jairus's daughter brought to life
Matthew 14 – Jesus walks on water
Matthew 14 – Feeding of the 5000
Matthew 15 – Feeding of the 4000
Luke 1 – Conception of Jesus Christ
Luke 17 – Healing of 10 lepers
John 2 – Water turned to wine
John 9 – Healing of a blind man
John 11 – Lazarus raised from the dead
John 21 – Jesus resurrected

So, what do you think? Is our God big enough to take care of our daily requests? Are there times we think that He's not able to do mighty and marvelous things? How big is our God? Does He care about our little things?

Ephesians 3:20 - *Now unto him that is able to do exceeding abundantly above all that we ask or think, according to the power that worketh in us.*

He Touched Me

Truth for Today – Matthew 8:2-4

At six years old, the small Haitian boy knew grief and loss. His mother and father had died from AIDS. In a country where 2% of the people are HIV+, the disease had earned a reputation for death.

He was given to a relative to raise, but soon he became ill. The relative nursed him through the illness, but it wasn't long until he became sickly again. After a few bouts, she suspected that he had "the disease".

She put him in the yard where he wouldn't infect her family. Placing his food and water on the ground she would retreat to the safety of her house. In the yard, he had little shelter from the rains so his health continued to deteriorate.

Though there were no up-sides to his young life, one of the things he missed the most was "touch". No one would touch him. In his misery and illnesses, there was no one to comfort him or hold him. He was an untouchable and he was only six.

Sadly, around the world, there are the untouchables. Whether resulting from AIDS, leprosy, discrimination or caste societies, many people know the stigma of being untouchable. Periodic rejection can be overcome, but a lifetime of rejection is a massive burden.

Jesus knew the power of touch. As God, He could have healed someone from the end of the universe, but He chose to do His healings up close and personal. Many times Jesus healed with a personal touch.

For instance, there was the man with leprosy in Galilee, a 12 year old girl in Capernaum, a man who was deaf in the Decapolis, a blind man just outside Bethsaida, a blind man in Jerusalem, a crippled woman in the synagogue, two blind men near Jericho, and the servant whose ear Peter cut off in Gethsemane.

> *Oh, He touched me, Oh, He touched me... And the joy*
> *that floods my soul... Something happened and*
> *now I know... He touched me and made me whole!*

Help?

Truth for Today – Genesis 2

I realize there are many opinions regarding the confinement of cattle, pigs, chickens, turkeys and rabbits. That being said, this is not about that debate, rather it is about a Biblical principle.

Years ago, friends of ours raised pigs. Not two or three, but hundreds. The pigs were housed in confinement facilities where all their needs were met with water, food, appropriate temperatures and ventilation. The pigs lived on slatted floors that permitted the pigs waste to drop into a watery slurry pit below.

One evening, some of the slats fell into the pit, along with some of the pigs which were ready for market. Though there was a sloping escape ramp at the edge of the pit, the pigs were unaware and were trying desperately to swim for their lives.

My friend heard the squealing of the pigs and shouted for his wife to call for help. She made the call and ran to the barn to find her husband in the manure pit pushing the porkers towards the ramp. Without hesitation, she jumped into the slurry pit to join her husband. Pushing and shoving them to safety.

God set up an institution called marriage between a man and woman at the beginning of time. He said several things which established the order of that relationship.

- Genesis 1:27 - *So God created man in his own image, in the image of God created he him; male and female created he them.*
- Genesis 2:18, 22, 23 - *And the L*ORD *God said, it is not good that the man should be alone; I will make him an help meet for him. And the rib, which the L*ORD *God had taken from man, made he a woman, and brought her unto the man. And Adam said, this is now bone of my bones, and flesh of my flesh: she shall be called Woman, because she was taken out of Man.*
- Genesis 2:24 - *Therefore shall a man leave his father and his mother, and shall cleave unto his wife: and they shall be one flesh.*

What would cause this wife to jump into a manure slurry pit? Clearly it was her desire to honor their "one flesh" relationship. He needed her help and she was his *Help-Meet*.

Helpless and Hopeless

Truth for Today – John 5:1-15

She was six years old, sitting in a tiny heap alongside a dirt street in Port au Prince, Haiti. Her tiny shoulders, exposed outside of her ragtag little shirt, moved up and down to coincide with her weeping. With a couple of extra hours on my hands I had taken a walk and found her all alone.

I went to her and asked her what was wrong. In the middle of her sobs she pointed to a plastic bag in the middle of the dirt street. Looking inside I saw that the bag had ripped under the load of five bottles of beer.

Then I realized that this sweet little girl was a restavek. She was a domestic servant-slave for a family. She was in a fix. She couldn't carry the five bottles to her master in her tiny hands, since the bag was broken. She would be beaten if she didn't return soon with the bottles. She was helpless, hopeless and she knew it.

I tied the bottom of the bag shut and nestled the five bottles into the now intact sack. I placed the bag into the hands of the girl and showed her how to put a hand under the sack to support it.

She took the bag and began walking away. She looked over her shoulder at me and I'll never forget the smile she gave in exchange for the new hope she had. No whipping was going to happen that day.

That experience made me think about how God picks me up in my desperate moments, dusts me off, equips and encourages me to get back on my journey.

She reminded me of the sick man at the Jerusalem sheep market pool who was helpless and hopeless until Jesus told him to, *"Rise, take up your bed and walk."*

How often am I on the road to Jericho and I see someone in need? The thieves robbed and beat a man 2,000 years ago, and the priest and Levite passed by the injured man. The Good Samaritan was a great example to us. In fact, so great that he is honored yet today. What will we do the next time we have the opportunity to be the hands and feet of Jesus?

Here Today and Gone Tomorrow

Truth for Today – Revelation 21:1-4

It was a day to remember! Finally becoming a winner of $16.2 million in the lottery, he was ready to fulfill his dreams. However, one year later he was $1 million in debt, and on food stamps.

She defied the odds. She won the lottery one year and then again the next year, resulting in $5.4 million. Sadly, she gambled it all away in Atlantic City.

He won $10 million and spent it all in seven years. Devastated, he took his own life.

The $15 million lottery winnings were going to finance his dreams. Unfortunately, his dreams were cocaine, parties, prostitutes and cars. Seven years later he was hoping to get his old job back at the garbage company.

Walking away with $114 million after tax from his $315 million lottery winnings, he felt great. Four years later it was completely gone.

Diminishing assets. Pursuit of happiness. Elusive wealth. Treasures seem to be made of dreams. We wonder what we'd do with a million dollars or much more. As believers we may think that we'd handle it well, and that charities and God would benefit, but history doesn't necessarily assure us of that. The temptation and pursuit of riches may be a curse.

But, there are no diminishing assets in Heaven. Time does not dull the warmth and depth of crystallized gold. The gems and precious stones in the walls and gates will not tarnish or dim. The mansions for God's tenants won't become outdated or rundown. Nothing loses value or beauty.

Time affects nothing, because there is no time. There will be no tracking of portfolios or stock markets, because everything is static and there is no money. Heaven is beautiful and Heaven is eternal.

Revelation 21:1,4 - *And I saw a new heaven and a new earth: for the first heaven and the first earth were passed away; and there was no more sea. And God shall wipe away all tears from their eyes; and there shall be no more death, neither sorrow, nor crying, neither shall there be any more pain: for the former things are passed away.*

Heroes and Heroines

***Truth for Today** – Matthew 25

She was two years old and fell 20' off a dock into the frigid 40° river. Her dad heard the splash and began running and jumped into the water after her. He went down and down and the crowd above watched. He emerged with his daughter in his arms. She was limp, motionless and silent and then suddenly, started crying. She was going to be fine. He was a hero.

The alarm went off at the fire station and the trucks headed to the house fire to find half the home already engulfed in flames. A firefighter saw the intense heat and knew that going into the home would be suicidal. Then he was told about an elderly lady inside. He jumped through a window into the bedroom and found her. She was barely responsive. Her foot was tangled in something and she couldn't be pulled out, nor could he see what it was due to the smoke. He wrestled her loose and got her out. He was relieved when he heard the words, "We have a pulse!" She fully recovered. He was a hero.

Someone once said, "I've never rescued a child from a burning building, but my bucket of water helped put the fire out." Often we think of heroes as being the rescuer in the burning house, doing a water rescue or doing the Heimlich maneuver.

Every day, there are millions of people who provide the charitable funds necessary to: Rescue girls from prostitution; snatch children from domestic slavery; pull children from the grips of child soldiering, exploitation or trafficking; place Bibles in the hands of those who have never heard the name of Jesus; provide food to the hungry; and drill wells so disease ridden people can have clean drinking water.

Without those funds, the work would not get done. The millions and millions of people providing the essential funds are a lifeline. They are heroes and heroines. People sacrifice to bring help to the last, least, lost and lonely. Matthew 25:34-35 - *Come...inherit the kingdom prepared for you from the foundation of the world: For I was an hungred, and ye gave me meat: I was thirsty, and ye gave me drink: I was a stranger, and ye took me in: Naked, and ye clothed me: I was sick, and ye visited me: I was in prison, and ye came unto me.* - Heroes!

Heroes

Truth for Today – John 3:16

On December 27, 1936, James was born in Australia. He has become a legend and a hero. What is it that makes some men and women heroes? Is it their physical ability to achieve great things in sports? Or possibly their high intellectual capabilities that make them great scientists? It's difficult to identify who will become legendary, heroic or renowned until events put individuals in a position for success.

For James, life started out as fairly normal. However, when he was 14, he developed lung issues that necessitated major lung surgery. Thirteen liters of blood (3.4 gallons) were required to get him through his surgery and subsequent three month recovery. Realizing that the blood saved his life, he committed to donating blood when he reached the legal age of 18.

In Australia at that time, 17% of pregnant women had an Rh Blood factor issue which caused the mothers immune system to attack that of her baby. Quickly it was found that his blood carried an extremely rare antibody which effectively fought the disease.

He began donating his blood when he turned 18 and has been donating every three weeks for 57 years since then. Now, having donated blood and plasma over 1000 times, his blood is credited as having saved the lives of 2.4 million babies. When his wife became pregnant it was found that she needed his antibody as well to prevent the loss of their baby girl. He literally saved his daughters life.

His arm has been nicknamed "the Golden Arm" and his life was insured for $1 million. He has received the Medal of the Order of Australia and was nominated for the Australian of the Year award. James is a hero.

That of course brings us around to the hero of all humanity. The one whose blood can save men and women from eternal death. Our Lord and Savior Jesus, the very Son of God. King of kings and Lord of lords. The Eternal One, before whom every knee shall bow and every tongue will confess that He is the Heroic Savior of mankind.

Hey, That's My Hay!

Truth for Today – Matthew 5

During what has become an exceptionally wet summer, we experienced an inordinate amount of rainfall in northeast Indiana. While normally receiving 4.2" of rain in June, we received a record breaking all time high of 11.98" in June of 2015.

Farmers planted and replanted corn with the hope that the rain would abate. Unfortunately, for most area farmers the replanting efforts were almost fruitless.

As I discussed the wet season with a farmer, he offered a perspective. He said, "Farmers control many things to assure a great harvest. They prepare the ground with great care. They are careful about field compaction; the ground condition when preparing the ground, as well as when they plant; the upcoming weather; the traditional weather patterns; when they spray their pesticides and insecticides; the cloud cover and wind direction; watchfulness for insects and disease; seed varieties; fertilizer components and percentages; and a hundred other things. But ultimately with all their control and caution, we've learned again that God is in control."

God is in control. I cannot imagine the faith of a farmer. So many factors and so many things that can go wrong. In the end, it is God who provides the yield or increase.

As I read the illustrations of Jesus related to how people handle the talents they've been given, or the laws of sowing and reaping, or how we are accountable for the efforts we put into a project, I realize there are things we can control and things we cannot.

I remember a preacher visiting with a farmer, with the conversation going something like this:

Preacher - "How's the farming going?"

Farmer - "It's been a tough week. It rained on my mowed hay in the field and that ticked me off!"

Preacher - "Why should you care if God decided to rain on His hay?"

Lord, help me to remember who owns the hay…

Hi, My Name is Howdy

Truth for Today – Ecclesiastes 7:1

So, what do the following real names of people have in common? Dyl Pickle, Filet Minyon, Bear Trapp, Angus Pattie, Howdy Ledbetter, Azalia Snail, Hans Ohff, Autumn Fogg, Felix Pie, Rockland Steel and Rip Torn. The commonality is that they all are odd, unusual or simply funny names.

Ecclesiastes 7:1 reminds us - *"A good name is better than precious ointment."*

A friend of mine told me that at birth, his mother spelled and recorded his name as Dog on the birth certificate. Later the mistake was caught and he had it changed to Doug. What's in a name?

Unfortunately in towns across America, the last name of a person can be tied to the antics, criminal activities and perversions of men and women two or three generations earlier. People remember and history lives on. Names can brand us.

But the good names live on as well. Our life creates a history, and people generations later, speak of various attributes and legacies of men and women long gone.

Philippians 2:10 says, *"That at the name of Jesus every knee should bow."* His attributes and name have been written about, whispered and shouted down through the course of 2000 years. His qualities, power, actions and merits live on and on.

He is the King of kings, Lord of lords, Prince of life, Prince of peace, Mighty Conqueror, Morning Star, Most Holy, Light of the World, Advocate, Almighty, Alpha and Omega, Amen, Arm of the Lord, Author, Finisher, Beloved, Blessed, King over all the Earth, Lamb of God, Lawgiver, Leader, Image of God, Jehovah, Judge, Just One, King, King of Israel, King of the Jews, Ruler, Salvation, Savior, Scepter, Seed of David, Servant, Shepherd, Son of God, Son of Man, Teacher, True Vine, Truth, Way, Witness, Wonderful and the Word.

What history is being written about us in the minds of men?

Hide and Seek

Truth for Today – Matthew 25:31-46

As young cousins, we spent many dark nights playing "hide and seek" and "kick the can". In both cases you have the "hiders" and the "seekers". Invariably you would hear a voice out of the dark saying, "Where are you?", or "Here I am".

In the world today there are diverse and huge problems in every corner of the earth. Many times we hear the question asked, "Where was God when that happened?" The obvious implication is that God is to blame for whatever the problem, issue or subject being talked about.

Sadly, I have been guilty of asking God that question - "Where were you when that happened?" I am inferring guilt, blame or responsibility on Him. I am in fact saying that He does not care, that He is too busy, or that He alone is responsible for taking care of the world.

Does that question apply to me? "Where are you?" Is there a possibility that disaster, trauma, hurt and tragedies are opportunities for me to get involved?

Isaiah 6:8 shares a dialogue between God and Isaiah. *"The voice of the Lord, saying, whom shall I send, and who will go for us?"* Then Isaiah said, *"Here am I; send me."*

I am convinced that instead of asking God where He is, I need to tell Him, "Here I am. What can I do to help?"

- Acts 20:35 - *I have shewed you all things, how that so labouring ye ought to support the weak, and to remember the words of the Lord Jesus, how he said, It is more blessed to give than to receive.*
- Matthew 20:28 - *Even as the Son of man came not to be ministered unto, but to minister, and to give his life a ransom for many.*
- Luke 10:36-37 - *Which now of these three, thinkest thou, was neighbour unto him that fell among the thieves? And he said, He that shewed mercy on him. Then said Jesus unto him, Go, and do thou likewise.*
- 1 John 3:18 - *My little children, let us not love in word, neither in tongue; but in deed and in truth.*

Hold My Hand

Truth for Today – Isaiah 41:13

Next time you're in a large department store, observe parents and grandparents holding the hand of their three to six year old child or grandchild. Elementary reasons as to why we hold the hands of young children might range from: To keep them from wandering off; to keep them from touching things; to simply enjoy the physical contact with someone they love; or possibly to be able to pull them along to keep up with the adults pace.

If I imagine God holding my hand throughout life, I can believe that He would do it for all the above reasons. After all, scripture would indicate that He wants us to stay out of trouble; to help us stay away from things that could do us damage; He enjoys contact with us; and He wants us to keep up with Him. However, I believe there is another aspect that is good for me to remember.

I've wondered about Isaiah 41:13 - *For I the Lord thy God will hold thy <u>right</u> hand, saying unto thee, Fear not; I will help thee.*

Specifically the Word mentions that God will hold our *"right hand"*. Why is it so specific as to mention the right hand? With 90% of the world's population being right handed, possibly that's a factor? Or possibly it's because the right arm and hand are considered the dominant limb in dexterity and strength?

Typically when I do something it is with my right hand. It is the most flexible, dominant and strongest limb I have. Instinct, habit and default put my right hand and arm to use.

Could it be that He holds our right hand to restrict its use? Is God constraining our strength, habits, instinct and default mechanism so He can show us His strength?

How often do we find ourselves failing in our efforts? How often is our brute strength not enough to fix a problem? Why do we tend to work hard at solving a difficulty before praying? If we let God restrict our efforts and strength, we will be surprised at His effectiveness to do things we cannot.

2 Chronicles 20:17 - *Ye shall not need to fight in this battle: Set yourselves, stand ye still, and see the salvation of the Lord with you.*

Holding Value

Truth for Today – 1 Samuel 16

She was only eight years old and tiny. Her eyes reminded me of a scared rabbit or kitten. Her hair was orange, matted and filthy. I could smell her from a few feet away. Her stomach was large compared to her small but dirty crusted hands and feet.

How do we measure value? Is value measured in what we see, smell, hear or touch? Is value measured by what a product can return on our investment? If so, this little girl would have little or no value.

Two months later, she was no longer an orphan but part of a family with a lifetime Haitian mom and dad and eleven sisters. Today, nine years later, she is vibrant, healthy, receiving an education, healthcare and the Gospel. Are we to assume that she has more value today than she did on that first day in 2007? Her value in Gods eyes was exactly the same then as now. He is not a respecter of persons and His love is unconditional and perfect.

I treasure a tattered dollar bill to remind me of "value". The bill is torn, dirty, frayed and wrinkled. On the surface it has just as much value in that condition as a new and crisp bill.

But I wouldn't give up my tattered piece of currency for $25.00. It has value that you cannot see. I've had it for fourteen years. I am attached to it for reasons other than currency value. There are memories within that particular piece of currency that are very meaningful to me. How do we put a value on a person or item?

- 1 Samuel 16:7 - *But the Lord said unto Samuel, Look not on his countenance, or on the height of his stature; because I have refused him: for the Lord seeth not as man seeth; for man looketh on the outward appearance, but the Lord looketh on the heart.*
- 2 Corinthians 4:16 - *For which cause we faint not; but though our outward man perish, yet the inward man is renewed day by day.*

Horribly Blessed

Truth for Today – Philippians 4:13

We've heard trite bumper-sticker sayings often throughout life. Sometimes they are applicable, while other times they make us angry:

- It's a blessing in disguise.
- Every cloud has a silver lining.
- Take one step back to take two steps forward.
- When God closes a door, He opens a window.
- Every rose has a thorn.
- No pain; no gain.
- You have to break a few eggs to make an omelet.

Jeni and I independently but mutually came to a common peace and commitment to become foster parents. What we witnessed and experienced in eight years of foster parenting was eye-opening for us, to say the least. Children who were abused, burnt, beaten and sorely mistreated were in our home and part of our family. Their childish joy, trust and emotions had been ripped from many of them. The tragedies to these children were difficult to witness, but we were committed to giving them love, security and emotional healing.

We would often say that those years were the most horrible years of our lives... but would follow up by saying that they were also some of our most blessed. We were truly "horribly blessed". Our hearts were broken again and again through those fostering years but we wouldn't trade them for anything. God used those years to break, mold and shape us in ways we could not have imagined. No regrets.

Though the trite sayings seem shallow and hollow at the time, they do speak of powerful principles outlined again and again in the Bible. Where would we be if Jesus had not sacrificed Himself for us? What would have happened if the disciples of Jesus had given up in their passion to bring the name of Jesus to the 1st century church?

As God's people are faced with horrible adversity, pain, grief, torture and loss, the temptation to give up is normal. God is so able to bring miraculous good from bad things! We can be horribly blessed.

Philippians 4:13 - *I can do all things
through Christ which strengtheneth me.*

How Fast is Fast?

Truth for Today – 1 Corinthians 15:52

It was a nice day for traveling and the couple in their 80's were enjoying their quiet time together. Then the rain started. Suddenly, there was a bright flash of lightning, their car lit up and everything shut down. Somehow managing to stop their car, they survived the lightning strike without injury.

Lightning strikes the earth an estimated 45 times per second. Approximately 24,000 people are killed by lightning each year worldwide with 240,000 injured. The odds of being struck in the U.S. by lightning in any particular year is one in 700,000, and only one in 3,000 in a lifetime.

Someone can be struck by lightning from a storm ten miles away with blue skies overhead. Lightning can occur in snowstorms, volcanic eruptions, nuclear explosions, forest fires and hurricanes. Lightning discharges as much as 100 million volts.

Lightning travels at the speed of light which is 186,000 miles per second. If lightning traveled around the world, it would circle the globe 7.5 times in one second. If it traveled from the earth to the moon, it would only take 1.3 seconds. What do those statistics and facts tell us? Quite simply, there is no escaping a lightning strike. You can't outrun it.

The Bible says in 1 Corinthians 15:52 - *In a moment, in the twinkling of an eye, at the last trump: for the trumpet shall sound, and the dead shall be raised incorruptible, and we shall be changed.*

What is a twinkle? How quick is a twinkling? Scientifically speaking, a twinkle is seeing a light reflection in someone else's eye. Literally it is the length of time it takes for light to travel the distance between the two people. In other words, as fast as the speed of lightning.

Is there any hope of escaping judgment? Is there any chance of being ready for the coming of Christ? Ephesians 2:8-9 provides the answer - *For by grace are ye saved through faith; and that not of yourselves: it is the gift of God: Not of works, lest any man should boast.*

How Good is That?

Truth for Today – 1 Samuel 16

I was reading in Genesis 1 about creation and read that on the 6th day *"God made the beast of the earth after his kind... and God saw that it was good."*

Recently I ran across a photo of a "naked mole rat" from East Africa and an Aye-Aye primate from Madagascar and thought how can these things be among the "good" that God created? They are, without a doubt, on the top ten list of the most ugly animals on earth. But He said they were good, so they are without doubt beautiful.

How quick are we to judge by outward appearance or certain traits and attributes? How quickly do we judge a lack of usefulness and beauty without knowing the gifting of the heart and soul? How often do we sideline someone who has great value and gifting because of our erroneous judgment?

If we used outward appearance to determine whether we wanted to know anything more about the naked mole rat, we would miss interesting facts. They have the most longevity of rodents, living up to 31 years. Their skin has no pain sensations and they are cancer resistant. Who knows, maybe they have the answers to cancer?

I think of Esther. Her parents died, leaving her as an orphan in a foreign country. Who would have guessed that God would use her to bring status, benefits and even redemption to her people?

We read about the prostitute Rahab and wonder why God would use her for strategic actions to benefit His people. The twelve Apostles didn't bring any great gifts to Jesus when they came. In fact, their list of negatives ran fairly long. Our Jesus wasn't someone who we would have taken a second look at. He was common.

Lord, help me to see others with your eyes and heart.

How Much are you Willing to Give?

Truth for Today – 1 Timothy 6:14-16

Betty had turned 17 just seven weeks earlier. Life for everyone was difficult in the undeveloped West Virginia territory in 1782. Living just 1/4 mile from the Ohio River had its blessings, but the Shawnee, Wyandot and Mingo Native American tribes harassed the settlers.

As the end of the Revolutionary War was approaching, the British used Indian tribes to attack the settlers. The early settlers had built a small fort to protect the men, women and children if an attack happened.

Then on September 11, 1782 the alarm sounded. The settlers rushed to the fort and prepared for the inevitable fight. The Indians and British attacked. Betty's father was shot and fell from the top wall of the fort and landed at her feet. Another man died. Then, word was passed that black powder for the guns was about gone.

Betty knew that in their cabin outside the fort was a stash of powder. She gathered her skirts and took off at a run to retrieve it. The Indians and British shot at her on her run. She arrived at the cabin and gathered the black powder in a tablecloth and began her run back to the fort. The attackers again began firing. They missed, except for one ball which flew through her flying skirt, leaving her uninjured.

The local settlers won the battle, with the Indians and British finally giving up their attack. Betty was an early American heroine. Today, a town is named after her. A poem about her heroism was penned. A book was written about her. Every year the town of Martin's Ferry, Ohio has a festival named the Betty Zane Frontier's Day Festival. She is remembered.

Some people do heroic things to survive or to help others. No one would minimize Betty's brave and daring run.

But, place the heroism of anyone from the beginning of time up against that of our Lord and Savior Jesus Christ. We then have a new definition of heroism. Giving your life for your persecutors and enemies and for the most evil and violent men of all time is beyond comprehension. He is the King of king's and Lord of lord's. His record will stand forever!

I Am Not What I Used to Be

Truth for Today – 2 Corinthians 5:17

As a bullied child through elementary and higher grades, I knew about failure and rejection. Not standing up for myself when bullied proved my cowardice.

Being small for my age, I knew the rejection of being chosen last for basketball teams and other games. Having girls chosen before me for those teams was evidence of my lack of ability.

Graduating 49 out of 76 in my graduation class affirmed my ingrained perception of being intellectually less than others.

Getting fired from my first job at age 16 assured me of my lack to measure up to expectations.

Failure and rejection in early years can create a lifetime of more failure and rejection. But God has other plans. He desperately wants us to look forward in hope, rather than back to a trouble-filled past. Philippians 3:13 says, *"...but this one thing I do, forgetting those things which are behind, and reaching forth unto those things which are before."*

Our past does not necessarily have to dictate our future. The experiences of our past can be powerfully used by God if we permit Him to use them. Acts 8:28 says, *"And we know that all things work together for good to them that love God, to them who are the called according to his purpose."*

God desires us to look to a future not predicted by our past. Our future is not limited, defined or dictated by who we used to be. 2 Corinthians 5:17 says, *"Therefore if any man be in Christ, he is a new creature: old things are passed away; behold, all things are become new."*

Paul, the disciples and countless others have proven that conversion and the born again experience produces new ideas, actions and a successful, predictable and eternal future.

1 Corinthians 15:10 - *But by the grace of God I am what I am: And his grace which was bestowed upon me was not in vain.*

I Can Carry That for You

Truth for Today – Isaiah 40

While driving in Haiti, I came upon a truck loaded with mattresses. Driving in Haiti is dangerous enough, but taking a photo while driving certainly crosses a line. Obviously I yielded to the temptation.

Seeing oversized loads in developing countries is common, and always amazing. Seeing this load immediately reminded me of what our Father does for us.

I often try to handle difficult and heavy things myself, but eventually I get to the point of asking Him to take care of them for me. He loves to help with the heavy and difficult problems of His children. Why is it I take so long in asking Him to help?

- 1 Corinthians 10:13 - *There hath no temptation taken you but such as is common to man: but God is faithful, who will not suffer you to be tempted above that ye are able; but will with the temptation also make a way to escape, that ye may be able to bear it.*

- Matthew 11:28 - *Come unto me, all ye that labour and are heavy laden, and I will give you rest.*

- Isaiah 40:28-31 - *Hast thou not known? Hast thou not heard, that the everlasting God, the Lord, the Creator of the ends of the earth, fainteth not, neither is weary? There is no searching of his understanding. He giveth power to the faint; and to them that have no might he increaseth strength. Even the youths shall faint and be weary, and the young men shall utterly fall: But they that wait upon the Lord shall renew their strength; they shall mount up with wings as eagles; they shall run, and not be weary; and they shall walk, and not faint.*

- 2 Chronicles 20:15 - *Thus saith the Lord unto you, Be not afraid nor dismayed by reason of this great multitude; for the battle is not yours, but God's.*

I Can Do This

Truth for Today – 2 Corinthians 11

One of television's main attractions in the past decade has been the reality show phenomena. There are many types of shows trying to realistically show competition and survival of the best or fittest. Shows related to singing, talents, cooking or merely surviving the elements draw in huge amounts of viewers.

The final episode of one series called *"Survivor"* drew in 51 million viewers. On this particular show, contestants were placed in hostile environments with minimal resources to determine their ability to work together and survive harsh conditions. Contestants were asked to create their own lodging, eat bugs and other things, endure the rain or drought, and come through it with a good attitude.

The winner of a particular series would win $1 million and even the last place contestant would win thousands. World acclaim awaited those who could survive. However, help was always near. Those injured or in jeopardy had their escape routes. Incentives of money, normalcy of life, and an end to their particular hazards soon being over, kept them in the contest.

As I read 2 Corinthians 11, I learn about another survivor. The list of the Apostle Paul's survival experiences is long: Five times he was whipped to near death with 39 lashes of a whip; three times he was beaten with rods; he was stoned to near death; three times he was shipwrecked, and for one and a half days he floated in the sea; he experienced many perils with thieves; betrayal by his countrymen; danger from heathen natives; hazards in the wilderness; being cold and naked; and ultimately death.

Paul had no earthly reward for his adventures. There was no audience, no guarantee of survival, and no monetary reward or acclaim awaiting his efforts. He was driven by a love for God and the Gospel. He was motivated by an eternal home called Heaven. He was a survivor!

Philippians 1:20-21 - *According to my earnest expectation and my hope, that in nothing I shall be ashamed, but that with all boldness, as always, so now also Christ shall be magnified in my body, whether it be by life, or by death. For to me to live is Christ, and to die is gain.*

I Couldn't Get Ahead

Truth for Today – John 10

"I couldn't get ahead of him, his legs were longer, his stride was better and his lungs were stronger." - 100 meter dash sprinter

"I couldn't get ahead of him. He had more horsepower and cornered better." - Race car driver

"I couldn't get ahead of her. She's brighter and more committed than I am." - Salutatorian about the Valedictorian

The United Nations has stated that, "for every $1 that the developing world received in grants, it spent $13 on debt repayment." It has been called the "poverty trap". They simply cannot get ahead.

It reminds me of another trap from which you cannot get ahead. Sin. There's a Gospel song that speaks about sin taking you farther than you want to go; keeping you longer than you want to stay; and costing more than you want to pay.

We as humans are destined for sin with the Adam nature we inherited. It seems to start small...

- White lies lead to deception, deceit and dark malignant lies.
- Benign and small lustful thoughts lead through the dark valleys of pornography and sexual perversion.
- An unresolved hurt can steadily take us up a ladder of anger, resentment, bitterness, hatred and murder.
- A desire to keep up with the Jones's can lead to jealousy, envy, a materialistic heart, selfishness and greed.

People say: I couldn't get ahead of it; sin had a grip on me that I couldn't break; satan had told me that the first look wouldn't hurt; it seemed like satan gave me an inch and then took a mile; I tried and tried to overcome it, but it was too strong for me; satan got his toe in the door and before I knew what happened, he was part of me... The testimonies of sinners go on and on.

But there is an answer. We cannot get ahead of sin. We don't have the strength to go head to head with satan. John 10:10 - *"The thief cometh not, but for to steal, and to kill, and to destroy. I am come that they might have life, and that they might have it more abundantly."* - Jesus is the perfect and only antidote for sin.

I Get the Point

Truth for Today – Proverbs 12:15

Tony had a lot of qualities and interests. He loved the outdoors, adventure, taking risks and new experiences. All of those exciting things came together for him one day in 1996.

As part of an initiation rite, Tony had an equally adventuresome friend try to shoot an empty beer can off his head with an arrow. Possibly the empty beer can gives us a clue as to why anyone would try a stunt like this.

His friend let the arrow fly and it entered Tony's right eye, penetrated his brain and stopped with the tip exposed at the back of his skull. In the ambulance, paramedics stopped Tony from trying to pull out the arrow, thus saving his life.

If the arrow had been one millimeter to the side, it would have cut a major blood vessel killing him instantly. The arrow was removed and Tony survived. At a news conference, Tony said, "I feel stupid!"

As I read the Bible, I try to learn from the experiences of others. It's difficult for me to imagine that I can learn from people who lived 2000 – 6000 years ago, but I'm finding that human nature is still the same. We learn from one another's successes and failures, but I still make my share of mistakes. Wise is the man who can learn from others, rather than believing he must experience things himself.

I've never been tempted to have someone shoot a beer can off of my head, but I've certainly used poor judgment in other things I've said, or decisions I've made.

What can we learn from David in the Bible regarding his poor choices? Is there anything beneficial we can learn about impulsiveness or lack of integrity from men like Peter?

On the other hand, what can we learn about the beautiful choices of Esther as she willingly sacrificed herself on behalf of her people? Or, lessons learned from people like Joseph and his choice to forgive and to let God have His way? Life is full of teachings and we are blessed in being able to learn from others.

Proverbs 12:15 - *The way of a fool is right in his own eyes: but he that hearkeneth unto counsel is wise.*

I Know Where the Stumps Are!

Truth for Today – Psalm 40

Jeni and I were leaving for a few days, so I asked our son Rick to mow our yard. During our time away, I received a text from him with a question. "Do you have another mower blade?" Those kinds of texts provoke questions!

He had been mowing our yard and hit a short stump hidden in the grass. The blade was bent and beyond repair. I asked him where the stump was located and he explained it to me. I said, "Oh, I know the one you're talking about. I know where the stumps are."

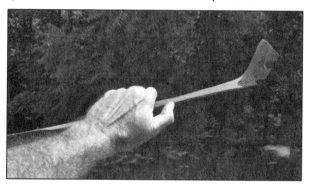

Of course, even though I knew where the stumps were, it wouldn't help him unless I communicated their location with him.

All of that caused me to reflect on God. He knows where the stumps are. But more importantly He knows where we are right now; what we are facing; the problems of tomorrow; the trauma of today; the hurt of the past; and the hairs of our head.

And most importantly, He cares deeply about it all and desires to help. He provides two essential tools to assist us in our daily walk.

- His Word, which of course is full of comfort and warnings; prophecy for tomorrow; healing for the past; and instructions for today.
- His Holy Spirit, living within us, comforting, convicting, leading and instructing us.

Our God knows where the stumps are. He's sharing. Are we listening?

I Know Who You Are

Truth for Today – Psalm 139

Walking into a hospital elevator, I was surprised when a nurse said, "Hi Jim, how are you."

Two weeks later I was at the local post office when a postal service employee said, "Hey Jim, I have your mail for you."

In both cases I informed them that I was "Ed" and asked them about Jim. They had both said that I looked like my cousin Jim and then they apologized. Actually no apology was necessary because Jim is five or six year's younger, slimmer and has more hair. I liked the comparison.

With 7.3 billion people on earth, we each have our unique identity. We like to protect it, preserve it, and we're thankful when people remember our names and faces. The last thing we want is for someone to steal our identity. However, it happens much more often than we might think.

- The odds of dying in a plane crash in any given year is 1 in 11 million.
- The odds of being struck by lightning in any given year in the U.S. is 1 in 700,000.
- The odds of being a victim of identity theft is 1 in 20.

It takes great effort to protect ourselves from identity theft. On the internet, there are viruses, malware, predators and phishing experts trying every minute we are on line, to learn our passwords, user-names and other information.

But our omniscient, omnipotent and omnipresent God knows who we are at all times, and in every place. He knows our identity. It reminds me of a few Bible verses assuring me of that fact.

- Jeremiah 1:5 - *Before I formed thee in the belly I knew thee.*
- Revelation 3:5 - *He that overcometh, the same shall be clothed in white raiment; and I will not blot out his name out of the book of life, but I will confess his name before my Father, and before his angels.*
- Proverbs 15:3 - *The eyes of the Lord are in every place.*
- Jeremiah 23:24 - *Can any hide himself in secret places that I shall not see him? Saith the Lord.*

I Love Ice Cream

Truth for Today – John 1

Soft, creamy, colorful, tasty, beautiful and patriotic. Any idea what fits that description?

In the 19th century in Naples, Italy, dessert makers had a product called spumoni. Made of layered ice cream, nuts and fruit it became famous. As Italian immigrants made their way to America, they brought along their great Italian cooking and desserts. In the 1870's, spumoni became Neapolitan ice cream.

Typically the three layers are made of strawberry, chocolate and vanilla ice cream. But, in the old country, the colors were green, white and red. Symbolically the three colors mimicked the Italian flag. Over the years the Italian dessert has evolved into an American delicacy.

What is the point of this trivia? All three ice creams are ice cream. Yet, each is distinctly different in color and taste. All three together create something distinctive in the ice cream world. Together they complement one another, but each are unique. Individually they are ice cream, but together they are more than ice cream.

I am always looking for practical illustrations that help me understand the Trinity of God the Father, the Son and the Holy Spirit. All are part of the same entity, but all are uniquely different. Each complement the other and together they point to something greater than themselves.

It almost feels sacrilegious to draw a parallel between the Trinity and Neapolitan ice cream, but with a simple mind, I need word pictures. Eating ice cream can almost become a spiritual experience... not that I need an excuse.

- 2 Corinthians 13:14 - *The grace of the Lord Jesus Christ, and the love of God, and the communion of the Holy Ghost, be with you all.*
- John 14:16 - *And I will pray the Father, and he shall give you another Comforter, that he may abide with you forever.*
- John 10:30 - *I and my Father are one.*

I Need That

Truth for Today – 1 Timothy 6:17

For Sale:
- *Diamond Dog Collar* – 18K white gold, platinum and crocodile leather - $3,200,000
- *Computer Mouse* – Covered with Swarovski crystals - $34,000
- *Poker Set* – 384 white gold 18 karat chips inlaid with stingray skin, platinum cards and a crocodile leather case. - $7,100,000
- *Gold Staples* – 25 gold staples for your standard stapler - $175
- *Haute Joaillerie from Chopard Watch* – Diamond studded wristwatch. - $25,000,000.
- *Jackson Pollock No. 5, 1948 Painting* - $140,000,000
- *Alberto Giacometti Bronze Sculpture "L'Homme Qui Marche I"* - $104,300,000.
- *Chopard Blue Diamond Ring* - $16,260,000
- *Manhattan Parking Spot* – Located in a luxury eight story condominium building - $1,000,000

Americans are considered wealthy by world standards. But the above items would only be purchased by a few of the wealthiest of the wealthy. Money can purchase almost anything imaginable, but what does the Bible say about wealth?
- Matthew 16:26 - *For what is a man profited, if he shall gain the whole world, and lose his own soul? Or what shall a man give in exchange for his soul?*
- Matthew 6:19-20 - *Lay not up for yourselves treasures upon earth, where moth and rust doth corrupt, and where thieves break through and steal: But lay up for yourselves treasures in heaven, where neither moth nor rust doth corrupt, and where thieves do not break through nor steal.*
- Mark 10:23-24 - *And Jesus looked round about, and saith unto his disciples; How hardly shall they that have riches enter into the kingdom of God! And the disciples were astonished at his words. But Jesus answereth again, and saith unto them, Children, how hard is it for them that trust in riches to enter into the kingdom of God!*

I Need to Catch That Call

Truth for Today – Psalm 37:27-29

She was anxious to rent out her available apartment in Beijing, China and was very thankful when a man asked to see it. All went well until he said, "Give me all of your money!"

No sooner had he said that, than her cell phone rang. She told the thief that it was an important foreign business call and she needed to take it. He permitted her. She began speaking in English to the caller and said, "A man is here to rob me, so please call the police."

Not understanding English, the thief had no idea what had just happened. Within minutes her home was surrounded and the man was arrested. He had orchestrated and carried out his own arrest and fate by permitting her to take the call.

It reminds me of the Persian story of Haman in Esther. Haman had been given position, authority and power from King Ahasuerus. All of the king's servants were to bow and give him honor when he was in their presence. Mordecai the Jew continually refused to bow and Haman felt slighted and dis-respected. In vengeance he built a set of gallows to hang Mordecai.

In a twist of fate, Mordecai was honored, Haman was dishonored and eventually hung from his own gallows. Esther 7:10 - *So they hanged Haman on the gallows that he had prepared for Mordecai.*

- Proverbs 21:15 - *It is joy to the just to do judgment: but destruction shall be to the workers of iniquity.*
- Romans 12:19 - *Dearly beloved, avenge not yourselves, but rather give place unto wrath: for it is written, Vengeance is mine; I will repay, saith the Lord.*
- Psalm 37:27-29 - *Depart from evil, and do good; and dwell for evermore. For the Lord loveth judgment, and forsaketh not his saints; they are preserved for ever: but the seed of the wicked shall be cut off. The righteous shall inherit the land, and dwell therein forever.*
- Isaiah 61:8 - *For I the Lord love judgment, I hate robbery...*

I Never Saw That Before!

Truth for Today – Revelations 21

Those around me know that I am "fashion challenged". For years Jeni has had to say, "Plaids and stripes don't mix", or "Those two colors don't go well together."

But recently in seeing a sunset, I realized that orange and purple go really well together. It seems that God has a different way of mixing things up. Does God have a special touch when it comes to beauty?

Every day we have occasions to see things we've not seen before: An opportunity to look through a telescope at the moon, stars or galaxies; a glimpse through a microscope at a housefly or living organism; a snorkeling adventure viewing the unseen world underwater; or maybe a newborn baby.

But God has only just begun in showing us His unseen treasures. I believe He is just like a dad who can't wait to surprise his children with a new swing-set in the backyard, or a Saturday trip to the zoo.

The Bible says in 1 Corinthians 2:9 - *Eye hath not seen, nor ear heard, neither have entered into the heart of man, the things which God hath prepared for them that love him.*

What will Heaven be like? Every day God is introducing newly arrived believers to the splendors and surprises of His Heavenly Kingdom. I can't wait to see His wonders. When the known colors are mixed together, there are almost infinite numbers of new colors. Can you imagine the colored light show He wants to show us? Colors we have never seen or experienced?

What about sound? We hear unusual sounds when we listen to the pulsing signals coming in from the stars or from the whales. But I am certain we cannot imagine the beautiful singing that will happen when he cranks up the volume and introduces new sounds for us in Heaven.

New smells, sights, sounds and tastes? It will take an eternity to take it all in. Not one surprise a day for a year, but infinitely new surprises every day for eternity.

I Remember Him

Truth for Today – Genesis 50:22-26

If you are as fascinated by world records as I am, you may find todays devotion, as one of interest.

Consider Matt Suter, a 19 year old senior from Missouri. He achieved a world record in 2006 when a tornado demolished his grandmother's mobile home. Trying to close a window during the storm, a lamp blown by the wind hit him on the head. Unconscious, he was sucked out of the home, carried over a barbed wire fence 600' away and dropped gently into a grass covered field. The National Weather Service officially measured 1,307' as the distance Matt flew through the air. Matt only needed a few staples to sew up his lamp wound.

Robert is all too familiar with broken bones and injuries. In his 69 years of life he suffered more than 433 fractures of 35 different bones. Crushing and breaking his pelvis three times was a start. He broke his back five times. Then breaking both ankles, every one of his ribs, breaking several toes, his shin, a knee, both wrists, sternum, both arms and collarbones, nose, jaw, fractured skull, tailbone and his hip finally put him in the record book. Most of us remember him as Evel Knievel.

An 18th century peasant from Moscow received recognition for fathering 87 children. The children consisted of many sets of twins and a few sets of triplets as well as quadruplets. His first wife had 69 births and his second wife 18.

Legacy can be defined as something left from one generation to another. It could be property or money, though it may also be a reputation. As we think about the legacy we leave to our children and grand-children, what does it consist of? How will we be remembered? Broken bones, surviving a tornado, prolific child-bearing?

Or will there be a spiritual legacy that supersedes everything else? I love reading the Old Testament histories of those early men and women of faith. They inspire me and propel me to greater heights. A truly memorable legacy creates inspiration and potential success for descendants. How will I be remembered?

I Should Have Done my Homework

Truth for Today – Luke 6:37

Douglas Adams in his classic novel, *The Hitchhiker's Guide to the Universe,* shares the fictional story of a massive fleet of spacecraft and aliens who attack earth. The aliens discover upon landing in a park that they've made a huge mistake. They failed to identify the relative size and scale of the earth and its inhabitants. The entire fleet was eaten by a small dog upon landing.

It is a vivid and almost comical reminder to me of how important it is to understand relative context when considering an issue. Though imagining an entire hostile fleet of aliens being eaten by a small dog may be comedic, it is rarely funny when I misinterpret someone else's motives, actions or inactions.

How often are we guilty of Monday morning quarterbacking? The phrase refers to people who criticize the actions or decisions of others, after the fact, and use hindsight to assess situations.

Possibly we fail to consider personality traits, culture, spiritual gifting, gender, fears, failures, experiences or how someone was raised when we criticize someone else's actions or decisions.

There is an old saying that reminds me of how important it is to communicate and listen before rushing to judgment.

Reasonable people, equally informed, seldom disagree.

The Sixth Amendment of the United States Bill of Rights relates to this subject. *"In all criminal prosecutions, the accused shall enjoy the right to a speedy and public trial, by an impartial jury of the State and district wherein the crime shall have been committed, which district shall have been previously ascertained by law, and to be informed of the nature and cause of the accusation; to be confronted with the witnesses against him; to have compulsory process for obtaining witnesses in his favor, and to have the Assistance of Counsel for his defense."*

- John 7:24 - *Judge not according to the appearance, but judge righteous judgment.*
- Luke 6:37 - *Judge not, and ye shall not be judged: condemn not, and ye shall not be condemned: forgive, and ye shall be forgiven.*

I Thought I Knew

Truth for Today – Hebrews 4:15

My dad passed away and we were at the funeral home. Many friends, family, and neighbors came through to extend sympathy and love. I had many thoughts and experiences through those two days, but one stood out.

As a pastor for fourteen years at that point, I had been given many opportunities to minister to those who had lost their father. I thought I could feel their pain and loss. But losing my own dad helped me understand that I had only thought I knew. Now I knew first-hand what losing a dad was like.

I didn't know the loss of a dad until I lost my own. I didn't know what traumatized families went through until our own son had a traumatic brain injury. I didn't know the anxiety of having surgery until I had a hernia repaired.

All of this teaches me that there are many things I've yet to experience. I've not experienced the loss of a child. I've not grieved the loss of a wife. I've not experienced excruciating or chronic pain. I've not been diagnosed with cancer or had a heart attack.

Maybe those things will be in my future, but my prayer is that, until then I can hold my tongue and opinions about things I know very little about. I pray that I can share silent love and compassion to those who are experiencing things I've not been touched with.

- I thought I knew hunger until I met a seven year old girl who ate dirt to fill her stomach.
- I thought I knew pain until I heard of a lone hiker who had to cut off his arm which was pinned under a large boulder.
- I thought I knew thirst until I read of men in a life-boat for weeks.
- I thought I knew hopelessness until I read about a kidnapped little girl later found dead.
- I thought I knew grief until I saw the weeping of a mother and father holding their full-term, still-born, long-awaited and only child.
- I thought I knew loss until I stood beside a man whose wife and child had just died in a tragic car accident.

Lord, give me ears to hear, eyes that see and a heart to understand.

I Wasn't Watching Where I was Going

Truth for Today – Revelation 12:9

The lioness was intent on her prey. A herd of antelope on the plain was unaware of her presence. She was within 100', hugging the dirt, nestled in the tall grass, and waiting for the right moment.

Then, she bolted from her prone position to a full out run, singling out one antelope. They seemed to be equal in speed with the lioness 20' behind the antelope. The antelope was leaping and running with a wary eye on what was pursuing him. The lioness was making no headway, though it appeared she could close the gap.

Suddenly in front of the antelope were three other lionesses. While he had been intent on the danger from behind he failed to see the other threat in front, and to his right and his left. The race was over. The trap had been set and the quarry became dinner.

Lions are unique in the cat family in several ways. They are the only cat species that form a social group. All other cats hunt alone. Lions work for a common goal.

Revelation 12:9 says, *"And the great dragon was cast out, that old serpent, called the Devil, and Satan, which deceiveth the whole world: he was cast out into the earth, and his angels were cast out with him."*

As believers we need to be aware of satan's tactics as he seeks to devour God's people. Satan has many associates and is certainly devious and cunning in his desire to overthrow the power of Jesus. If we condition ourselves to watch only one area of our lives, we may open up vulnerability in another. Awareness of satan's tactics is vital.

In another respect, just as the lions work together in a pride for common goals, we as believers have the same opportunity. The Bible says in James 5:16 - *Confess your faults one to another, and pray one for another, that ye may be healed. The effectual fervent prayer of a righteous man availeth much.*

Likewise in Hebrews 10:25 - *Not forsaking the assembling of ourselves together, as the manner of some is; but exhorting one another: and so much the more, as ye see the day approaching.*

God's family has the privilege of watching one another's back.

I Wish I Would Have Stopped...

Truth for Today – John 16:13

"I wish I would have stopped!" Regrets. How many of us have said...

"I wish I would have stopped before that first puff."
"I wish I would have stopped while the beer was still in the bottle."
"I wish I would have stopped when I was still a virgin."
"I wish I would have stopped and just said no to that first joint."
"I wish I would have stopped before opening that porn-site."
"I wish I would have stopped before saying that."
"I wish I would have stopped texting while driving."
"I wish I would have stopped at the stop sign."

I was sitting in a small restaurant in Port au Prince, Haiti enjoying my fish dinner when a man asked if he could join me. He was an American helicopter pilot who was helping with emergencies right after the January 2010 earthquake.

He ordered chicken and rice. While we talked about the tragedy of the earthquake, we ate.

Suddenly he stopped eating and pushed his plate away. I asked him what was wrong. He said, "When you get to the cold part of the chicken you need to stop!" I looked at the pink meat in front of him and realized that this was a man who recognized warning signals.

Do we have our eyes and ears open, or our brains tuned into the clues surrounding us as we make everyday choices? We can save ourselves trouble and regrets by listening to the Holy Spirit.

John 16:13 - *Howbeit when He, the Spirit of truth, is come, He will guide you into all truth: for He shall not speak of Himself; but whatsoever He shall hear, that shall He speak: and He will shew you things to come.*

I'll Fly Away

Truth for Today – 1 Thessalonians 4:15-18

Armen gathered as many vulture feathers as he could find. He attached them to his body and constructed two wings for his arms. Then he jumped from a tower and promptly crashed. Observers said that Armen failed because he didn't have a tail. That early recorded jump happened in 852 AD and indicates man's early desire to fly.

Over the centuries, men courted injury and death in their pursuit of flight. Man-powered bicycles with wings; tightly wound spring operated carts; and rotors powered by steam continued to move man closer and closer to the 20th century.

Finally, on December 17, 1903, Orville Wright made a 120' flight that lasted for 12 seconds in Kitty Hawk, North Carolina. The one hundred plus years since that time has seen the advancement of unbelievable technology and accomplishments. Man can fly.

The Russian aircraft known as the Antonov An-225 can lift off a runway and fly, weighing in at 640 tons (1,280,000 pounds). That is the equivalent of 85 of the world's largest elephants.

Consider the rocket that NASA intends to launch in 2018, the Solar Probe Plus. It is designed to be the fastest rocket ever launched, achieving orbital speeds of 450,000 miles per hour.

In May of 1991, a Boeing 747 had seats removed to maximize the number of passengers to be transported from Ethiopia to Israel. A total of 1,122 people were loaded and successfully transported to create a new world's record. Interestingly, it was a clandestine operation to transport Ethiopian Jews to their homeland of Israel.

As I think of those Ethiopian Jews leaving their clothing and belongings behind to get to their promised land, I think of the Bible's promises about flying away to Heaven. It will be the flight of all flights!

> 1 Thessalonians 4:16-17 - *For the Lord himself shall descend from heaven with a shout, with the voice of the archangel, and with the trump of God: and the dead in Christ shall rise first: Then we which are alive and remain shall be caught up together with them in the clouds, to meet the Lord in the air: and so shall we ever be with the Lord.*

I'll Pass on the Dessert

Truth for Today – Romans 8:26-27

I'm pretty sure I know what I'm eating, most of the time. I do remember one experience in Haiti when I thought I was eating macaroni's in a red sauce. However, I learned halfway through the meal that in reality it was goat small intestine. In any case, it was good.

But recently I learned that we may be ingesting items we are unaware of. For instance, in many food items such as chicken nuggets, boxed waffles and other things, the cellulose on the ingredient listing is tree-pulp. It's used to keep shredded cheese from clumping, keeping low-fat ice cream creamy, and milk shakes smooth.

What do some strawberry yogurts and red candies have in common with beetles, which inhabit the prickly pear cactus? More than you'd like to know. The beetles are dried and crushed to make a bright red fluid which of course is processed for food coloring.

Ever wonder what happened to all that hair on the floor of barber shops? An amino acid is harvested from human hair and duck feathers to make an ingredient used for making pizza dough, cookies and various other pastries.

We love the shiny covering we see on many chocolate candies, jelly beans and other foods. It's called shellac. It is manufactured from a secretion of the female lac bug.

Knowing these little tidbits of information probably creates questions about what we ingest without thinking. We return a dish of spaghetti to the restaurant kitchen with great fanfare, when we find a hair. But in reality, we probably ingest worse without knowing.

On another note, what are we ingesting into our minds? Our eyes and ears are the funnels by which we channel great amounts of information to our brains. Do we have filters? Do we trust society to dictate what it is we should listen to or watch?

I'm thankful that the Holy Spirit with His still and small voice provides guidance, caution and direction. We can be assured of pure, natural and perfect ingredients as we open our Bibles and learn through the counsel of God's Spirit.

I'm a Failure Because I Failed

Truth for Today – Matthew 5

After graduating from high school I learned that I was ranked academically, 49 out of the 76 graduating seniors. It was fairly easy to feel that I had failed. I would tell myself, "You could have done better. You should have done better. You should have studied more. If only I would have paid more attention in class."

A failure can overwhelm our minds with negativity. A single occurrence of failure can put us quickly on the path of more failures. One singular failure can define us, if we don't take steps to find a new path.

So, how do we find a new path to success? We can be inspired by famous people who failed along their paths to success. Abraham Lincoln lost nominations to various government offices at least eight times before becoming president.

Michael Jordan once said, "I have missed more than 9,000 shots in my career. I have lost almost 300 games. On 26 occasions I have been entrusted to take the game winning shot, and I missed. I have failed over and over again in my life. And that is why I succeed."

Winston Churchill had to repeat a grade in elementary and failed the entrance exam to the Royal Military Academy.

Thomas Edison's school teacher stated that, "He is too stupid to learn anything." Later, Thomas made 1000 attempts to invent the light bulb.

Albert Einstein's teacher said that he was, "mentally slow, unsociable, and adrift forever in foolish dreams."

The Bible is the greatest record of the utter failures of mankind, and also the greatest book of hope.

- Philippians 4:13 - *I can do all things through Christ which strengtheneth me.*
- Romans 8:28 - *And we know that all things work together for good to them that love God, to them who are the called according to his purpose.*

Success is stumbling from failure to failure
with no loss of enthusiasm. - Winston Churchill

I'm Gonna Live Forever...

Truth for Today – John 5:28-29

One of my less desirable high school subjects was American History. A memorable topic we studied was the Spanish conquistador and explorer Ponce de Leon.

Born in 1474, he joined Christopher Columbus' three ship armada in 1493 at the age of 19 to search for the New World and a western passage to Asia. Later he was commissioned to explore the new lands found in the America's. It had been rumored that there was a "fountain of youth" in what is now Florida, where anyone entering the water would never age. He searched but obviously never found it since he died in 1521 at the age of 47.

A few days ago, I read two news articles, by two different authors, in two different newspapers. The one author stated, *"A battle with death can't be won."* The other author said, *"You can conquer your body's mortal limits."* Certainly two different perspectives! Ponce de Leon would have been confused.

However, God takes away the confusion when He speaks about mortality, death and eternal life.

- Ecclesiastes 12:7 - *Then shall the dust return to the earth as it was: and the spirit shall return unto God who gave it.*
- John 11:25 - *Jesus said unto her, I am the resurrection, and the life: he that believeth in me, though he were dead, yet shall he live.*
- John 3:16 - *For God so loved the world, that he gave his only begotten Son, that whosoever believeth in him should not perish, but have everlasting life.*
- John 5:28, 29 - *Marvel not at this: for the hour is coming, in the which all that are in the graves shall hear his voice, and shall come forth; they that have done good, unto the resurrection of life; and they that have done evil, unto the resurrection of damnation.*
- John 14:3 - *And if I go and prepare a place for you, I will come again, and receive you unto myself; that where I am, there ye may be also.*
- Matthew 25:46 - *And these shall go away into everlasting punishment: but the righteous into life eternal.*

I'm Talking Now

Truth for Today – Isaiah 40:28

We found two empty pork and bean cans and cut the tops off. The edges were jagged. Using a nail and hammer we poked a hole in the closed end of each can. Then we unwound the balled up string I had used for a kite.

As ten year olds, we were always looking for new things to try. We had heard that stretching a string tight between two tin cans could work like a telephone. So we stuck the ends of the string through the can and secured them with a washer. Then we headed to the hay mow of our barn. Stretching the string tight we were able to talk and listen to one another with the 40' span. Great communications!

A mere 55 years later, communications are vastly superior and almost supernaturally different. What do communications look like in the 21st century?

- Currently it is estimated that there are more cell phones in the world than people.
- Internet permits us almost immediate communication with others around the world.
- 42.3% of the world's population are using internet connections.
- In 2013, there were a reported 3.9 billion email accounts.
- It is expected that there will be 4.9 billion email accounts by 2017.
- 191 billion emails were sent or received per day, worldwide, in 2014. That equates to 2.2 million emails flying around the world per second.

The Bible tells us that God is omniscient. He is infinitely aware of everything, everywhere at any time. Isaiah 40:28 says, *Hast thou not known? Hast thou not heard, that the everlasting God, the Lord, the Creator of the ends of the earth, fainteth not, neither is weary? There is no searching of his understanding.*

When we begin to doubt God's ability to handle the situations, issues or hurts in our lives, we need to research and understand His infinite strengths and abilities.

Impossible Possibilities

Often we need reminders of God's faithfulness, His strength, power and His desire to fight our battles. The Bible is full of stories illustrating the concept. Reminders are good for me.

They decided to build their building out of logs. The loggers began by cutting down trees with their axes. While chopping the logs, the axe head flew off of one man's handle and fell into the river next to him. He was frustrated because he had borrowed the axe and he knew he would have to face the owner. According to 2 Kings 6, *"the man of God said, where fell it? And he shewed him the place. And he cut down a stick, and cast it in thither; and the iron did swim."*

The slaves were escaping their owners. It had been so long since they had known freedom and their hopes were growing. Then they came to a body of water. It was too large and too deep to swim across and they didn't have the time to consider going around. Then... *"Moses stretched out his hand over the sea; and the LORD caused the sea to go back by a strong east wind all that night, and made the sea dry land, and the waters were divided. And the children of Israel went into the midst of the sea upon the dry ground: and the waters were a wall unto them on their right hand, and on their left."*

The children of Israel looked up at the formidable walls of Jericho and knew that no human strength or will would permit them access to their enemy's city. *"So the people shouted when the priests blew with the trumpets: and it came to pass, when the people heard the sound of the trumpet, and the people shouted with a great shout, that the wall fell down flat, so that the people went up into the city, every man straight before him, and they took the city."*

- 2 Chronicles 20:15 - *Thus saith the Lord unto you, Be not afraid nor dismayed by reason of this great multitude; for the battle is not yours, but God's.*
- Philippians 4:13 - *I can do all things through Christ which strengtheneth me.*
- Isaiah 41:10 - *Fear thou not; for I am with thee: be not dismayed; for I am thy God: I will strengthen thee; yea, I will help thee; yea, I will uphold thee with the right hand of my righteousness.*

Indicators

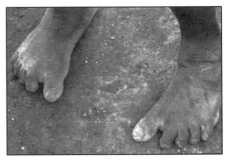

She was 83 years old and her feet looked like they had been everywhere. In reality she had never been out of Haiti and maybe never to Port au Prince. She had never owned a bicycle and her life had been spent in a dirt floored, thatched hut with a tin roof.

In her 80 years of walking to market, to the river several times a day to retrieve water, in the fields picking Congo beans and corn, and visiting friends down the road, she had probably averaged a conservative five miles a day of walking. That is a total of almost 150,000 miles on those hard, calloused, flat but solid feet.

150,000 miles. With an earth circumference of 25,000 miles, those feet would have walked the equivalent of six times around the world.

Our physical appearance is an indicator of what has happened or is happening in our lives. We see anger in someone's eyes at a restaurant; we see tears rolling down the cheek of a homeless person; the fearful, sad and skittish eyes of a five year old child; the wrinkles on the forehead of a miner; the missing fingers of a carpenter; the 4" scar on someone's arm; and the worn torn feet of a great-grandmother in southwest Haiti. They are all indicators of life-stories.

As I think of Jesus, there are things that give us indications about His life. We picture Jesus weeping as He looked over Jerusalem; looking into the eyes of the woman taken in adultery; or the sadness in His eyes as He looked at the widow who had lost her only son.

But to me the greatest gauge of Jesus was indicated in Luke 22:44 - *And being in an agony he prayed more earnestly: and his sweat was as it were great drops of blood falling down to the ground.*

He was facing the heaviest trial of His young thirty-three years of life. I would not have wanted to walk a mile in His shoes, but I am glad that He walked a lifetime in mine.

Intimidation

***Truth for Today* –** 1 Thessalonians 5:11

Walking down an aisle at the grocery store I heard a mother tell her young son, "I don't know why I always have to tell you that. You're worthless." My heart broke for the boy whose value, confidence and self-worth were being pulled out of him.

As a bullied child I know how quickly a child can feel last, least, lost and lonely. People with strong and aggressive personalities can do much damage to people with quiet and introverted natures. Mothers and fathers without compassion, love and a nurturing spirit can unwittingly teach children to become withdrawn.

Do we permit our physical stature, strong voices, gender type, personality, financial status, age, position or demeanor aggressively intimidate those who are smaller or weaker? The below image graphically speaks volumes to me.

1 Thessalonians 5:11 instructs us to encourage one another and build each other up. In our culture we have many opportunities to practice self-control, esteem others, as well as lifting one another up.

A few years ago, a good friend said to me, "There's not much I can do for you, but I am happy to stay in the background and try to do things that make you look good."

His self-sacrificing attitude was humbling and challenging to say the least. It reminded me of the life of Jesus. Taking a back seat. Lifting others up. Doing the heavy lifting. Doing the dirty work. Accepting blame when it wasn't deserved.

Jesus, help me to have your heart, mind and spirit.

Is Good, Good Enough?

Truth for Today – Genesis 1

I'm not sure what existed before God started creating the heavens and the earth, but fortunately we have an accurate accounting of what came later…

- Day One – Light and dark; night and day.
  - God looked at it all and said "It was good."
- Day Two – Water, dirt, sand, mud and heavens.
  - God looked at it all and said "It was good."
- Day Three – Dry land, seas, grass, herbs, trees, and their fruit.
  - God looked at it all and said "It was good."
- Day Four – Stars, seasons, time, sun and the moon.
  - God looked at it all and said "It was good."
- Day Five – Everything that lived in the water and in the air.
  - God looked at it all and said "It was good."
- Day Six – Every animal, insect, reptile that was on the earth.
  - God looked at it all and said "It was good."

And then at the end of Day Six, *God created man in His own image, in the image of God created He him; male and female created He them.*

We get a glimpse of God's level of fulfillment and enjoyment after all the butterflies, waterfalls, canyons, zebras, amoebas, crawdads, boas and eagles were made, when God said – *"It is good!"*

Then and only then, man was made in God's image and in His likeness. Man didn't create anything, nor had he accomplished anything. Man merely existed and God looked at it all and said *"it is **very** good!"*

Can we imagine, the entire creation prior to man was only "good"? After man was created it went to "very good". Why? Pretty simple – We are made in the image and likeness of God and we have a living soul. He loves all His creation, but we are His crowning glory.

Do we live our lives knowing who we are in His eyes?

Is That a Tree?

Truth for Today – Mark 8

Perry, a friend of mine and farmer, was 25 years old in 1959, when an anhydrous ammonia accident caused total blindness in his right eye. Then one year later, a battery exploded and he felt irritation on his face. He checked his remaining good eye carefully but found nothing in it. He kept working until a week later when the pain took him to his eye doctor.

The doctor found an ulcer on his cornea, created by a microscopic bit of battery acid from the explosion. The cornea ruptured and a transplant was necessary, but the transplanted cornea rejected and a second transplant was done. Again, deterioration took place and Perry's vision was still very poor. A decision had to be made whether to be thankful for the very poor vision he had, or risk a third transplant. Feeling God's direction, he made the decision to go ahead.

A long two year healing process took place and at one time his vision was so poor he couldn't see the food on his plate, see the characteristics of people, and had to feel his way through the house. He now knew the disappointment of unrealized expectations.

I'm reminded of the blind man in Mark 8:22-24 - *And (Jesus) cometh to Bethsaida; and they bring a blind man unto him, and besought him to touch him. And he took the blind man by the hand, and led him out of the town; and when he had spit on his eyes, and put his hands upon him, he asked him if he saw ought. And he looked up, and said, I see men as trees, walking.* - What a disappointment! I'm sure the blind man had high expectations that he would receive sight from this man Jesus. But Jesus wasn't finished, as we read in verse 25 - *After that (Jesus) put his hands again upon his eyes, and made him look up: and he was restored, and saw every man clearly.*

Back to Perry. Doctors decided to try a new miracle contact lens. He was measured, fitted and received near perfect vision. He looked at his wife and said, "You have more wrinkles than I remember," and then said, "I'm kidding." The most exciting part of all of this is Perry's statement, "I had learned contentment with whatever God wanted for me." Contentment, faith and miracles. God is good all the time.

Is the Bible Enough?

He was a husband, father and a Christian believer. I met him in a city north of Delhi, India. I was intrigued by how he came to know Jesus in a country that is less than 1.5% Protestant Christian.

He said it began when someone gave him a small Bible to read. I asked him if he went to a church for teaching at that time and he said, "No". I asked him if he had gone to a Bible study and was mentored or discipled by someone. He said, "No, it was only the Bible."

Fascinated, I listened as he shared his testimony. "I began reading in the book of John. When I got to John 14:6, I was captivated by the words of Jesus saying - *I am the way, the truth and the life. No man cometh unto the Father but by me.* - I accepted that truth and the Gospel of Jesus."

Why am I fascinated by that story? I shouldn't be. God's Holy Spirit, His Word and His Son are enough. He is truly an awesome, perfect and complete God!

- 2 Timothy 3:16-17 - *All scripture is given by inspiration of God, and is profitable for doctrine, for reproof, for correction, for instruction in righteousness: That the man of God may be perfect, thoroughly furnished unto all good works.*
- Joshua 1:8 - *This book of the law shall not depart out of thy mouth; but thou shalt meditate therein day and night, that thou mayest observe to do according to all that is written therein: for then thou shalt make thy way prosperous, and then thou shalt have good success.*
- Psalm 119:105 - *Thy word is a lamp unto my feet, and a light unto my path.*

It Can't Be!

We draw conclusions about people, things, and situations or in this case, animals and insects based on perception. Sometimes it is difficult to believe some facts, simply because we've believed fiction for so long. Consider the following facts about animals and insects.

- Centipedes – Though the name would insinuate that this insect has 100 legs, they do not. In fact it is impossible for a centipede to have 100 legs as they always have an odd number of pairs of legs. Some may have as few as nine pairs and some as high as 149, but no centipede has 100 legs.
- Camels – Though many live in hot climates, camels do not sweat. Their body temperature can rise to 120° Fahrenheit.
- Pigs – Though often they are considered "not-so-bright", they are in fact quite intelligent. In many cases, pigs pitted against human toddlers win in the areas of object recognition and manipulation.
- Sheep – We develop an opinion of the intelligence of sheep based on their ability to be deceived (by wolves in sheep's clothing), or how they blindly follow one another. However, their intelligence level is high in relation to others in the animal world.
- Bulls – We tend to believe that the color "red" angers or attracts bulls. In fact, they are drawn to the motion of a cape rather than the color. Red is no more attractive to a bull than other colors.
- Wolves and Coyotes – Do they howl at the moon? No, they howl to communicate with one another. They howl more at night because they are more active after dark.
- Camels – They do not store water in their humps. The humps are a storage place for fat, which can be converted to water in dry seasons.
- Toads – A human cannot get warts from touching a toad. Human warts are caused by a human virus.

Of course this list could go on and on. This exercise is merely to point out that not all things are as we've learned, thought or been taught. It applies equally in the human world. How many times do we discriminate against others due to our prejudiced perceptions?

It Could Have Been Worse

Truth for Today – Matthew 27

I got out of bed, wiping the sleep from my eyes as I headed into another day. A good morning for me is to slowly and methodically move from inaction to action. *Special emphasis on the slow and methodical.* But on this particular morning as I entered a dark room, the middle toe of my left foot solidly thumped into one of my parked shoes.

I went from inaction to action immediately as pain lit me up. We all know the feeling as we stub our toe, jam a finger or get a finger pinched in a car door. It is instantaneous and unforgiving.

I was angry at myself for not turning on the light or watching where I was going. The end result was a middle toe turning shades of black, blue, red with tinges of green.

In the middle of my pain and throbbing toe woes, I thought of a farmer I know. It was forty years ago, late fall, unseasonably cold and he still had corn to pick. Without a cab on his tractor, his feet were getting colder and colder. Then he had the idea of climbing on top of the hood of his tractor, dangling his feet over the side, and resting them on the warm engine block.

Unfortunately, he inadvertently stuck his foot into the fan blade of the motor. He lost the middle toe of his foot.

As I thought about the farmer's pain and loss, my pain started to subside. There is therapy in thinking about how others have had it worse than me. I was immediately thankful that I still had my toe and that it was going to be okay.

On another note, the farmer who lost his toe told me, "When I lost my toe I wasn't happy. But then I thought of my brother-in-law who lost his arm in a corn-picker accident. Then I realized it could have been worse."

It could have been worse... but, someone, somewhere, sometime, experienced the absolute worst case scenario. There is someone who endured more physical, emotional and spiritual agony than anyone else ever. Who was that?

I would say it was our Jesus. Torture, pain, agony, forsaken, unjustly accused, with the weight of the world on His shoulders.

It Isn't What it Seems

Truth for Today – 2 Corinthians 12

At 12 years old the obsessive practicing began. Though she had loved swimming prior to that, it was now that the hard work began. From the age of 12 to 19 she put in 8,840 hours of training. That is 3.5 hours per day. At 19 she won two Olympic gold medals.

The Russian four year old boy was given a miniature violin. From the beginning it seemed like a natural part of who he was. Practicing seven hours a day on his violin, he gave his first recital at age five. His family would eat their evening meal at 8:00 P.M. and he would take lessons until 4:00 A.M. He was traveling abroad at age 10 and at 15 he won his first international competition. Today he is a professor of music in London.

Yet another young boy began playing piano at age two. At age three, at his first recital he played a G major sonatina by Beethoven. He practices up to eight hours a day as he pursues his dream of becoming a world class pianist.

We are taught that hard work and effort brings rewards. In fact the Bible tells us that *"the workman is worthy of his meat,"* and that we are to *"study to shew thyself approved unto God."* But, in the reality of living out our daily walk with Him, we are called to not trust in our intelligence, flesh and strength.

Rather we are told that the eternally good things come as a gift, not by our strength and power. It becomes a difficult thing to process eternal things in a manner that is different than our culture teaches. In the end we live by faith and trust of someone we've never seen, heard or felt. A God who has our backs and wants us to rest in His arms and power. Can we do that?

- 2 Corinthians 12:9 - *My grace is sufficient for thee: for my strength is made perfect in weakness. Most gladly therefore will I rather glory in my infirmities, that the power of Christ may rest upon me.*
- Psalm 71:16 - *I will go in the strength of the Lord God.*
- Ephesians 6:10 - *Finally, my brethren, be strong in the Lord, and in the power of his might.*

It's Just a Rock

Truth for Today – 1 Samuel 16:7

It was just a rock. It had bumps and ridges. There was dirt and mud still clinging to it. It was, of course, created by God, but there was no beauty associated with it. After all, it's just a rock... or is it? Are things just as they appear?

How many times do we judge beauty by external factors as we observe someone? What is beauty based upon? The right size nose or ears? Color of skin or hair or eyes? Lips with an appropriate contour or size? Weight? Height? Age? The list of factors we use to determine beauty goes on and on.

1 Samuel 16:7 gives us a glimpse into how God judges beauty - *But the LORD said unto Samuel, Look not on his countenance, or on the height of his stature; because I have refused him: for the LORD seeth not as man seeth; for man looketh on the outward appearance, but the LORD looketh on the heart.*

God used Jesus as a standard. In Isaiah 53:2 we read about the outward appearance of Jesus - *He (Jesus) hath no form nor comeliness; and when we shall see him, there is no beauty that we should desire him.*

So, back to the rock. It's just a rock, or is it? A chisel and a hammer open the rock to show the crystals and beauty!

I keep this geode around to remind me that inside each of us are qualities, value and beauty that are not always apparent on the outside. I am thankful that He knows who and what we are. We are created by Him and for Him.

It's Just H₂O

***Truth for Today** – Matthew 3

We drink it, swim in it, boil it, ski on top of it, freeze it, bathe with it, and the list goes on. It's just water. But the word "just" doesn't seem to do it justice. Water is such a part of our lives that we sometimes fail to recognize its unique qualities.

- 71% of the world's surface is covered with water.
- 97% of the world's water is salty; 2% is frozen in icecaps; 1% is available for drinking.
- Hot water freezes faster than cold water.
- If you throw boiling water into sub-zero air, the water immediately turns to snow.
- 85% of the world live in the driest half of the earth; 783 million people don't have access to clean water; 2.5 billion don't have access to adequate sanitation; and 3.4 million die annually due to water related diseases.
- 80% of a newborn's weight is water.
- It takes 2900 gallons of water to make one pound of coffee.
- For every glass of water served in a restaurant, it takes two cups to wash and rinse the glass.
- In theory, all the water that was ever created is still in existence today, in one form or another.
- 338 gallons of water are used to produce one serving of beef.
- It takes 880 gallons of water to produce one gallon of milk.

Water has been with us from day one of creation. Its significance is vitally important to every living organism. Under pressure it creates caves and underground rivers. With volume it changes river boundaries and borders. With volume and intensity it creates waves that can devastate nations.

However, there was one usage of water that Jesus specifically encouraged His followers to utilize. Baptism. Jesus was baptized in water and encouraged us to follow His example. Symbolically we experience baptism to indicate faith and a renewed spirit and life. Of all the usages of water, there seems to be none of greater importance than what Jesus encouraged us to experience.

Just As I Am

Truth for Today – 1 Corinthians 12

She was about twenty years old and had lived with the ramifications of Cerebral Palsy from her premature birth. There were speech and physical issues that created many challenges for her. However, many admired her ability to love Jesus, remain independent, active and known as an encourager. Then, one eventful evening, she was invited to someone's home for time with friends.

Upon arrival she met a man she had not known before. Towards the end of the evening the gentleman told her, "I have the faith to believe that you can be freed from the challenges you have. With enough faith you can be healed and made whole. Can I pray with you so you can be delivered from these problems?"

She left and arrived at my home weeping. Through tears she shared the episode with me. Then I heard one of the most profound faith-filled statements ever. "I am happy with who God has made me to be. I don't want to be changed from what He wants. I've accepted who and what I am. Why can't others accept me for who I am? I am whole and complete, in spite of what others may think."

As humans we have ideas as to what we consider as whole, complete, perfect and flawless. She taught me a profound truth that evening. Her faith was and is still deep, twenty-four years later.

Paul was flawed with a thorn in his flesh based on 2 Cor. 12:7; history would indicate that Paul was short, bald-headed and bow-legged; Jesus lacked beauty and comeliness according to Isaiah 53:2. Moses was not gifted with public speaking. Esther was an orphan. Joseph was a slave. David and Solomon had their issues.

We are made in the image and likeness of God. We were found "very good" without having done anything at all. Good enough to be entrusted with a living soul that is able to bring glory, honor and pleasure to the Creator of the universe.

- 1 Corinthians 12:18 - *But now hath God set the members every one of them in the body, as it hath pleased him.*
- Exodus 4:11 - *Who hath made man's mouth? Or who maketh the dumb, or deaf, or the seeing, or the blind? Have not I the* LORD*?*

Keep on Keeping on...

Truth for Today – 2 Timothy 4:6-8

Merriam Webster Dictionary defines "stamina" as – *Great physical or mental strength that allows you to continue doing something for a long time.*

We know and admire stamina when we see it. It is one of the qualities that sets the super-athletes apart from the athletes. Let's try to gain perspective.

- Horses can have a maximum speed of 54 mph. If they ran a 26.2 mile marathon, they would average 10.5 mph and complete it in 2.5 hours.
- Humans can reach a maximum speed of 27.45 mph with an average speed in a marathon of 12.7 mph and completion in 2.0 hours.
- Sled dogs can run at 25 mph, with an average speed of 15 mph with a marathon completion in 1.34 hours.
- The ugly, ungainly, awkward ostrich is a high performer in the stamina department. Reaching a maximum speed of 55 mph, they could average 30 mph in a marathon and complete it in a record 45 minutes.

So, what's the lesson regarding the ostrich? Outward appearance doesn't make a difference in performance? Don't judge a book by its cover? Don't taunt an ostrich in open country and expect to get away?

Stamina. It is a defining quality that I see in many aged believers. Though frail, fragile, weak and elderly, I admire their determination, grit, courage and strength. Stamina is not just about speed and ground distance, it is about perseverance and fortitude. It is about the ability to stay in the race, to fight to the end.

Many people are encouraged by Paul's life-end statement in 2 Timothy 4:6-8 - *For I am now ready to be offered, and the time of my departure is at hand. I have fought a good fight, I have finished my course, I have kept the faith: Henceforth there is laid up for me a crown of righteousness, which the Lord, the righteous judge, shall give me at that day: and not to me only, but unto all them also that love his appearing.*

Knees in the Dirt

***Truth for Today* – Acts 16**

Walking along the blue water of the Caribbean, I had several companions. A Haitian pastor, visitors from the U.S. and a ragtag group of several children who lived nearby. We left the beach and entered a small village of the poorest of the poor. In the U.S. this stretch of beach would command exorbitant real estate prices, but in Haiti it is home for the poorest squatters.

As we visited several families, a man invited us into his small yard. Flying over his home were flags signifying his role as a voodoo houngan or priest. Immediately I noticed his altar and ceremonial pole.

Three months later on another visit to the village, this time with two Haitian pastors and others, the voodoo priest invited us to visit once again. However, the visit took a different turn as the Haitian pastors challenged the priest in his work of voodoo. It wasn't long until the priest dropped to his knees in the dirt of his voodoo yard. He wanted to know what he needed to do to walk away from his voodoo life and follow Jesus.

It reminded me of the scripture in Acts 16 when Paul and Silas were in bondage in a prison in Philippi. An earthquake struck, the foundations shook, the doors opened and the chains fell from Paul and Silas. As the head jailer saw the inevitability of his prisoners potential escape, he asked Paul the ultimate question – *"What must I do to be saved?"* Paul's response was, *"Believe on the Lord Jesus Christ, and thou shalt be saved, and thy house."*

Fortunately for us, the Bible is clear on what it takes to be a follower of Jesus:

- Acts 16:31 - *Believe on the Lord Jesus Christ, and thou shalt be saved.*
- John 3:3 - *Except a man be born again, he cannot see the kingdom of God.*
- Acts 3:19 - *Repent ye therefore, and be converted, that your sins may be blotted out.*

Knowing My Place

Truth for Today – 1 Chronicles 29:11-12

South American Indians, or Papua New Guinea natives are acutely aware of the sun. It is their companion every day, breathing life into their families. At night, they watch the moon make its trek across the sky. They think that the two balls in the sky are the same size.

We however, due to science, telescopes and technology know that the sun has a diameter that is 400 times larger than the moon. The sun is also 400 times farther away from the earth's surface than the moon. Those two facts create an illusion that they are equal in magnitude. It is an amazing thing that two objects so enormously different from one another appear to be the same size.

The concept is yet another reminder to me that not all things are as they seem. That is true for my relationships with others, as well as my relationship with God.

How often do I judge another person's decisions, actions or inactions from my own viewpoint? Am I aware of all the issues, factors or experiences the other person used to make their decision?

It is rather easy to judge others. It seems to be human nature to critique after the fact. Rarely are situations as black and white as they seem. If I think that I can second guess another's situation, am I possibly arrogant in my limited judgment?

How often do I question God's sovereignty? Do I give Him the right to be God and Creator of all things? In my humanness and lack of understanding do I ask Him "why"? Is there a chance that He sees things differently than me? Is there a possibility, given His ability to see all and know all, He might have a better idea on what is happening?

1 Chronicles 29:11-12 - *Thine, O Lord, is the greatness, and the power, and the glory, and the victory, and the majesty: for all that is in the heaven and in the earth is thine; thine is the kingdom, O Lord, and thou art exalted as head above all. Both riches and honor come of thee, and thou reignest over all; and in thine hand is power and might; and in thine hand it is to make great, and to give strength unto all.*

Left Behind

Truth for Today – Psalm 25:4-5

He was five years old and was certainly enjoying the zoo with his kindergarten class. But unfortunately, when the bus left the zoo for school, he wasn't on it. He had been left behind.

She was only two months old, wrapped in a blanket and left alone on a step in a small yard in a remote mountain village of southwest Haiti. She had been left behind.

The couple was enjoying their sunny, nine day vacation getaway in Mexico. At their home in Illinois, the smoke alarm in their home malfunctioned. Their nine year old daughter who was tending the home called 911. It was then that the fire department found out that the nine year old girl and her four year old sister had been left behind to care for themselves.

The "No Child Left Behind Act" of 2001 deals with resources, assessment, equity and testing to make sure that disadvantaged and other children are not left behind.

There are books and movies characterizing the Biblical end-time concepts of the Rapture and what it may be like to be left behind.

But, I do wonder how often God feels left behind? When I make choices in my life that are selfish and self-serving, does God feel left behind?

When I fail to share with the last, least, lost and lonely, does God feel left behind? When I arrogantly go places and do things without asking God for guidance, does He feel left behind?

- Psalm 32:8 - *I will instruct thee and teach thee in the way which thou shalt go: I will guide thee with mine eye.*
- Proverbs 3:5-6 - *Trust in the LORD with all thine heart; and lean not unto thine own understanding. In all thy ways acknowledge him, and he shall direct thy paths.*
- Psalm 25:4-5 - *Shew me thy ways, O LORD; teach me thy paths. Lead me in thy truth, and teach me: for thou art the God of my salvation; on thee do I wait all the day.*

Lord, help me to make sure I am always looking at your tail-lights.

Lend Me a Hand

Truth for Today – Isaiah 41:10

As a professional carpenter, Richard Van As from South Africa was working on a project for a customer. A distraction, and a moment later, his table saw had amputated four fingers on his right hand.

With doctors unable to reattach the fingers, Richard started using his time to research and hopefully find prosthetic fingers. Unable to find what he needed at an affordable price, he joined up with Ivan Owen in the U.S. to engineer and develop something that could work.

Together they came up with prosthetic fingers. Utilizing 3D printers, stainless steel, aluminum and specialized plastics, they have accomplished the miraculous. Working fingers that can move, flex and pick things up. Beyond that, they are making the technology available at no cost to many others around the globe who can print their own parts, assemble them and have working hands again.

One of Richard's highlights was watching his first customer, a five year old boy born without fingers on his right hand. Almost immediately he was picking things up and showing his excitement. The creative engineering and generosity of Richard and Ivan will provide thousands of fingerless people around the world an opportunity to experience life in a fuller measure.

Richard's loss has certainly turned into huge blessings for many others. There are many trite sayings that characterize his situation:

- No pain, no gain.
- Let your situation make you better, not bitter.
- Champions don't quit.
- Winners never quit and quitters never win.

God talks about the subject in another way. Romans 8:28 - *And we know that all things work together for good to them that love God, to them who are the called according to his purpose.*

Should you shield the canyons from the wind-storms,
you would never see the true beauty of their carvings.
Elisabeth Kubler-Ross

Let Me Drive

Truth for Today – Psalm 46:1

During the 20th century, it seemed that we experienced a transition in technology. In the first 50 years, new inventions surprised the general public on an intermittent basis. In the last 50 years of the 20th century, it seemed that technology began moving much faster.

On July 20, 1969 humans landed on the moon. Many believe that the technology required to bring that to pass propelled mankind into a new era. One only needs to follow the common telephone or computer to understand how quickly current technology is replaced by the next generation. A phone or computer can become obsolete within a year or less!

We were amazed to learn that the first driver-less automobiles were being tested on America's highways. States have legalized their presence on their roads. What will the next years bring?

As believers we shouldn't be overly concerned as we think about the concept of a driver-less car. We try to live our lives with God in control. A bumper sticker from some years ago said - *God is my Co-Pilot.* A subsequent one stated – *If God is your Co-Pilot, Change Seats.*

As believers we try to become relaxed and comfortable in God's hands. We trust Him to lead us. We know that He does a better job of guiding our lives than we ourselves. Can we become comfortable in taking a back seat?

- Isaiah 40:29 - *He giveth power to the faint; and to them that have no might he increaseth strength.*
- Psalm 46:1 - *God is our refuge and strength, a very present help in trouble.*
- Isaiah 41:10 - *Fear thou not; for I am with thee: be not dismayed; for I am thy God: I will strengthen thee; yea, I will help thee; yea, I will uphold thee with the right hand of my righteousness.*
- Isaiah 43:2 - *When thou passest through the waters, I will be with thee; and through the rivers, they shall not overflow thee: when thou walkest through the fire, thou shalt not be burned; neither shall the flame kindle upon thee.*

Let Your Imagination Roll

Truth for Today – Genesis 1

      I like to let my mind wonder as I try to imagine what those days of Creation were like. There was nothing, and then something. The first five days rolled by and then the morning of the sixth day arrived.

      The environment was set in place. Just the day before, God had filled the skies with birds and the waters with fish. Now He was ready to populate the land. Did He rub His chin as He pondered what to create next? Possibly He was like an artist with an empty canvas in front of Him, or as a sculptor with a granite rock waiting to reveal a masterpiece? Then He began.

      His creation that day revealed the zebra, horse, cow, chameleon, groundhog, squirrel, armadillo and the list went on. Each were unique and different in their sizes, colors, habits, instincts, skin or scales. Then His imagination began to soar.

      What if you started the next animal with the feet and bill of a duck? Then added a beaver's tail? What if you added the body and fur of an otter? What if you had this furry animal lay eggs? How about making it a mammal and giving her the opportunity to nurse her young? Might as well add venom to this hybrid. How about getting really creative and putting the venom in the heels of this animals rear duck feet? There we have it. Now for a unique name... platypus! Project completed – time to move on to the rhinoceros.

      What a Creator God we serve. I can't imagine the fulfillment and pleasure God had in those first days of Creation. It reminds me of being in first grade and having a blank piece of paper and a box of crayons in front of me. Taking home those colorful scribbles to my mom and dad was special, fulfilling and their positive comments brought pleasure to my creativity.

      Then He started creating men and women in His image and His likeness. There have been billions of uniquely different human beings. We use words like omniscience, omnipresent and omnipotent to describe God's ability to be all knowing, present everywhere and all powerful. Possibly we should add omni-imaginative.

Let-down

Truth for Today – Revelation 21:4

The keynote speech in Washington D.C. was over. The standing ovation indicated the audience's acceptance of the speaker's passion to find ways in which faith based organizations could receive grants from the federal government.

As the audience began leaving, the speaker, President George W. Bush remained on the stage to shake hands with a hundred or so people lined up along the edge.

As he worked his way around the stage, he reached down and shook hands with one after another. There was no room for me, so I went to the very end and waited. Finally, he was ten people away, then five, then two and then our eyes met; our hands extended and a man abruptly pushed me aside and grabbed the president's hand. My great opportunity to shake hands with a president was gone.

The experience caused me to reflect on the experience. There had been no doubt that I was anxious to meet the president if only for a brief five seconds. There had been anticipation. I was nervous. I was excited to know that I could tell others that I had shaken hands with the President of the United States! I was upset with the man who had robbed me of my chance.

Then I thought about my God, the Creator of the universe. He has made it possible for me to join Him for eternity. How exciting is that! No shortage on opportunities for quality time with Him.

We seem to have unrealized expectations on earth along with disappointments or anti-climactic events. But Heaven will have none of those. All of our expectations will be exceeded.

- Revelation 21:4 - *God shall wipe away all tears from their eyes; and there shall be no more death, neither sorrow, nor crying, neither shall there be any more pain: for the former things are passed away.*
- John 14:2 - *In my Father's house are many mansions: if it were not so, I would have told you. I go to prepare a place for you.*
- 1 Corinthians 2:9 - *But as it is written, Eye hath not seen, nor ear heard, neither have entered into the heart of man, the things which God hath prepared for them that love him.*

Life is in the Blood

Truth for Today – Hebrews 9:22

The Masai tribe in central Africa live in Kenya and Tanzania. They are semi-nomadic and rely on cows as one of their primary livelihoods. Milk and meat are an integral part of their diet, but blood from their cows supplements that diet.

Blood is a source of high protein to the tribe. Mixed with milk it provides nourishment to the sick and recovering; provides hangover relief to intoxicated elders; and a protein kick to others. Blood has unusual uses and characteristics.

- In the U.S. it is donated by type and sold into the hospital markets at about $230 per pint.
- Donated blood is sold on the open market and is a $4.5 billion U.S. industry.
- A newborn baby has about one cup of blood in its body.
- Most black printer ink is more expensive than blood.
- There are 100,000 miles of blood vessels in an adult human body.
- A person's heart will pump approximately 1.5 million barrels of blood over the course of a lifetime.
- Pregnant women have about 50% more blood at week 20 than they did before conception of their baby.
- A red blood cell can make a complete circuit of your body in 30 seconds.
- 1.3 million pints of blood spoil per year due to a 40 day shelf life.

Blood donated by one person and given to another can be a life-saver. Jesus knew the concept and was a willing donor. We give a pint at a time while He gave it all. Someone gets $230 per pint of ours. He received nothing. Giving His blood killed Him. Yet there are those today who say, "I know I need His blood and I know that I'll die eternally without it, but I refuse it." As Robert Lowry said in 1876 in the old traditional hymn...

What can wash away my sin? Nothing but the blood of Jesus.
What can make me whole again? Nothing but the blood of Jesus...

Lifetime Warranty

Truth for Today – Ephesians 5:22-33

When we buy products today we look at the warranty, guarantee, and return policies. What if we don't like the item? Is there a money-back guarantee? Who pays the shipping on the return? Is there a re-stocking charge?

What if I open the package and don't like the color, performance or size? What if it doesn't perform as promised? What if my needs change from the time I ordered it until I received it? What if the product becomes outdated or simply doesn't fit?

Is there anything certain or predictable about anything we acquire?

What if I found something I desired and had to make these promises?

- Will you promise to take care of it for as long as you live?
- Will you promise to love it for as long as you live?
- Will you promise to not abuse or treat it in a demeaning manner?
- Will you promise to never throw it away?
- Will you promise to never get something similar to it as long as you possess it?

When God brought Jeni and me together 46 years ago, I had to think through the vows I would soon share on her behalf. I was, without reserve, willing to promise faithfulness to her and love her, in spite of financial, health, physical, emotional, mental changes as long as I lived. I would seek, cherish, nourish or love no other woman as long as we both lived.

The *"for better or worse"* thing was an enormous promise! At 20 years old, Jeni and I had no comprehension of what that meant. Children came, jobs changed, illness arrived, grief was experienced, wrinkles adorned, disappointments happened, and the list goes on.

If we accepted marriage with the same restrictions and expectations we place on our purchases of cars, homes, smartphones, computers, loaves of bread and milk, would we have the courage to say, *"I do?"* I'm thankful for a God who partnered with Jeni and me in our marriage.

Light a Candle

Truth for Today – Matthew 5:16

This morning as I was reading the news I felt a variety of emotions arising.

Horror as I read the story of a husband convicted of murdering his wife with cyanide. Sadness as I thought of their six year old daughter now having no mother and a father in prison.

Anxiety as I read of new alliances being developed between Russia and China. Dark memories of the Cold War that the world engaged in during the last half of the 20th century flooded back to the forefront of my mind.

Anger as I thought about the incinerated remains of 43 college students allegedly found in Mexico. Fear as I thought about how evil can somehow escalate and many times hold authorities captive.

Sadness as I read the account of funeral services for three 13 year old girls killed by a hit and run driver in California while they were trick-or-treating. Anger at the alcohol that impairs people and does so much damage.

Sorrow as I thought about a five year old girl gunshot while sitting on her grandfather's lap in a home. Two men had approached the home and opened fire, striking the little girl.

Concern as I read about a "swarm" of mini-earthquakes hitting northern Nevada over the last four months. The strongest was just recent and registered as 4.6. The chance of a much larger one are growing.

As I think about the things beyond our control, I realize that our temporary world is a "dark place", but our God is busy lighting candles. Though we can be overwhelmed at times by the darkness, it is good for me to pay attention to the beautiful, wonderful, glorious and blessed things that are happening all the time everywhere. He is busy lighting candles to illuminate this dark world.

What am I doing today and every day to make a difference for others and for His Kingdom?

Matthew 5:16 - *Let your light so shine before men, that they may see your good works, and glorify your Father which is in heaven.*

Lightning Storm

Truth for Today – John 8:12-59

We have all seen the magnificent yet brutal flashes of light that fill the sky. The electrostatic lightning discharge occurs within a cloud, between two clouds or between a cloud and the earth.

Around the world, lightning discharges approximately 40 – 50 times per second or 1.5 billion times a year. The flashes last about 30 millionths of a second.

Psalms 97:4 says, *"His lightning's enlightened the world."* That verse strikes me (no pun intended) as I think about all the people I know who are making a difference in their personal mission field. I love the passion of God's children who are sharing their gifts, talents, personalities, time and money in putting the Gospel in front of darkness. Children of God who are being lights in a very, very dark world.

Just as lightning lights the world, the Gospel brings light to the world. The Bible says in Matthew 5:14-16 - *Ye are the light of the world. A city that is set on an hill cannot be hid. Neither do men light a candle, and put it under a bushel, but on a candlestick; and it giveth light unto all that are in the house. Let your light so shine before men, that they may see your good works, and glorify your Father which is in heaven.*

- John 8:12 - *Then spake Jesus again unto them, saying, I am the light of the world: he that followeth me shall not walk in darkness, but shall have the light of life.*
- Luke 8:16 - *No man, when he hath lighted a candle, covereth it with a vessel, or putteth it under a bed; but setteth it on a candlestick, that they which enter in may see the light.*
- Psalm 119:105 - *Thy word is a lamp unto my feet, and a light unto my path.*
- 2 Corinthians 4:6 - *For God, who commanded the light to shine out of darkness, hath shined in our hearts, to give the light of the knowledge of the glory of God in the face of Jesus Christ.*
- 1 Thessalonians 5:5 - *Ye are all the children of light, and the children of the day: we are not of the night, nor of darkness.*

Lights and Bugs

Truth for Today – 1 Corinthians 10

Students in Haiti are passionate about going to school and learning. It is a lifeline of hope for not only their future, but also that of their families. Their study in many cases is limited by the number of daylight hours, so it is not uncommon to see them using public lights to study after dark.

Unfortunately, they share those lights with many tropical bugs, critters and bats. But their thirst for learning is a higher priority than personal comfort.

That visual image reminds me of a saying, *"Where there's lights, there's bugs."* As believers we can count on the fact that our lives as Christians will draw criticism and the disapproval of others.

But we are reminded in Matthew 5:16, *"Let your light so shine before men, that they may see your good works, and glorify your Father which is in heaven."*

Though the criticism of non-believers can annoy me at times, I am thankful for God's command to let my light shine, as well as understanding the reality that disapproval from others is normal.

How do we handle disapproval, unwarranted criticism and sometimes ignorant statements regarding Christianity? Are we able to let it slide off our backs? How thick is our skin or how broad are our shoulders? Do we back away from confrontation on difficult subjects for fear of persecution?

There are a variety of verses that give encouragement to us to handle the inevitability of criticism as well as what appears to be an increasing volume of it.

- Philippians 4:13 - *I can do all things through Christ which strengtheneth me.*
- 2 Chronicles 20:15 - *Be not afraid nor dismayed by reason of this great multitude; for the battle is not yours, but God's.*
- 1 Corinthians 10:13 - *There hath no temptation taken you but such as is common to man: but God is faithful, who will not suffer you to be tempted above that ye are able; but will with the temptation also make a way to escape, that ye may be able to bear it.*

Look at Me!

Truth for Today – Hebrews 12:2

War is not glamorous. Countless millions have died during wars leaving untold widows and orphans. Aside from the devastation of lives lost, cities and civilizations destroyed, PTSD, and economies ruined, there are always the wounded.

During the Civil War, 620,000 men were wounded in battle. In World War I, there were 204,000 Americans wounded and two short decades later, another 670,000 U.S. soldiers suffered wounds.

The Korean War added another 105,000 as did the Vietnam War with 304,000.

Shrapnel and bullets created devastating injuries to our American troops. As medics rushed to their sides and began caring for them, those injured soldiers who were conscious would sometimes scream and cry from what they saw as they looked at their torn body and wounds. Some medics would say, *"Don't look at the wound, look at me"*, in an effort to calm the soldiers.

Most of us will never be in a war nor suffer from battlefield injuries. But, all of us in God's family know about injuries and wounds. Disappointments, disease, grief, depression, abuse, betrayal, failure, desertion, gossip, infidelity of a spouse, abandonment and regrets, all create horrific injuries not easily mended. Most leave lifetime emotional scars we carry to death.

But I believe that Jesus offers the same advice to us as we contemplate our wounds. *"Don't look at the wound, look at me!"*

- Jeremiah 30:17 - *For I will restore health unto thee, and I will heal thee of thy wounds, saith the Lord...*
- Isaiah 53:5 - *But he was wounded for our transgressions, he was bruised for our iniquities: the chastisement of our peace was upon him; and with his stripes we are healed.*
- Hebrews 13:5 - *...for he hath said, I will never leave thee, nor forsake thee.*
- Hebrews 12:2 - *Looking unto Jesus the author and finisher of our faith; who for the joy that was set before him endured the cross, despising the shame, and is set down at the right hand of the throne of God.*

Look at That!

Truth for Today – Luke 6

We were driving on the interstate in Indiana with three grandchildren in the back seat. I pointed out the window to a field and said, "Look! There's an elephant!"

It was a game I played with them for years to see how many would look. I still catch them off guard today to their dismay. That being said, I find it amazing how easily I can be distracted from the things I have in front of me.

I remember in the mid 1950's when I was six years old and learning how to ride a bicycle in our backyard. I was distracted by my grandpa arriving for lunch and I fell. Tangled in the bike and having scraped my arm, I got up crying as my grandpa walked up to me and asked what was wrong.

I pointed to my elbow. He immediately spit on my arm. I was so shocked, I quit crying. It was a gross and unique way of taking care of my arm and of course I wouldn't do it today, but that was his method. He had raised 14 children and seemed to have learned a few things.

In 1985, Jeni and I were part of a short term mission and work team trip to Haiti. The two week trip was shocking to say the least, as we experienced a different culture that was filled with poverty. That culture shock rocked my world as I thought of the materialistic mindset that I had developed in 35 years of life. It was life changing.

Sometimes we need our worlds rocked. Jesus shocked His culture 2000 years ago by out-of-the-box methods that rocked the status quo. Are we open to the Holy Spirit's methodology in the 21st century? Are we open to change? Are we willing to let God introduce diversity to our lives?

What were some of the shock and awe methods Jesus used in His day? A few come to mind in learning about the sinless Jesus.

- Jesus healed on the Sabbath.
- Jesus permitted the disciples to pluck corn on the Sabbath.
- Jesus ate with publicans and sinners.
- Jesus spent time with a harlot.
- Jesus spent time with an adulterous woman.

Looking Forward

***Truth for Today** –* John 14

First grade is a great time to learn new things and to develop friends. Unfortunately, after a few months in school I contracted viral pneumonia. My life centered on a cough, chills, fever and eight weeks out of school.

The days were long. I was in bed for days on end, waiting for the symptoms to leave and the strength to return.

The teacher sent homework so I could keep up with the rest of the class. Then one day a large box was delivered to our home along with my new homework. Mom said that it was a "sunshine box". There were forty or fifty small wrapped gifts inside given by my classmates.

The concept was simple. Each day I was permitted to open one gift to help my days go more quickly. It certainly worked, but it accomplished something much more important. It generated hope, expectation and anticipation for the next day. I was looking forward, not backward or pitying myself any longer.

As I think of the life of Jesus, it seems He was always looking ahead. While He lived in today, He was looking forward towards those things He would create; towards the crucifixion; towards His resurrection; towards His ascension; towards seeing His Father again; and now for coming again.

Philippians 3:13 - *...but this one thing I do, forgetting those things which are behind, and reaching forth unto those things which are before.*

Looking Good

Truth for Today – Jeremiah 18:3-6

A young man and his girlfriend were riding a subway in England. They were minding their own business when another young man approached them. The young man snatched the girls silver bracelet and necklace and threatened them. Feeling helpless, they could only watch as the thief walked off with their possessions.

As the not-so-brilliant thief left, he paused in front of a closed circuit television security camera for 15 seconds. He put on the necklace and admired himself in the camera lens reflection. That 15 second pause of vanity was enough to incriminate him.

I am amazed at the love God has for His creation. In Romans 5:8 we read - *But God commendeth his love toward us, in that, while we were yet sinners, Christ died for us.* That verse indicates that sin does not deter God in His quest to bring us to Him.

If the young thief had been aware of Psalm 119:37, he might have decided to not try the robbery. *Turn away mine eyes from beholding vanity.*

Apparently the young man was also unaware that the CCTW camera would incriminate him. What he failed to recognize is the truth of Proverbs 15:3 - *The eyes of the Lord are in every place, beholding the evil and the good.* God is watching everything, everywhere at all times.

Last but not least, the young robber would have benefited from learning this scripture when he was a boy. Numbers 32:23 - *...and be sure your sin will find you out.*

Often our personal desires, lusts, and pride get in the way of remaining pure before God. We serve a God who desires to mold, shape and change us into a pottery piece worthy of His use.

Jeremiah 18:3-6 - *Then I went down to the potter's house, and, behold, he wrought a work on the wheels. And the vessel that he made of clay was marred in the hand of the potter: so he made it again another vessel, as seemed good to the potter to make it. Then the word of the Lord came to me, saying, O house of Israel, cannot I do with you as this potter?*

Looking in the Mirror

Truth for Today – Matthew 7

My friend from Paris and I were having discussions about politics and religion. We had very different perspectives on many things but we both enjoyed the mind-expanding dialogue.

I brought up the subject of the 800,000 African slaves which his country-men, the French, enslaved in Haiti during the 18th century. My friend listened as I shared some of the shocking and factual stories of how slaves were treated by the French. Then he asked a simple question. *"Tell me stories of how the American slave-owners treated their 3.2 million African slaves on your U.S. plantations."*

I hit the proverbial brick wall. There was nothing to be said. How often do we find ourselves so intent on pointing out another's faults, failings and sins while ignoring or hiding our own? Two dictionary definitions may help us understand human nature:

- Hypocrisy - *The practice of engaging in the same behavior or activity for which one criticizes another.*
- Judgmental – *The tendency to harshly judge people too quickly and critically.*

If there are two sins in the New Testament which we see Jesus addressing most often, it may be the sins of hypocrisy and wrong judgment.

- Matthew 7:1-2 - *Judge not, that ye be not judged. For with what judgment ye judge, ye shall be judged: and with what measure ye mete, it shall be measured to you again.*
- Romans 2:3 - *And thinkest thou this, O man, that judgest them which do such things, and doest the same, that thou shalt escape the judgment of God?*
- Matthew 7:3-5 - *And why beholdest thou the mote that is in thy brother's eye, but considerest not the beam that is in thine own eye? Or how wilt thou say to thy brother, Let me pull out the mote out of thine eye; and, behold, a beam is in thine own eye? Thou hypocrite, first cast out the beam out of thine own eye; and then shalt thou see clearly to cast out the mote out of thy brother's eye.*

Lost and Found

***Truth for Today* – Matthew 6**

Englishman Peter was doing repair work in a field and lost his hammer. After fruitless searching he asked his friend Eric, the owner of the farm to help search. Instead of the hammer, they found 15,000 Roman coins and 200 other artifacts, including extremely rare Roman jewelry. Peter and Eric received $2.9 million for their find in the field.

Terry was doing treasure hunting in a field in England. He found a few promising finds and kept searching. His search yielded 11 lbs. of gold, 3 lbs. of silver, golden animals, jewelry, sword hilts and rings. Total value was $5.4 million.

Joe, often on wintry Sunday afternoons, was searching for Native American artifacts turned up by farmers and their plows.

Finding the usual flint flakes, he saw something that got his heart racing. One of the enviable finds for every arrowhead hunter. A banded slate bird stone! A $4,000 find.

Treasure. Where is it found? How do you establish a value? Who owns the treasure once found? The short answers to those questions can be complex. But, when we think about the treasure being the peace and security that comes with salvation in Jesus Christ, the answer is simple. Anyone, anywhere at any time can find the priceless treasure and own it for eternity.

- Mark 10:21 - *Then Jesus beholding him loved him, and said unto him, One thing thou lackest: go thy way, sell whatsoever thou hast, and give to the poor, and thou shalt have treasure in heaven: and come, take up the cross, and follow me.*
- Matthew 6:19-20 - *Lay not up for yourselves treasures upon earth, where moth and rust doth corrupt, and where thieves break through and steal: But lay up for yourselves treasures in heaven, where neither moth nor rust doth corrupt, and where thieves do not break through nor steal:*
- Luke 12:34 - *For where your treasure is, there will your heart be also.*

Lost

Between naps on the long flight to Mumbai, India, I had the opportunity to dialogue with a young Indian man. We discussed family, politics and religion. He was a devout Hindu and explained the differences between three of his gods, Ganesha, Shiva and Rama.

I had the opportunity of sharing the reality of The One God Deity and the Trinity. He had a difficult time understanding how it was possible to have a close and personal relationship with God.

We landed in Mumbai and everyone in my party had located their suitcases on the luggage belt. As more and more passengers found their belongings, I noticed that only myself and my seatmate were remaining and waiting. I was getting anxious and it was then I decided to pray that my luggage would come around the bend.

Within ten seconds I saw it and was elated. I went to my seatmate and told him, "I was getting concerned that my luggage was lost, so I prayed to my God and within ten seconds it appeared." He smiled and kept looking for his as we walked away.

What are the take-aways from my experience? Probably, that I waited too long to bring my need to God. Or, that God is interested in answering prayer. It likewise tells me that God wants to show Himself to those who do not know about Him.

For years I felt that the small things were too small for God to care about. I still fail at times in bringing the small things to Him quickly, but I am learning. With 7.3 billion people to keep an eye on, does He care about one suitcase on a luggage belt in Mumbai? I know He does!

- Deuteronomy 3:22 - *Ye shall not fear them: for the LORD your God he shall fight for you.*
- Deuteronomy 31:8 - *And the LORD, he it is that doth go before thee; he will be with thee, he will not fail thee, neither forsake thee: fear not, neither be dismayed.*
- John 16:23 - *Verily, verily, I say unto you, Whatsoever ye shall ask the Father in my name, he will give it you.*

Love in Action

Truth for Today – 1 Corinthians 13

Early in my ministry, I saw love in action. A young couple in our congregation was on the receiving end of a tragedy. The father was driving on a country road with his three year old son. A young lady failed to stop at a stop sign and broadsided the father and his son. The little boy had his short life taken in an instant.

I had never met the young lady, but because I knew she had to be going through a very difficult time, I went to visit her. The horrendous guilt she was experiencing was obvious. The weight she was carrying was huge for having taken a child's life.

The funeral for the little boy was going to take place the next day. For her future welfare, I encouraged her to talk to the parents of the little boy. I knew their hearts and I knew their faith. I knew it would be a positive experience for the guilt-ridden young lady.

The girl reluctantly agreed to meet them and went with me to the funeral home. When we arrived, the grieving couple saw us coming, left the side of the casket, came over and wrapped their arms of love around the young lady. They comforted her while she poured out her grief and sobbed. I will never forget the scene as we witnessed the three of them intertwined.

The weeping young woman was engrossed in such obvious guilt, shame and grief. The parents were tenderly sharing their love and giving comfort to her. She was the recipient of their mercy, grace and love. Her life would never be the same because of the tragedy, but equally so for receiving the unconditional love of the parents whose son's life had been taken. The wonderful love Jesus gives His people can soften even the harshest realities of life.

It seems like our lives have a steady stream of hurt. Are we responding to those hurts in a Christ like manner? Are we extending love, mercy and grace even when it is undeserved?

Jesus certainly knew about hurt and accusations. When we follow Jesus as our example, we'll be handling things in a right way.

Philippians 2:5 - *Let this mind be in you, which was also in Christ Jesus.*

Loving Hands

***Truth for Today** – Hebrews 12:1-13*

The Biblical commandment of Deuteronomy 5:20 was clear – *Thou shalt not bear false witness.* My dad's mandate was just as clear, "Never lie to me."

What the lie was on that particular day, I don't remember. But it was clear to my eight year old mind that the lie I had been caught in would warrant discipline from my dad. As he and I headed to the bathroom, I knew what was next. Up close and personal with his hand.

He sat on the edge of the bathtub and instructed me to lie down on his knees with my bottom side up. My whimpering began before the action began, but I will never forget what happened next. I looked up at his face in a meager attempt for undeserved mercy and saw tears rolling down his cheeks.

It was on that day I learned that love, mercy, compassion and discipline must be intertwined to be Biblical and to be effective. I saw that combination on my dad's face. I received my justified discipline that day, but the lesson I learned about love was far greater.

What is our perception of God's discipline? Can we see His love through the pain? I know the tears of my dad became a treasure on that day. It forever changed how I viewed discipline on both the receiving and the giving end.

When tough times come or when we are challenged by unforeseen difficulties, do we wonder why God would let it happen? Do we wonder what the purpose is behind complicated troubles? That may be the time to search for God's face and tears to more clearly understand His heart.

Hebrews 12:5,6,11 - *My son, despise not thou the chastening of the Lord, nor faint when thou art rebuked of him: For whom the Lord loveth he chasteneth, and scourgeth every son whom he receiveth. Now no chastening for the present seemeth to be joyous, but grievous: nevertheless afterward it yieldeth the peaceable fruit of righteousness unto them which are exercised thereby.*

Making a Wrong Turn

Truth for Today – Galatians 6:7

There is an old African proverb that speaks of *"Running from a lion and meeting a gorilla."* Often, our fears can cause us to jump from the frying pan into the fire.

I recently read about a man who hopefully learned the lesson well. He had been stopped by police for a minor traffic violation of not using a turn signal. Suddenly he put his car in gear and tore away from the police officers. They pursued him. In an effort to evade the officers, the man smashed through a gate into a parking lot in a last minute effort to escape.

The gate he smashed and the parking lot he found himself in was the Toledo, Ohio Correctional Institution. Trapped inside the prison parking lot, he was arrested.

Now charged with his minor traffic violation, the additional charges started piling up. Vandalism of government property and drug possession. Fear of having his drugs found in the traffic stop probably created enough fear to cause him to try to escape. He bumped into the gorilla.

Temptation can lead to sin; sin leads to guilt; guilt brings fear; fear leads to impulsive actions; impulsive actions lead us to justice. As one song states, *"Sin will take you further than you want to go..."*

The Bible has countless examples of men and women who followed those paths to destruction. Sadly, we know those paths as well. God wants us on a better path of purity and holiness.

- Galatians 6:7 - *Be not deceived; God is not mocked: for whatsoever a man soweth, that shall he also reap.*
- Numbers 32:23 - *But if ye will not do so, behold, ye have sinned against the Lord: and be sure your sin will find you out.*
- James 4:17 - *Therefore to him that knoweth to do good, and doeth it not, to him it is sin.*
- Romans 6:23 - *For the wages of sin is death; but the gift of God is eternal life through Jesus Christ our Lord.*
- Romans 3:23 - *For all have sinned, and come short of the glory of God.*

Making Do

Truth for Today – Matthew 14:14-21

Cultures and societies around the world each have their own unique characteristics. Citizens of one country tend to develop perceptions about citizens of other countries. Those perceptions may be accurate, but generally they are not.

As a for instance, some think that the people of Haiti are ill-prepared to be inventive, entrepreneurial or progressive. However, I've found exactly the opposite to be true. They, along with many other developing countries have an inherent ability to do a lot with a little. In fact, little is ever wasted in those countries.

In Haiti, there is a Haitian Creole word that means literally, "to make do", or to "do a lot with a little". The word is degaje (deg-ah-jhay). Anyone traveling in Haiti will see many examples of the term. Farmers make-do by cutting an old worn-out tractor tire and turning it into a feed or water trough for their livestock.

The absence of department stores and toy stores, along with the abject poverty gives children a great opportunity to degaje. They rise to the occasion and are as proud of their invented toys as a U.S. child is of his new video game.

One of the exciting characteristics of God is that nothing He created was second best. None of it was simply "making do" because He had wrongly planned something. There was, and is purpose to everything He has done and created. While he did a lot with a little when He fed the 5000 with five loaves and two fishes, we see His obvious plan to show a miracle. It was not second best or making do.

I'm encouraged to know that He knows my tomorrow before I get there, and He's prepared me for it today.

Masterpieces

Truth for Today – 1 Corinthians 6:19-20

Every middle school student enjoys a field trip. What's not to like about a day away from school? The twelve year old boy was no different. He was enjoying his trip to the art museum admiring early paintings. As he walked past an oil on canvas work from the 17th century, he tripped and steadied himself with his right hand hitting the painting. He punched a fist through the canvas.

Painted in 1660, the painting was renowned and fragile. Valued at $1.5 million, the damage was significant. Fortunately it was insured, but it will never be the same.

The boy isn't alone in doing damage to valuable pieces. In 2006 a man in England tripped over his shoelaces and knocked over three Chinese vases that were 300 years old. In 2010 a woman in New York tripped and fell into a Picasso painting, creating a six inch rip.

The list continues about men and women who purposely or accidentally did damage to very expensive pieces by Monet, Picasso and others.

We cringe when we think about works of art being damaged by people. I wonder what God thinks about His works of art. As we look at Genesis chapter one we see that the entire universe was filled with His masterpieces. Are we carefully protecting His work?

A collision at sea ruptures an oil tanker, spoiling beaches, and killing aquatic fowl, fish and sea-life. Pollution-spewing chimneys fill the atmosphere with haze and dirt. Heavy metals pollute streams, creeks, rivers and our blood streams. Abusive parents damage children with negative and non-affirming rhetoric.

Alcohol, drugs, nicotine, fat and carcinogens pollute our bodies and minds. Profanity does damage to hearers. Pornography does damage to viewers. The list goes on. Am I damaging God's masterpieces?

Lord, help me be a caretaker of your Creation.

Maybe Another Day

Truth for Today – Luke 16:19-31

They had been sailing for 70 days. Excitement had been building aboard ship because of a promise King Ferdinand and Queen Isabella of Spain had made. They had promised a lifetime pension to the sailor who would first sight land in the New World.

Finally, at 2:00 A.M. on October 12, 1492, Rodrigo de Triana yelled, "Tierra! Tierra!" as he sighted an island in the Bahama's. One can only imagine his excitement, knowing of his financial dreams being realized.

However, it wasn't long until Christopher Columbus told the crews that he had sighted it four hours earlier but didn't want to say anything "because it was so indistinct that he did not dare to affirm it was land." Christopher claimed the pension.

Unrealized expectations. Have you ever been short-changed in receiving credit for an accomplishment? Have you been disappointed when others were rewarded for the blood, sweat and tears you put into an effort or person? When someone else's success occurs at your expense, what do you feel?

We can take comfort in knowing that "God knows." The rewards for Kingdom work rarely get paid in our lifetime. Believers look forward to a Heavenly inheritance and reward system.

Ironically, Rodrigo de Triana had his day. It wasn't in 1492, but rather 1998 (506 years later) that NASA developed a Deep Space Climate Observatory satellite and named it Triana, giving Rodrigo his moment of fame. Again, ironically, it was renamed GoreSat some years later to honor Vice President Al Gore who came up with the idea of the satellite. Fame is fleeting, it seems.

So, are we waiting for someone to honor us? Are we awaiting our ten minutes of fame? Are we designing and securing our legacy? We probably shouldn't wait on a fickle society to meet our expectations. We will be disappointed. On the other hand, God has promised golden streets, golden crowns and a mansion for His children. That's not ten minutes of glory, but rather an eternity of glory that will never end!

Measuring Bravery

Truth for Today – Philippians 2:7

It was another average workday morning for the plumber. He was getting ready for another day when he heard a woman's screams. Running outside, he saw his 37 year old neighbor on the ground with a pit bull and three other dogs on top of her. She had just returned from her morning jog when attacked.

Decision time. Call 911? Wait for someone else to help? Stay inside? He ran into the fray without thinking. The dogs turned on him, but he grabbed her and began dragging her the 40' to his van. He managed to get her inside the van in spite of the dogs attacking him and her.

She had been bitten through to the bone on her ankles and elbows, bitten on her face and had lost a significant amount of blood. He likewise required surgery to repair his injured elbow.

Bravery. Merriam-Webster Dictionary defines bravery as, *"the quality that allows someone to do things that are dangerous or frightening."* I think the plumber fit the description well. He is a brave man.

All of us have experienced pain and we've learned enough to know that we avoid it at all costs. It is not normal for people to willingly endure pain if there are ways to avoid it. Bravery is what put the plumber's legs in motion.

As the Son of God, Jesus had the opportunity to watch, as His creation experienced pain. No one has witnessed more pain than our Jesus. For thousands of years He had a front row seat to wars, tragedies, murders and accidents. He saw the agony. It may be accurate to say that our desire to avoid pain is in direct proportion to how much pain we witness. The more we see, the less we want to experience it.

Not so for Jesus. He obediently took on the flesh that would include nerve endings and pain. Though He witnessed the depravity of man in inflicting pain on others from the beginning, He still chose to become a man. Though He knew His ending, He meekly and submissively arrived on earth. He might have been God on the inside, but He was all man on the outside. Our Jesus was a brave man.

Men-Catchers

Truth for Today – Luke 5:10

As a West African tribal chief, he felt honored to sit in the visiting European's tent. The liquor warmed him. When he was asked if he'd like to tour the ship in the harbor, the tribal leader willingly agreed. Once aboard, he was captured and his village was available for conquest. He would became one of 200 men, women and children from his tribe heading to the New World and slavery.

Estimates reveal that 15% would die on board ship, and that up to 40% died enroute from their villages to the seaport ships.

In 300 years of the Atlantic slave trade in the 16th to 19th century, it is estimated that over 20 million Africans had been captured and 12 million of them were transported to New World slavery.

The Atlantic slave trade is only one snapshot of the slavery that has plagued humanity from almost the beginning of time. Money, power, greed, lust and pure evil drove men to become men-catchers. Jesus Christ had His own group of men-catchers. In Luke 5:10, *Jesus said unto Simon, Fear not; from henceforth thou shalt catch men.*

Men-catchers. I wonder what Peter thought as he heard Jesus say those words? He most certainly was aware of the slave trade active during that time. I am certain that Peter learned quite a lot over the next three years which He spent as a Jesus follower. Ultimately Peter would give His life for the principles of love and peace which Jesus would preach and teach. What were the principles regarding men-catching that Jesus taught?

- Matthew 28:19-*20 - Go ye therefore, and teach all nations, baptizing them in the name of the Father, and of the Son, and of the Holy Ghost: Teaching them to observe all things whatsoever I have commanded you: and, lo, I am with you always, even unto the end of the world.*
- *Matthew 9:37-38 - Then saith he unto his disciples, The harvest truly is plenteous, but the labourers are few; Pray ye therefore the Lord of the harvest, that he will send forth labourers into his harvest.*

Messes

***Truth for Today** – John 10*

We were expecting guests for dinner and Jeni was busy preparing the food. She had a large bowl of red cherry jello that was still in liquid form that she needed placed in the downstairs refrigerator. I carried it down the carpeted steps to our finished and carpeted basement and tripped on the bottom step. Do you have any idea how difficult it is to get bright red, cherry jello out of carpet? It was a mess!

Jeni and I were babysitting for our youngest grandchild Carter. He was two years old and a pleasure to have around. Then things became too quiet. "Carter, where are you?" Silence. Jeni went into the den, started laughing and called me. Carter was sitting on the floor next to his "mess".

Scattered on the floor were nine puzzles and three board games. He smiled with little idea that he had made a mess. He still smiles at the photo today.

Messes. We all make them. Certainly, some of our messes are easier than others to fix or clean up. Some are sprinkled with funny components, others are filled with tragedy.

One mess that needed to be cleaned up was in the Garden of Eden several thousand years ago. It was a gorgeous environment with a perfect future. A place where God Himself took walks in the cool of the day. Adam and Eve had sinned. Their sin of disobedience had occurred and had to be dealt with. The consequences of their sin were severe. Eviction, hard work, thorns and thistles, no more walks in the Garden, and a diminished relationship with God.

A few thousand years later we find ourselves still creating messes. But we have a Savior who is willing to fix those messes if we let Him. Thank you Jesus for having our back.

More on the Sidelines

Truth for Today – 1 Samuel 17

One of the most memorable experiences I had during a trip to Israel was in the valley of Elah. A beautiful hour drive southwest from Jerusalem brings you to the eastern end of a beautiful valley. It stretches east to west with a flat bottom and large hills climbing up the north and south boundaries.

While there I climbed the north hill at the west end. Getting to the top I met a shepherd with sheep and immediately thought of another shepherd from 3000 years ago on that same hill. David as a young shepherd found himself in that area with Saul and the army of Israel. They were overlooking the Elah valley and heard the booming voice of Goliath, a nine foot giant of immense strength. Goliath was intimidating and cursing Saul and his army.

Accepting the challenge to fight Goliath, David scrambled down the hill to a creek. I did the same, and at the bottom of the hill I found a creek and began holding its round rocks in my hand. David had picked five smooth stones for his sling from quite possibly this very creek. We know the story of how he slew Goliath with one stone. But why did David pick up five stones?

Some say, he had little faith. Some say he was only getting prepared for a long battle with Goliath or with the Philistines if they chose to attack. Who knows for sure? Perhaps it's related to another reason buried in 2 Samuel 21.

Four additional giants were killed by the Israelite army as recorded in verses 16, 18, 19 and 20. Verse 21 states, *"These four were born to the giant in Gath."*

Is it possible that David was aware of four sons of Goliath as he picked up four additional stones? Did he think Goliath's sons might revenge the death of their father? It's a question I'd like to ask David someday. If the theory is accurate, my admiration for David's courage has grown by leaps and bounds. Meeting one giant is huge, but realizing that four more may enter the field of battle is quite another.

2 Chronicles 20:15 - *Be not afraid nor dismayed by reason of this great multitude; for the battle is not yours, but God's.*

Moving Mountains

Truth for Today – Psalm 37

I was sitting at my gate in Fort Lauderdale, Florida waiting to board my flight to Port au Prince, Haiti. The airline desk attendant approached me and asked for my passport which I provided. He said, "I'll bring it back shortly." Confused and concerned, I waited. Ten minutes later he returned with my passport and a newly issued first class ticket and told me I could board right away.

Settling into my first class seat with a minor degree of guilt, I soon had an orange juice in my hand along with cashews. Life was good and I thanked God for the unexpected blessing. But, anyone who serves the God of the universe soon finds out that God always has a bigger plan than simply making us comfortable.

As I relaxed, I was thinking about some of the complexities facing our organization in Haiti. We had just purchased a small mountain on which to build a campus for orphaned children, as well as a church and school. There was no road to the top and we had a mountain of work to accomplish. I was racking my brain as to how we could create a road to the top and get the infrastructure finished.

I struck up a conversation with a gentleman across the aisle. Asking him what he did for work in Haiti, he said, "I have a rental business." Asking him what he rented, he said, "Construction equipment, like earthmoving equipment such as bulldozers and trucks." A business card now in my hands, we had our answers for levelling the mountain, the difficult job of making a road, and constructing the sites for the nine buildings waiting to be built.

Anyone who has spent time in a developing nation knows the complexities of finding reliable equipment, efficient operators, finalizing contracts, and successfully completing projects. There is no doubt that it was a miracle. I wasn't seated in first class for my comfort. God truly cares about the fatherless and orphans.

- Proverbs 3:5-6 - *Trust in the Lord with all thine heart; and lean not unto thine own understanding. In all thy ways acknowledge him, and he shall direct thy paths.*
- Psalm 37:4 - *Delight thyself also in the Lord: and he shall give thee the desires of thine heart.*

Moving Mountains – Part 2

Truth for Today – Romans 8:28

Getting moved to first class on an earlier flight to Haiti, for no apparent reason, and then finding an answer to moving a mountain, had taught me about God's surprises. When the unexpected happens, it's good to look around and see what God is either teaching me, or how possibly He is maneuvering me into a position for His purpose.

So, two months after the bulldozer and earthmoving miracle, I was again heading to Haiti. Sitting in the gate area, an airline desk attendant approached me and asked me for my passport. I was excited because now I knew what was happening. What's next, Lord?

She brought my passport back with a first class ticket and invited me to board. Upon boarding, I looked across the aisle and noticed a Haitian business man. He had no idea what was coming. I asked him, "What do you do in Haiti?" He said, "I have a cement business. I import cement and truck it by semi to worksites."

Now that we had a mountain-top prepped for construction, we needed materials. This man sold cement by the semi-load and delivered it economically on-site. God is good all the time. I now had a business card in my hand and we were off and running.

I am still amazed at how often I take blessings for granted. I thank God for the blessings I receive and believe that I've either earned them or He simply loves me so much He wants me to be blessed. Sadly, I've taken advantage of blessings in a selfish manner over the years. I'm gradually learning that blessings aren't just about me. They are about Him. His planning and His strategy are for Kingdom purposes. Too often I've made them about me.

Gradually, I'm learning to look at delays, detours, disappointments and blessings in a Kingdom manner. What is God teaching me with this circumstance? What chess game is God playing as He made this move?

- Romans 8:28 - *And we know that all things work together for good to them that love God, to them who are the called according to his purpose.*
- Isaiah 55:8 – *For my thoughts are not your thoughts, neither are your ways my ways, saith the Lord.*

Moving Mountains – Part 3

Truth for Today – Isaiah 42:8

I was gradually becoming used to God putting me in the first class section on my trips to Haiti. Two different times He had moved me from economy class to first class so I could accomplish His purpose. So, again, I was sitting at my gate in Fort Lauderdale waiting for the desk attendant to approach me and give me a first class ticket. It didn't happen. Late in the boarding process I finally made my way almost to the back of the plane and took my seat.

Disappointed in God not using me in first class I decided to look across the aisle. A very elderly Haitian lady smiled at me, so I settled in for a quiet trip to Port au Prince. Then, the stewardess came to me and said, "There's a mix up on tickets. Would you be willing to move forward a few aisles?" A bit aggravated, I gathered all my belongings and moved a few aisles forward. Settling in, I looked across the aisle and noticed a distinguished Haitian businessman.

I said, "I have no idea why I've been moved to this seat, but I've learned from experience that when God moves me on a plane, He has a plan. Why did He seat me beside you?" He laughed and said, "Why don't you tell me what you do in Haiti."

I did, and then he told me what it was he did in Haiti in the investment, banking and financial grants arena. That ongoing relationship will glorify God.

God has taught me that though His surprises may come in the form of blessings, it is not always the case. Those are easy to receive, as we enjoy the blessing part. But there are times when His changes are not convenient, not comfortable and not understood. If we fail to see Him working in all areas of life, we will miss the teachings and blessings He has in mind.

Are we watching Him? Are we so adapted to His blessings that we fail to see why He blessed us? When He invests in us, He has a bigger plan in mind. What return is He getting on His investment? In situations that are either good or bad, convenient or inconvenient, He is still God of the Universe and good all the time.

Isaiah 42:8 – *I am the Lord: that is my name…*

Muddy Boots

Truth for Today – Philippians 4:6

What do you get when you mix Indiana farm ground clay with water? You get a muck and sludge that sticks to anything it touches. The antidote is a water hose and brush.

When God created mud, he also created something to wash it off. Psalm 40:2 says it another way: *He brought me up also out of an horrible pit, out of the miry clay, and set my feet upon a rock, and established my goings.*

God has a million ingenious ways to take care of His creation. Though we may feel hopeless and helpless at times with our seemingly impossible situations, He is watching.

An old African proverb says, *"When God gives me an itchy skin rash, He also gives nails on my fingers."*

There is no end to the resources God has at His disposal to carry out His role as our Provider. It seems that God waits for us to get to the end of ourselves, until finally we fall to our knees and ask for His help. When difficult times come, how quickly do we get on our knees? Too often it seems like my default is to fix it myself. I would think that as I get older I would learn to get on my knees sooner rather than later.

Job 7:6 says, *"My days are swifter than a weaver's shuttle, and are spent without hope."*

An old Pennsylvania Dutch proverb states, *"Vee get too soon oldt, und too late schmart."*

- Philippians 4:6 - *Be careful for nothing; but in everything by prayer and supplication with thanksgiving let your requests be made known unto God.*
- Mark 11:24 - *Therefore I say unto you, what things soever ye desire, when ye pray, believe that ye receive them, and ye shall have them.*

Multi Purpose Tool

***Truth for Today** – John 16:5-15

The pile had paper, cardboard, wood scraps and a couple of paper sacks full of trash. All of it was heaped on the burn pile at our farm and my dad and I were standing by it.

We knelt down by the pile and he pulled a matchbook out of his pocket. He moved a piece of wood here and put a sack there and piled paper around it all. When he was done, there was a neat little pocket about 6" deep and 6" wide.

He said, "The wind is your enemy when you start a fire, so keep the wind away from your match." He struck the match and the fire started.

Then after the fire started burning he said, "The wind becomes your friend after the fire is burning. It keeps the fire going."

It was difficult as a young boy to imagine how one thing, like wind, can have multiple functions.

The Holy Spirit is equally complex.

- Convicts of sin – John 16:8 - *And when he is come, he will reprove the world of sin...*
- Teaches us – John 14:26 - *But the Comforter, which is the Holy Ghost, whom the Father will send in my name, he shall teach you all things...*
- Lead us – John 16:13 - *Howbeit when he, the Spirit of truth, is come, he will guide you into all truth...*
- Comfort us – John 14:16 - *And I will pray the Father, and he shall give you another Comforter, that he may abide ith you forever...*
- Helps us to pray and intercede for us – Romans 8:26-27 - *Likewise the Spirit also helpeth our infirmities... the Spirit itself maketh intercession for us with groanings which cannot be uttered....*

The infinite power and flexibility of the Holy Spirit is phenomenal. He is truly a friend in every way to God's children.

My Heart Hears

Truth for Today – Romans 8

She was six years old and was watching cousins, uncles and friends play baseball at a family park picnic. She along with others were sitting on top of a baseball dugout. She fell, received a concussion and skull fracture.

One of the complications to the skull fracture was meningitis and one of the complications of the meningitis was full hearing loss.

In the years since that accident, I've watched her grow up to become a Godly woman, wife and mother. Everyone who knows her finds her incredibly encouraging and full of joy. She can't hear a word but you'd never consider her challenged in any way. She is an adept lip reader and carries on a great conversation.

A few years ago I was sharing devotions with a group of 80 women who were going to record a CD of great hymns. After we finished the devotions, they began practicing. It was phenomenal and I was touched to tears. As I exited the room they were in, I bumped into the young woman who was challenged in her hearing.

Without thinking, I said, "Wasn't that incredible? Their harmony was beautiful." She smiled at me and said, "Ed, did you forget that I can't hear? But I heard the singing in my heart anyway, and it was beautiful!" Then we both shed tears.

That was a profound day for me that I'll never forget. It brought new meaning to the words in Romans 8:26-28 - *Likewise the Spirit also helpeth our infirmities: for we know not what we should pray for as we ought: but the Spirit itself maketh intercession for us with groanings which cannot be uttered. And he that searcheth the hearts knoweth what is the mind of the Spirit, because he maketh intercession for the saints according to the will of God. And we know that all things work together for good to them that love God, to them who are the called according to his purpose.*

The Holy Spirit is able to speak for us and take care of anything we are unable to accomplish on our own. Matthew 11:5 says it well - *The blind receive their sight, and the lame walk, the lepers are cleansed, and the deaf hear, the dead are raised up, and the poor have the gospel preached to them.*

My Heart is Racing!

Truth for Today – John 3

It was a very hot and humid day. I was doing the usual Saturday chores of getting the yard mowed, trimming around the house, trees, shrubs and flower-beds, and a few more odd jobs.

I was thirsty so I grabbed a Coke and headed back to work. The kids and grandkids came for supper that evening and as I leaned back in my recliner I realized that something wasn't right. I was feeling hyper and at the same time very tired.

I checked my pulse. 180 heart-beats a minute! Something was wrong as it should have been 60 or 70. I checked again. My pulse was 180. I checked the third time. 180! My heart was racing.

I went to the emergency room and received IV's which slowly started to deal with the dehydration of the day. I learned a bit more that night about the benefits of water and of course that the Coke's caffeine didn't help the dehydration issue.

A few months later I was doing a study on the effects of Christianity in the world. I learned statistics that troubled me. You can do your own math, but my study established that there are 70 people dying every minute without Jesus. That of course requires some judgments, but that's what I concluded.

Now, back to the heart-rates. When I put my finger on my pulse, for every heart-beat I feel, another person is meeting eternity without Jesus. That has had a profound impact on my life. I can lay in bed and feel my heart beat. I am reminded again and again of those who die without Jesus. My heartbeat prompts prayer for the unsaved.

I remember years ago asking God to break my heart for the unsaved. I asked Him to give me a heart that would never forget them. I believe those prayers were answered as He reminds me daily with my heart-beat.

Thump... thump... thump... my heart is beating and breaking.

My Way, Your Way or What?

Truth for Today – Proverbs 12

Many years ago I heard an old minister say, "We need to be careful about how strong we hold to an opinion in discussions with others. There are always three ways of looking at an issue. My way; your way; and the truth."

I have thought about that many times since. The advice has compelled me to try to listen to others more often with a desire to actually hear what they have to say. Rarely in life is anything exactly as I perceive it to be.

We are instructed in the Bible to listen and receive opinions from others. Proverbs 11:14 says, *"Where no counsel is, the people fall: but in the multitude of counselors there is safety."*

Over the years I have learned the difficulty in resolving a conflict via email or letters. Those types of communications do not provide the back and forth interchange necessary to learn the hearts of those we are communicating with. Dialogue brings us understanding and generally closer to truth.

Much can be said for face to face communications as well as an attitude of Philippians 2:3 - *Let nothing be done through strife or vainglory; but in lowliness of mind let each esteem other better than themselves.*

If we truly believe that we have all the answers, we would be in violation of Biblical principles:

- We do not have everything figured out – Isaiah 55:8 - *For my thoughts are not your thoughts, neither are your ways my ways, saith the Lord.*
- We can and should learn from others – Proverbs 19:20 - *Hear counsel, and receive instruction, that thou mayest be wise in thy latter end.*
- A man who does not seek advice is a fool – Proverbs 12:15 - *The way of a fool is right in his own eyes: but he that hearkeneth unto counsel is wise.*
- Our solitary wisdom brings disaster – Proverbs 14:12 - *There is a way which seemeth right unto a man, but the end thereof are the ways of death.*

Natural or Supernatural?

As a child, I remember hearing of magicians turning doves into rabbits as part of their act. Doves in a cage were lowered into a box. When the magician pulled the cage out, the doves were gone and replaced by rabbits. Amazing!

I've been intrigued by the notion of turning a worn out van with many miles on it into a van with leather upholstery, captain's chairs, entertainment systems and refrigerators. That idea created a brand new concept, the conversion van era.

Helping in the garden as a child, I remember the dreaded tomato worm. Bright green and larger than my fingers, I hated them. Then my dad told me they would eventually become a moth. Later he showed me the Sphinx moth and I couldn't believe that a worm so ugly could actually transition into something so beautiful.

Not so long ago, my grandson caught a tadpole. I've seen hundreds of tadpoles over the years and of course knew that they'd become a frog. But I had never seen a tadpole in transition until then. I was amazed in seeing a frogs head and feet, yet having  a tail in what looked like some sort of alien creature.

Conversion. Transition. Change. There are many illustrations in nature that astound us. But there is nothing more incredible than the conversion, transition or change that miraculously happens to someone who comes to faith in Christ.

The Biblical concept is illustrated in the words "repent" and "converted". The original Greek indicates that we *"change our minds"*, *"turn around or go back"*, *"change"*, *"change direction"*, *"change our minds"* and *"accept the will of God."*

Never Ever Hungry

Truth for Today – John 6

Marie was only seven years old but knew what it was like to lose a mom and a dad. Alone, she went to live with her elderly grandmother. Hearing there were interviews being conducted to find 12 orphaned girls to begin a new lifelong family, grandma brought Marie for the potential opportunity.

She was tiny, her hair was turning orange from malnutrition, and she had sores and was incredibly shy. She was among the poorest of the poor. It wouldn't be long before grandma would need to give Marie away to another family to become a domestic servant and slave.

I asked grandma if Marie was healthy and got the reply "No, she gets sick in her stomach." I asked how frequently it occurs and grandma said, "Whenever Marie eats dirt, she gets sick." I asked the inevitable question of "Why would she eat dirt?"

The haunting response will be with me forever, "She eats dirt when there is nothing else to eat and she needs to fill her stomach."

I learned on that day about hunger. I had thought I knew what hunger was, but now I heard about it in a much deeper way.

Mud cookies are sold in Haitian markets for the poorest of the poor. Marie didn't even have those to eat. She ate the dirt under her tiny and bare feet. Needless to say, Marie was among the twelve chosen on that day for her new family and home.

That experience makes me think about Jesus' words in John 6:35 – *And Jesus said unto them, I am the bread of life: he that cometh to me shall never hunger.*

When Jesus provides what we need spiritually, there is no more need. He paid the price! There is a hunger that will never be filled, unless Jesus provides the everlasting nutrition.

No Potholes in Heaven

Truth for Today – Revelation 21

When I read 2 Chronicles 3, I am amazed at the vast amounts of gold that came to King Solomon each year. Approximately 60,000 pounds! When I read of Aztec, Mayan and Inca history, I am astonished at their reported great accumulations of gold.

We hear of the huge gold reserves around the world hidden in concrete bunkers and banks, as well as the gold rings and other jewelry worn by millions. Just how much gold is there?

Though estimates differ, there seems to be a loose agreement that since the beginning of time only 182,000 tons of gold has been mined. That would be 364 million pounds or 302,325 cubic feet of gold.

Interestingly enough, that gold would only fill three and one-half Olympic swimming pools! I'm not sure how it strikes you, but that is far less gold than I would have ever imagined. No wonder it is rare.

Then I thought about Heaven where the streets will be paved with pure gold. Revelation 21:16 says, *And the city lieth foursquare, and the length is as large as the breadth: and he measured the city with the reed, twelve thousand furlongs. The length and the breadth and the height of it are equal.*

The size of Heaven according to scripture is approximately 1500 square miles and 1500 miles high. That sounds like a lot of roads, streets, avenues and boulevards to me, and that's a lot of gold under our feet.

The 48 U.S. states have 3.9 million miles of roads. If we assumed that Heaven would have a similar grid-work of roads, that would be 2.925 million miles of road, just on one level! If Heaven's boulevards were 20' wide with 1" of gold paving, all the gold ever mined on earth would cover only 34 miles of Heavenly highways.

Of course this is all subjective and open to great debate. But it does give us an indication where all the gold is!

Revelation 21:21 - *...and the street of the city
was pure gold, as it were transparent glass.*

No Reprieve for Jesus

Truth for Today – Mark 15

In 1995, Dubaku was arrested for an armed robbery in his African country which had occurred in 1988. He was tried, convicted and sentenced to death.

He had been on death row for 19 years awaiting execution. Then the fateful day arrived when he and four others were taken to the gallows. He watched in terror, as his four fellow prisoners were hung. He was told, "You're next."

Then, seconds away from hanging, his execution was halted. Someone noticed that he had been sentenced to death by firing squad, not hanging. They were not prepared to carry the sentence out so he went back to his cell with his sentence now being investigated.

I think of another man at another time and place. His name was Barabbas. He had been arrested and convicted of insurrection and murder. However, while on death row it was determined he would go free and another prisoner, Jesus, would be killed.

While we know most guilty men receive their carried out sentences, we also know innocent men are sometimes wrongfully convicted. We also know that some men elude justice by hiding their wrongful deeds. Justice and truth can be a bit evasive at times.

But in Jesus' case, He was 100% innocent and pure. Not guilty, but arrested, sentenced and executed for the wrongful actions and sins of others. A tragedy? Yes, beyond comprehension. But as always, God is able to redeem tragedy, wrongdoing and disaster. The death of Jesus opened the way for prison and jail-house doors to be opened and the guilty to be proclaimed innocent and free.

- Romans 5:7-9 - *For scarcely for a righteous man will one die: yet peradventure for a good man some would even dare to die. But God commendeth his love toward us, in that, while we were yet sinners, Christ died for us. Much more then, being now justified by his blood, we shall be saved from wrath through him.*
- 1 Peter 2:22 – *(Jesus) who did no sin, neither was guile found in his mouth.*

Not all Quacks are Ducks

Truth for Today – 1 Corinthians 15:1-4

I had freckles as a young boy and detested them. Someone told me that rubbing them with a penny and then throwing the penny over your left shoulder would remove the freckles. I tried it… it didn't work.

Mankind has always looked for an easy fix to a problem. I am amazed at how quickly we try the unproven quick fixes. Sometimes those cures are dangerous, other times they are downright funny.

- In the 1800's and early 1900's, hot springs were reputed to cure illnesses. Today we know that some contained radioactive radium. People bathed in it and drank it. It was marketed in items like beauty cream and toothpaste. When promoters of the products began dying at early ages, customers connected the dots.
- In 1905 there were more than 28,000 patented snake oil elixirs available on the market to cure almost any illness. Subsequent research found that the liquids were generally 99% mineral oil and 1% beef fat, with traces of red pepper and turpentine.
- In the 19th century, a baldness cure was sold to many men troubled with hair loss. Unfortunately, the primary ingredient was lead which had many side effects to the men using it.
- For centuries and up until 1920, blood-letting was a medical practice used by doctors, quacks and barbers. Incisions were made into veins and arteries to release blood and impurities.
- The list goes on and on revealing what we used to believe about electromagnetism, ozone, magic belts, vacuum tubes and all types of remedies for our illnesses and problems.

The greatest malady is sin, with only one known cure:

1 Corinthian 15:1-4 - *Moreover, brethren, I declare unto you the gospel which I preached unto you, which also ye have received, and wherein ye stand; By which also ye are saved, if ye keep in memory what I preached unto you, unless ye have believed in vain. For I delivered unto you first of all that which I also received, how that Christ died for our sins according to the scriptures; And that he was buried, and that he rose again the third day according to the scriptures.*

Obedience 101

Truth for Today – Galatians 6:7-10

While in the army during WWII, my dad learned much about duty, obedience, submission and sacrifice. His experience in basic training was indicative of that.

Obey, obey, obey without thinking, and then, again, obey. He told me once, "I wouldn't pay a plug nickel for basic training again, but I wouldn't take a million dollars for the lessons I learned."

He told me several times that going to the army in WWII taught obedience and discipline principles applicable for the rest of his life.

Some of those lessons were learned through being taught, while others were gained through experience. He told me of one of those life lessons. While in the Philippines, he and the other American G.I.'s shared the jungles with the Japanese. Though a guarded perimeter had been established around their tents one night, they still needed to be cautious, as snipers were always looking for a target.

They had been taught again and again to be quiet and to keep lights out. Dad had received a few letters from home and wanted to reread them. He lit a small candle knowing that it would be dim and insignificant. Suddenly a shot rang out and a bullet whipped through his tent. Needless to say, he extinguished the candle.

His WWII experiences were very difficult for him to talk about, but I'm thankful he shared some of them with me. His life lessons also became life lessons for me.

As I think about my dad's experience, I have learned that disobedience and taking short-cuts in life can bring consequences. The more self-discipline I practice, the less grace and mercy I will need.

Jesus reminds us in Matthew 4:7 by quoting from the Old Testament, that we should not tempt the Lord our God. That would translate in those Hebrew texts as "Do not test the Lord."

Disobedience puts God in a position of potentially needing to supply grace, protection and mercy.

What is our obedience level? Are we doing things that create open doors for satan to come into our minds, relationships, hearts and lives? Or, are we learning the difficult lessons of obedience?

Of Mice and Women

***Truth for Today* –** 1 Corinthians 13

Our son, Rick, had a Boa Constrictor snake as a pet. The snake ate mice, but our source for mice was a pet shop 30 miles away. Since Rick did not get there often, the job of bringing mice home, went to Jeni as a duty on her shopping trips.

You need to understand three things about Jeni. First, she hates mice. Second, she hates snakes. Third, she loves Rick. Getting hated mice for a hated snake is asking a lot from a mom. But, Jeni would do it for Rick.

Once, on her drive home with six young mice, one particularly stormy night complete with thunder, lightning and rain, the mice chewed a hole in their box and got loose in the car.

Can you picture the scene? Ten miles from home, late at night, lightning, thunder, rain, and six loose mice in a car with a woman terrified of mice. Jeni stopped the car along the side of the road in the middle of the storm. I still do not know how she did it, but she captured every one of those critters and got them back into a secure box!

Love in action. That illustration makes me think of Jesus. In the Garden of Gethsemane just prior to his upcoming trial and crucifixion he prayed - *Father, if thou be willing, remove this cup from me: nevertheless not my will, but thine, be done. And there appeared an angel unto him from heaven, strengthening him.* Luke 22:42-43

Jesus' experience in the Garden teaches me three things:

- When I am faced with a fearful and daunting situation, I need to talk to Him about it.
- I need to eventually accept the task in front of me.
- He will give me the strength to handle

One plus One Equals a Thousand

Truth for Today – 2 Corinthians 5

Yellowstone National Park was registered in 1872. The 3,500 acre park was known for its geysers, rugged terrain, wolves, buffalo, elk, deer and other wildlife. By 1926 the wolves were virtually gone from the park. The deer and elk population began to increase and grazed the park's grasses and valleys dramatically.

In 1995, wolves were re-introduced into the park after being absent for 70 years. A phenomenon began occurring. The wolves began killing the deer. The deer and elk began avoiding their old pastures and valleys and went to new areas. Their old places began regenerating.

The bare places became forests of willows, aspen and cottonwood. Existing trees quintupled in height within six years. Then the birds started moving in. The beaver population increased as they created ponds and lakes which became home for otters, ducks and amphibians.

The wolves killed coyotes. The rabbits and mice began increasing which meant more hawks, weasels, foxes and badgers. Eagles, bears and ravens increased as they fed on the carrion of the wolves.

More vegetation meant more shrubs and more berries, which increased the bear population. The improved vegetation on the river and creek banks meant less erosion and a more stable and predictable environment.

The wolves brought balance to the eco-system of Yellowstone. Not only did it impact the wildlife, birds, insects and vegetation, it also dramatically changed the rivers and creeks.

When I think about how God affects the lives of people I see similarities to what happened at Yellowstone. When God takes over our lives, there are small changes that begin to happen which affect other things. Those things have an impact on other things and over time there is a transformation. God can indeed change the world.

2 Corinthians 5:17 - *Therefore if any man be in Christ, he is a new creature: old things are passed away; behold, all things are become new.*

Painful Healing

Truth for Today – Hebrews 4

Jeni had spent several hours working in her flowerbeds. Her hard work and efforts paid off with really beautiful posies, or whatever they are called. As she sat at the kitchen table, she asked me if I would massage her shoulders and neck. I began to work on those muscles and within ten seconds, she cried, "Ouch! That hurts so much, but keep it up."

In 2002, Great Britain reported success in utilizing an unusual method of treatment for some types of wounds. They found some wounds would not respond to conventional dressings and antibiotics. They began to test and use an ancient method of healing - maggots. When maggots were applied to some wounds, they would eat the diseased and deadened flesh leaving pink, healthy tissue.

I remember being in a hospital burn unit visiting a young man who had been burned and was going through skin grafting. While talking to him we heard a scream and shrieks from another room. I saw pain and fear in my friend's eyes as he knew that someone was getting their burns cleansed and scrubbed. This young man knew first hand that healing would only come with pain.

There are many disappointments, traumas, relationship issues, hurts, betrayals and grief we all experience in life. Those experiences are painful to endure. But sadly, the pain of the experience is only the beginning of healing and more pain.

Often, there is pain in confrontation, intervention, challenges, seeking forgiveness and granting mercy and grace. Healing for the challenges and hurts of life comes with a price. The application of antibiotic and moisturizing ointment to a burn victim is painful. Loving, probing fingers massaging sore muscles is painful. Maggots in an open wound would seem to be painful. Such is the healing that goes into the traumas of life. Physical, emotional, mental, relational, financial and spiritual healing is essential, life-giving and painful.

Our Jesus knew about the pain of healing. Our lives will experience the same. Hebrews 4:15 - *For we have not an high priest which cannot be touched with the feeling of our infirmities; but was in all points tempted like as we are, yet without sin.*

Painful Processes

Truth for Today – Hebrews 4:13-15

I recently watched a video showing the manufacturing of high pressure gas cylinders used to store various gas products such as propane and acetylene. With my background of manufacturing I was captivated at the complexities that went into the making of the five foot tall and twelve inch diameter tanks.

The tanks begin as a round slab of steel approximately 24" in diameter by ½" thick. The slabs are immersed in a chemical bath for 36 hours at a temperature of 1346°. Then they are soaked in five heated chemical baths to give flex qualities to the steel.

The slabs then go into dies and presses that extrude the steel slabs into seamless cylinders. 800 tons of force begin the process of stretching and expanding. Four additional press operations each expand the cylinder as much as 60%. A cutting operation cuts off the excess steel from one end of the cylinder. That end is super-heated and forged into a round curved shape. That end is then formed and later threaded for the valve.

The cylinder is dropped into a chemical bath for 90 minutes at a temperature of 1652°. Then they are plunged into a cooling bath for six minutes and quickly dropped into another 1202° bath for heating again. After all the heating and cooling baths, the cylinders are pelted with tiny steel pellets to clean them. The cylinders finally undergo rigorous testing to assure they are safely able to handle their high pressure environment.

The process reminded me of a few Bible verses describing the molding and shaping process God uses to turn me into a usable product for earth's harsh and high pressure environment.

- Isaiah 64:8 - *But now, O LORD, thou art our father; we are the clay, and thou our potter; and we all are the work of thy hand.*
- Job 23:10 - *But he knoweth the way that I take: when he hath tried me, I shall come forth as gold.*
- Isaiah 48:10 - *Behold, I have refined thee, but not with silver; I have chosen thee in the furnace of affliction.*

Peaceful Freedom

Truth for Today – 1 Thessalonians 5:18

It's peaceful to wake up in the morning with good health and another day to live. Having a bed, a roof over our heads and a home that is warm in the winter and cool in the summer are blessings.

Knowing there is hot coffee and breakfast ready to take us into our new day is comforting. The list goes on and on as we count the daily blessings God provides for us.

Thankfulness is always easy when things are going well. How much praise is in our hearts when there is trouble in our life? Do we thank Him for the highs and the lows? Sometimes it's good to consider what the rest of the world is going through. For today, we will think about our fellow earthlings who are displaced or in prison.

There are approximately 52 million men, women and children who are not able to live in their homes. They are displaced. They are refugees due to civil war, religious or race persecution, discrimination and a myriad of other reasons by which one group of people control others.

There are 11 million men and women in prisons worldwide. They are there for a variety of reasons. Some are imprisoned due to their own choices, others due to persecution and political control.

That is a total of 63 million people not in their own beds or homes. 63 million people knowing loneliness, displacement, unfamiliar, difficult and dangerous environments.

My thankfulness is increased as I see my blessings in a new way. My compassion for others less fortunate also increases, as my knowledge of others grows. We are blessed, are we not?

1 Thessalonians 5:18 - *In everything give thanks:*
for this is the will of God in Christ Jesus concerning you.

Perfect Gifts

Truth for Today – James 1:17

As I grew up, I was blessed to have parents who tried to provide birthday and Christmas presents that met my expectations. I tried to reciprocate by getting them appropriate gifts.

As Christmas approached in 1960 when I was eleven, I knew that my dad had a hammer with a broken handle. I also knew that he used dynamite for a few of his projects on the farm. So, with hard earned money in my pocket I went to the local hardware store and bought what I needed. I wrapped them up and anxiously awaited Christmas day.

Finally the time came, and I was excited to watch my dad's excitement in receiving my gifts. He began opening the first present. A wooden hammer handle. Then the second present, my sticks of dynamite. As he opened it, he looked at the red sticks and I could see confusion. What I thought were sticks of dynamite were only red flares used by truckers when their trucks broke down. As it turned out, the hammer handle was also the wrong size. I had failed with both gifts.

Dad didn't show disappointment because he knew the effort and love that went into my two gifts. For that I was thankful, though I felt a bit ashamed about my gifts to him.

The experience reminds me of how God provides gifts to His children. Sometimes we want things that aren't reasonable or good for us. But everything we receive from Him is just right and the timing is flawless. His blessings are perfect.

- James 1:17 - *Every good gift and every perfect gift is from above, and cometh down from the Father of lights, with whom is no variableness, neither shadow of turning.*
- Matthew 7:11 - *If ye then, being evil, know how to give good gifts unto your children, how much more shall your Father which is in heaven give good things to them that ask him?*
- Ephesians 5:20 - *Giving thanks always for all things unto God and the Father in the name of our Lord Jesus Christ.*

Perseverance

***Truth for Today* –** Hebrews 11

Antarctica is the fifth largest continent and roughly twice the size of Australia. 98% of its 5.4 million square miles are covered in ice. Within the ice lie the larvae of a tiny insect which is smaller than a flea.

The larvae of the wingless Midge live in the ice for up to two years before emerging and hatching. They undergo frigid freezing temperature as well as intense ultraviolet rays from the sun, without dying. In a test, the larvae have been subjected to immersion in liquid nitrogen at a minus 321° for three days without killing it.

It is a phenomenal example of survival. God calls the believer to the same level of survival. We need not marvel at the ability of the Midge larvae in their ability to withstand horrific environmental odds.

I read of the perseverance of Christian martyrs during centuries of persecution. I am amazed at their faith and desire to overcome.

- Revelation 2:7 - *To him that overcometh will I give to eat of the tree of life, which is in the midst of the paradise of God.*
- Revelation 2:17 - *He that hath an ear, let him hear what the Spirit saith unto the churches; To him that overcometh will I give to eat of the hidden manna, and will give him a white stone, and in the stone a new name written, which no man knoweth saving he that receiveth it.*
- Revelation 2:26 - *And he that overcometh, and keepeth my works unto the end, to him will I give power over the nations.*
- Revelation 3:21 - *To him that overcometh will I grant to sit with me in my throne, even as I also overcame, and am set down with my Father in his throne.*
- 1 Corinthians 15:58 - *Therefore, my beloved brethren, be ye stedfast, unmoveable, always abounding in the work of the Lord, forasmuch as ye know that your labour is not in vain in the Lord.*
- Hebrews 3:14 - *For we are made partakers of Christ, if we hold the beginning of our confidence stedfast unto the end.*
- Hebrews 4:16 - *Let us therefore come boldly unto the throne of grace, that we may obtain mercy, and find grace to help in time of need.*

Perspectives

Truth for Today – Isaiah 64:4

He first felt the ground shaking and knew something very, very large was coming towards him. It was getting closer and closer. He looked up at the sky through the foliage and leaves which were moving with the wind, or was it the trembling ground? Then the ant saw a blur of fur as the dog ran past.

In an ant's world, dandelions are like oak trees to us. Blades of grass to an ant seem like a bamboo forest to a human. To an ant, a dog would seem like a huge elephant to us. Ants measure their world on what they can see.

Understandably, his world would be incredibly tiny. A dog's world would be larger than an ant, but again, it would be very small compared to the world of a human being.

Our personal world is only as large as our technology permits us to experience it. Astronaut Neil Armstrong's world became enormous when he set foot on the moon. Our personal worlds get much larger when we experience air travel to the Grand Canyon or to international locations in Europe, Africa or Asia.

It seems like God has been strategically letting us get glimpses of the larger picture over the centuries. Technology has given us previews of things larger or smaller than ourselves. The microscope in 1580; the telescope in 1608; first bicycle in 1817; first airplane and flight in 1903; the molecular structure of DNA in 1953; and the Hubble space telescope in 1990.

Is there any end to what God would like to show us? Man thinks that his developing technology is opening the door to the unknowns. God permits miniscule discoveries to be made, to keep man learning and guessing. God tells us in Isaiah 64:4 - *For since the beginning of the world men have not heard, nor perceived by the ear, neither hath the eye seen, O God, beside thee, what he hath prepared for him that waiteth for him.*

God sets the boundaries on man's knowledge and He will take great pleasure in showing us what we cannot see today.

Pick Me, Pick Me!

Truth for Today – John 17:20-22

Being about a year younger than most in my elementary, middle and high school classes, as well as being a late bloomer, created difficulties for me while growing up. Thus, I was usually the last chosen for teams, whether it was red-rover, baseball or basketball. I knew the hurt of not being chosen or wanted.

In 2006, we began a search for four orphaned boys to place in a Loving Shepherd Ministries Home of Hope in southwest Haiti. Word had been passed around to various villages for children to be considered. We already had eight boys but needed four more.

I arrived at the mountain home for the interviews and went into the small school. I was startled to see forty-three children and their caretakers waiting for an interview. I found out that some had walked eight hours for the opportunity. Needing only four boys at that time, all the girls left and four boys were ultimately selected from the group.

Two years later at another location we were interviewing twenty-five girls to select twelve for a new Home of Hope. The twelve were selected and the remaining girls left. But, one little girl remained, sitting on a wall. Our missionary looked at her and she said, "I know what you are doing." Rich said, "What do you mean?"

She said, "I saw this happen once before at another home." It was then we found out that she had been in the 2006 earlier interview as well. This little girl was now rejected two times. As an orphan, she was a child slave for a family and said, "I can't carry any more water. I am so tired and I can't work anymore."

As things transpired over the next few days, one of the twelve girls chosen for the girl's home was HIV+ and was put into our HIV home for girls. That left an open spot and the twice rejected child slave now had a family, home and a bright future full of hope.

This little girl knew the hurt of not being chosen. Sometimes there are happy endings, other times not. God is not a respecter of persons and desires every soul He created to be with Him in Heaven.

1 Timothy 2:4 – (God) who will have all men to be
saved, and to come unto the knowledge of the truth.

Pigs as Teachers

Truth for Today – Proverbs 4

I had a very full day of business in Indianapolis. It had taken longer than I had expected and I knew I'd be late getting home. Leaving the last appointment, I merged onto I-465 circling around the north end of Indy and ground to a stop in heavy traffic.

Frustrated, I felt my blood pressure rise and my stress increasing. I knew I'd be late for supper and I wasn't happy about it. I prayed that God would teach me something through it.

I lowered the front two windows of my car and thought I may as well get fresh air while sitting in traffic. The traffic started moving. The lane to my right opened up and was filled almost immediately with a semi full of squealing pigs. My car filled up instantly with the aroma of one of Indiana's cash crops. My windows went up, but it was too late. I lived with the porker smell for quite a few miles.

So, was it a prayer answered? I laughed out loud as I realized that I'm not in control. What were the lessons learned? Life can always get worse... pig aroma can last for a long time in a car... I was thankful for a microwave at home that would warm up my late dinner.

I'm thankful for a God who hears and answers prayers in ways that are unorthodox, unexpected and even funny.

Psalms 32:8 - I will instruct thee and teach thee in the way which thou shalt go: I will guide thee with mine eye.

Poor Decision

Truth for Today – Numbers 22:21-41

It was a very hot and dry 95° at Grand Canyon. My son Rick and I had hiked to the bottom of the canyon and were spending a few days exploring the power of the Colorado River, the beauty of the hidden canyons and the magnificence of God's creation.

We knew of course that we needed lots of water for our day hikes. So we loaded our backpacks with H_2O and headed to a distant canyon. Halfway there I decided to cache about a third of our water behind rocks along the trail. Rick wasn't sure it was a good idea but I had the deciding vote. Caching the water lessened our load. We arrived at the canyon and explored for a few hours.

Knowing I had plenty of water cached for our return trip, we drank nearly all of our remaining supply. We headed back to our campsite which was miles away. Up ahead I saw what I thought were the rocks where I had cached our water. No water! It seemed like all the rock piles were looking alike. We searched and searched and never found our water.

It was a long, dry and dangerous trip back. Earlier we had noticed U.S. Park Service signs warning that there have been deaths due to sunstroke and dehydration. Of course, I had regrets. I shouldn't have left the water. I should have made a marker to find the cache. I should have listened to Rick. I shouldn't have been so careless.

Isaiah 5:21 challenges me about my perceived wisdom – *Woe unto them that are wise in their own eyes...* I may have age and I certainly have some experience, but I can still make wrong choices and decisions. I'm thankful for a God who has me in His hands.

Pushing a Rope Uphill

Truth for Today – 1 Corinthians 13

Kelly was in high school and worked part time at a fast food restaurant. One Saturday afternoon he was working in the grill area as usual, flipping his burgers.

Intent on his cheeseburgers, his leg hit the fire extinguisher button. Immediately the fire retardants white powder covered the hamburgers, cheeseburgers, and anything else it could reach.

Needless to say it took several hours to get the restaurant back to normal operations.

The damage done at the fast food restaurant is illustrative of what a word or words can do. Actions and consequences. The law of sowing and reaping. Words and responses.

The Bible reminds us often of talebearers, as well as those who gossip and backbite. Once harsh words are spoken or a gossipy tidbit is shared, it's almost impossible to get it undone. It would be similar to pushing a rope uphill, getting a cat into a bag or putting fire retardant powder back into a fire extinguisher.

- Proverbs 26:22 - *The words of a talebearer are as wounds, and they go down into the innermost parts of the belly.*

- Ephesians 4:29 - *Let no corrupt communication proceed out of your mouth, but that which is good to the use of edifying, that it may minister grace unto the hearers.*

- Titus 3:2 - *To speak evil of no man, to be no brawlers, but gentle, shewing all meekness unto all men.*

Putting on my Judge Robes

Truth for Today – John 8:1-11

I settled into my church bench to begin listening to a Sunday morning message from the pastor. Midway through the sermon I noticed a young man about ten benches ahead of me who was obviously distracted.

He was looking to the right, to the left, then down and finally blankly staring at the front wall. He was watching people and things and not watching the minister. Finally, after watching him with frustration for five minutes, I decided to quit watching him.

I wondered as to why someone came to church if they weren't going to listen to the message. It was then I realized that I had been doing the same thing. I had just missed five minutes of a sermon.

Sadly, I had to acknowledge the sin of hypocrisy and of judging another. The Bible clearly lays out the sinfulness of those actions and the Holy Spirit is quick to point out our humanness.

I had to think of the scenario 2000 years ago when the Pharisees brought a woman to Jesus who had been caught in the act of adultery. Though many lessons were taught that day, clearly a lesson on judging others, as well as hypocrisy were at the top of Jesus' list.

Likewise, the great illustration Jesus used in Matthew 7 helps us understand how we, with a log in our eye, are quick to judge someone with a splinter.

It seems to be a human tendency for us to judge others more harshly and more quickly than we judge ourselves. Our tendency is to hold others to higher standards than what we hold for ourselves. I'm thankful for the Holy Spirit and the Word to provide the teachings I need.

- Matthew 7:1 - *Judge not, that ye be not judged.*
- Luke 6:37 - *Judge not, and ye shall not be judged: condemn not, and ye shall not be condemned: forgive, and ye shall be forgiven.*
- John 7:24 - *Judge not according to the appearance, but judge righteous judgment.*
- Romans 14:13 - *Let us not therefore judge one another anymore.*

Qualifications

Truth for Today – Psalm 139

Growing up as a "country boy" on a farm in the '50's and '60's was great, but it sheltered me from the "big city". Shortly after I graduated from high school, I received notice that I was being given the opportunity to be interviewed for a Machinist-Toolmaker apprenticeship position with General Electric in Fort Wayne, Indiana. It was everything I wanted, so with anticipation I confidently walked into the interview room.

The manager began the interview. He had a folder and papers laid out on his desk. It grew quiet as he read them and then he said, "As I look at your school records and transcripts, I see nothing here that would make me want to hire you. You graduated 49 out of 76 in your graduating class; you missed a lot of classes; and you were in trouble multiple times. Can you give me one good reason why I should even consider you for a position?"

Devastated, with my opportunity heading south, I said the only thing I could think of. "A couple of months ago, I gave my heart to the Lord and I am a new person." The look on the managers face changed as he said, "That sounds interesting. Where do you go to church?"

I told him and he said, "I know that church. A good friend and neighbor of mine goes there. I will give you a chance based on how Jack lives his life and we'll see if you can turn out as good as he did." I got the job because of Jack's faith and life!

That experience has taught me so much about God. There is nothing about me that makes me desirable for a relationship with Him or even to serve Him. In fact there would be a thousand or a million things that would make me undesirable or unqualified. Yet, He accepts me because of Jesus. I cannot fathom the mercy, grace and love He has for His creation, but I am elated that He has accepted me.

Ephesians 3:17-19 - *That Christ may dwell in your hearts by faith; that ye, being rooted and grounded in love, may be able to comprehend with all saints what is the breadth, and length, and depth, and height; and to know the love of Christ, which passeth knowledge, that ye might be filled with all the fullness of God.*

Quiet Time

Truth for Today – Psalm 46

Going to church as a child brings back many beautiful memories. Warm memories of close family, singing, neighbors, worship, prayer, lunches and Sunday School.

Of course as a boy filled with energy, impatience and youth, it was always easy to get into a bit of trouble. I remember sitting with my mom in a church service as a child, becoming disruptive and the inevitable results.

Judgment, along with her follow-up action was swift. It came in the form of a pinch to the thigh and the sternly whispered, "be still". That was one of the painful memories of going to church.

I always knew that the pinch and warning needed to be heard and obeyed. If I didn't obey, there would be consequences. More pinches or possibly a later encounter with the loving discipline of my dad's hand.

Psalm 46:10 - *Be still, and know that I am God...* God's message to the Israelites is just as meaningful to us today. In fact, maybe even more so. In this technological age of gadgets, phones, computers and the associated social media, it's difficult to have quiet time to think about Him.

How can we know that He is God? Reading His Word, meditation, contemplation and reflecting are all avenues in getting to know Him. In a world saturated with noise, it takes determined and focused effort to find a "still" place.

Various commentaries add depth to the *"be still"* phrase. Phrases such as – *be silent, be quiet, be calm, don't tremble, be relaxed, don't exert, cease from war...* clearly define the expression of "be still". We would all agree that it takes effort to accomplish that. But learning how to be still brings fulfillment to the concept of getting to know God.

Railroads without Tracks

Truth for Today – Galatians 4:3-4

One of the saddest times in the history of the United States is the enslavement and exploitation of African men, women and children. A small group of sympathetic men and women decided to help slaves find their way to the northern states and into Canada.

One of the earliest recorded instances of someone in the north assisting a slave to escape the south was in 1786. George Washington had complained that one of his escaped slaves had been aided by *"A society of Quakers, formed for such purposes."* Scenarios such as that were the early beginnings of the Underground Railroad. Over the years, the movement grew and had a focal point in Fountain City, Indiana, only 60 miles from our home. Levi and Catherine Coffin are reported to have rescued over 3,000 slaves in the early years of the 19th century.

The Underground Railroad had a simple yet effective system. Homes and businesses stretching north became "depots" or "stations" with the owners being called "station-masters." When a slave arrived at a "station" after having escaped his southern owner and plantation, they would be escorted by a "conductor" to the next station. And so it went until they reached safety in the northern states or Canada.

Many techniques of disguise and deception were used to facilitate rescues. One of the most famous was of Henry Brown who had a friend ship him in a wooden crate to the north where he found freedom.

Escaping from slavery became a desire of virtually all slaves. They all desperately wanted the same thing - *FREEDOM.*

Freedom from physical slavery was a priority. But more importantly to mankind is our freedom from spiritual slavery. The early Quaker's were instrumental in delivering slaves to freedom. How passionate are we today in the 21st century in being part of the conduit by which unbelievers can become believers?

Lord, place a burden on my heart for those
who are enslaved in spiritual bondage.

Reach For the Sky

Truth for Today – Psalm 36

We as Indiana Hoosiers are known as living in a flat state that has a lot of corn, bean fields and pig farms. I wonder sometimes why God chose to be disproportionately excessive in pouring out canyons, mountains and abundant scenery in so many places around the U.S.A. and seemed to short-change Indiana. But, I am realizing that is God's business, so I will let it go.

However, in southern Indiana there are gullies, hills, lakes and scenery that give us a small taste of His beauty.

Hiking in Shades State Park in southern Indiana, we ran across a 5" diameter, 60' tall tree. It was tall, spindly and reaching for the sky. It was straight as an arrow.

The tree reminded me of Psalm 36:5 which teaches us that God's mercy and love reaches to the heavens and His faithfulness reaches to the clouds.

I am utterly amazed at the Bible's definition of God's love being perfect and unconditional. I am touched by His mercy and compassion being new every morning. His love and mercy never run out, as they reach to the heavens and climb to the clouds. They are deep, wide and high.

That is almost beyond comprehension, but not quite. We have become the recipients of His love and mercy every day, and thus know from a first-hand account.

"Thank you, Lord, for saving my soul. Thank you, Lord, for making me whole. Thank you, Lord, for giving to me thy great salvation so rich and free."

Reading, Writing and Multiplication

Truth for Today – Psalm 1

If you are able to read this page, you are more fortunate than 1.23 billion others around the world. 17% of people above the age of 15 cannot read or write.

Reading and education are one of the keys to a vibrant economy, hope for the future, as well as helping us become successful individuals and families. Without reading skills and education, poverty continues and people struggle in their daily existence.

Reading opens doors to a larger world and permits individuals access into other people's lives and experiences.

- "A reader lives a thousand lives before he dies, said Jojen. The man who never reads lives only one." - George R.R. Martin
- "The more that you read, the more things you will know. The more that you learn, the more places you'll go." - Dr. Seuss
- "A great book should leave you with many experiences, and slightly exhausted at the end. You live several lives while reading." - William Styron

Reading, education and knowledge are important. But, there is something much more important:

- Mark 8:36 - *For what shall it profit a man, if he shall gain the whole world, and lose his own soul?*
- Psalm 1:2 - *But his delight is in the law of the LORD; and in his law doth he meditate day and night.*
- John 8:32 - *And you will know the truth, and the truth will set you free.*
- 2 Timothy 3:16 - *All Scripture is breathed out by God and profitable for teaching, for reproof, for correction, and for training in righteousness.*

Sharing the Gospel is essential for the eternal welfare of the world. The ability to read can add huge amounts of value to understanding and absorbing truth. The ability to read and write, multiplies exponentially the ability to get the Gospel to the world.

Reality vs. Expectation

Truth for Today – 1 Corinthians 2:9

It's been said that the two best days of owning a boat are the day you buy it and the day you sell it. Why is that?

Most people who have purchased their dream boat understand the significance of that statement. Bent propellers, engine problems, being stranded on a lake and hitting a stump are hints for you non-boat owners.

I can relate to the issues surrounding boat ownership. I've owned two small fishing boats over the years and though they made sweet memories, the reality didn't live up to my expectations. Life got easier after the boat moved on to another owner.

As another illustration, one of my dreams was to have a lake. The bulldozer and equipment came and went and I had my hole in the ground. God filled it with water. I stocked it with channel catfish, bluegills, hybrid sunfish and largemouth bass.

Then the first curse of small lakes arrived. A few fish-loving birds or frogs brought cat-tail seeds to my long awaited and beloved lake.

When the cat-tails first emerged they were beautiful, but they populate quickly and in abundance. Then the second curse. Muskrats. They love to burrow into lake banks which then weaken the dam. They are similar to cat-tails, in that they multiply quickly and in abundance.

Then the third curse. Getting rid of the cat-tails is hot and hard work. Pulling them out, cutting them off and burning the piles. The work seems to be unending.

Then, of course, there was the mowing around the lake to keep it presentable. Trying to maintain the population of the right fish in the right proportion took additional time. Finally, there is almost no time to actually fish. I guess I'm not a lake person, especially when reality is different than my expectations.

I am excited to know that God's reality exceeds all my expectations. He says in 1 Corinthians 2:9 - *Eye hath not seen, nor ear heard, neither have entered into the heart of man, the things which God hath prepared for them that love him.*

Red Flags

Truth for Today – Matthew 24

There are things I enjoy doing and things I dislike doing. Thirty five years ago I was invited to go ice fishing with a friend. It was a very cold day and a wind was blowing as we walked onto the lake. Boring a hole through five inches of ice got a sweat going which created a chill a bit later.

Then, the fishing began. Many more holes and two very cold hours later, there were no fish to take home. It had been a bad experience, but being an avid fisherman, I decided it was just one of those days. So, a year later, not wanting to give up, I tried again, with yet another bad experience. I haven't ice fished since.

But one thing I did learn was the concept of "red flags". Small flags are rigged to the ice fishing poles. Since you generally fish with multiple holes and poles, the fisherman needs to know when a bite occurs. When the pole dips down from a biting fish, the red flag goes up to alert the fisherman.

The Bible is full of red flags as God doesn't want us to be surprised by things we are unaware of.

I've always been intrigued by the "signs of the end-times". God shares an enormous amount of end-time hints and clues. Not only do those scriptures help us be prepared, it also increases our personal passion to assist others to be ready. Ephesians 5:15-16 says it well. *See then that ye walk circumspectly, not as fools, but as wise; redeeming the time, because the days are evil.*

- 2 Timothy 3:1-5
- Matthew 24:1-51
- Mark 13:32
- Luke 21:11
- Revelation 13:16-17
- Joel 2:28-32
- Revelation 3:3
- 1 Corinthians 6:9-10
- Luke 21:36

Reflections

Truth for Today – Isaiah 42:8

In Genesis we read about God's creation work. At the end of each day, God reflected on what He had done, *"And God saw that it was good."*

On the sixth day, God created man and at the end of that day, *"God saw everything that he had made, and, behold, it was very good."*

When God paused at the end of each day, he reflected upon all that had been created. God reflected. He paused. He admired.

Genesis 1:26 says, *"And God said, Let us make man in our image, after our likeness."* I am convinced that God made us to "look" like Him and to "be" like Him. How special is that?

So, when I look in the mirror at my reflection, what do I see? Am I concerned or ashamed of my image? Are there things I would like to see different? Am I proud of what I see? Or, rather, do I comprehend that I was made in the image of God? In other words, I am physically and emotionally a reflection of Him, the Creator of the universe.

Recently I was standing by a pond and amazed at the stillness of the water. Then I noticed the reflections on the water. It struck me then that God wasn't satisfied to show me the beauty of His creation one time, He  had to show me twice. When we take photos of anything, they are merely reflections of what God has created. At the risk of sounding sacrilegious, and trusting that you understand, I believe God is showing off when He created reflections. He's allowed to do that. After all, He is God. We are reminded of that when He states 162 times in the Bible, *"I am the Lord."*

Isaiah 42:8 - *I am the Lord: that is my name: and my glory will I not give to another, neither my praise to graven images.*

Reluctant Leaders

Truth for Today – Matthew 16:24

In 2008, $5.3 billion was spent by candidates, political parties and independent groups on federal elections. $2.4 billion was spent on the presidential race alone, with the balance on congressional and senatorial campaigns.

Between the years of 2000 and 2012, there were five U.S. Senate campaigns with individual expenditures above $59 million and as high as $82 million. I read in the news recently that a heated senate race had already spent over $200 million with weeks still to go before election. Where will it stop?

Of course money needs to be expended to find and elect competent men and women of integrity for public office. What is an appropriate cost for that process?

As we think about the disciples of Jesus, we found Him selecting men with varying credentials and abilities. The men were diverse, with some considered common and others deemed influential. But, all were drafted for service by our Lord. What are the principles which Jesus defined about who would lead others?

- Matthew 16:24 - *Then said Jesus unto his disciples, If any man will come after me, let him deny himself, and take up his cross, and follow me.*
- Philippians 2:3 - *Let nothing be done through strife or vainglory; but in lowliness of mind let each esteem other better than themselves.*
- Luke 9:48 - *...for he that is least among you all, the same shall be great.*
- Matthew 5:5 - *Blessed are the meek: for they shall inherit the earth.*
- Matthew 20:26-27 - *But it shall not be so among you: but whosoever will be great among you, let him be your minister; and whosoever will be chief among you, let him be your servant.*
- 1 Peter 4:10 - *As every man hath received the gift, even so minister the same one to another...*

Reprieved or Not?

***Truth for Today** – John 3

Born in 1921, in spite of having good parents, he chose a dishonest, immoral and corrupt path in life. Robbery, kidnapping, assaults and rapes became the norm for him. In 1948 at the age of 27, he was sentenced to die for his crimes.

While on death row, he filed countless appeals and succeeded in barely evading eight execution deadlines. Then on May 2, 1960 he headed to the gas chamber. Everything was in place and his time had come, but his attorney was making one last effort to get a reprieve. He succeeded in getting a judge to issue the execution reprieve. One minute before the cyanide tablet was to be dropped into the chamber, the judge's secretary started dialing her phone to stop the execution.

Being nervous, she dialed a wrong number. By the time she dialed correctly and got through, the cyanide had been dropped and the process could not be stopped. The execution was finalized.

The history lesson causes me to reflect on God's judgment of mankind. What does the Bible say about sinful men and women who do not choose a personal relationship with Jesus Christ? What does the Bible say about reprieves and stays of execution?

- John 3:3 - *Jesus answered and said unto him, Verily, verily, I say unto thee, except a man be born again, he cannot see the kingdom of God.*
- Revelation 20:15 - *And whosoever was not found written in the book of life was cast into the lake of fire.*
- 2 Corinthians 5:10 - *For we must all appear before the judgment seat of Christ; that every one may receive the things done in his body, according to that he hath done, whether it be good or bad.*
- John 5:24 - *Verily, verily, I say unto you, He that heareth my word, and believeth on him that sent me, hath everlasting life, and shall not come into condemnation; but is passed from death unto life.*

John 3:16 - For God so loved the world, that he
gave his only begotten Son, that whosoever believeth
in him should not perish, but have everlasting life.

Response to a Pinch

Truth for Today – Job 1

He was 40 years old in 1960 and worked hard as a local farmer. Corn harvest had begun and he was operating a corn picker in a remote area. The pinch rolls plugged so he stopped the tractor to clear them but failed to disengage them. Pinch rolls have almost no room between them and they caught his fingers and pulled his arm into them until they stalled out.

Caught in the pinch rolls of a corn-picker was a tragic place to be. There was no way to open the roller assembly in the cornfield so someone drove the tractor four miles to a mechanic while he laid on the machine.

The mechanic thought they could use a cutting torch to open the machine to release him, but the corn chaff and stalks started on fire. So they brought out a hack saw to cut the machine away. A tourniquet stemmed the blood loss from the arteries and veins, but he still lost his arm near his shoulder. He never passed out.

No cowboy or astronaut was ever more of a hero to me. I was only 10 years old when it happened but I will never forget hearing about it. Watching him for the next 40 years was impressive. I never heard him complain about his loss or tragedy.

How do we handle adversity or tragedy in our lives? Our response at those times can be an encouraging inspiration to others, or it can be a discouragement. I'm thankful for those men of God who choose to inspire others.

I think of Job in the Bible when in one day, he lost his children, 7,000 sheep, 3,000 camels, 500 donkeys, and his servants. Job's response is recorded in Job 1:20-22 - *Then Job arose, and rent his mantle, and shaved his head, and fell down upon the ground, and worshipped, and said: Naked came I out of my mother's womb, and naked shall I return thither: the Lord gave, and the Lord hath taken away; blessed be the name of the Lord. In all this Job sinned not, nor charged God foolishly.*

Resting Easy

Truth for Today – John 14:1-3

As a grandpa there's nothing sweeter and more memorable than one of your grandchildren giving you special attention. As I was relaxing in my recliner, six year old Emma jumped onto my lap and said, "I need some cuddle time."

With a smile on my face and Emma snuggling in, she said, "I need something squishy for my head to lay on."

Thinking she'd run off to get a stuffed bear or pillow, she promptly laid her head on my well-fed stomach.

I can't help but wonder how our Father feels when we give Him special attention? Does He need it? Does He enjoy it?

Does He encourage us to communicate with Him? Does He want us to rest in His arms and in His strength? Is He pleased when we simply think about Him? Does He take pleasure in giving us what we need? Does He enjoy giving us more than we ask?

The Bible gives us hints about the soft side of our Fathers heart.

- Philippians 4:6 - *In everything by prayer and supplication with thanksgiving, let your requests be made known unto God.*
- Luke 11:9-13 - *And I say unto you, Ask, and it shall be given you; seek, and ye shall find; knock, and it shall be opened unto you. For every one that asketh receiveth; and he that seeketh findeth; and to him that knocketh it shall be opened. If a son shall ask bread of any of you that is a father, will he give him a stone? or if he ask a fish, will he for a fish give him a serpent? Or if he shall ask an egg, will he offer him a scorpion? If ye then, being evil, know how to give good gifts unto your children: how much more shall your heavenly Father give the Holy Spirit to them that ask him?*
- Matthew 11:28-29 - *Come unto me, all ye that labor and are heavy laden, and I will give you rest. Take my yoke upon you, and learn of me; for I am meek and lowly in heart: and ye shall find rest unto your souls.*

Run the Race

Truth for Today – Hebrews 11

It was Valentine's Day, February 14, 1962 when little Sarah Covington Fulcher was born in New Jersey. She was born with congenital hip dysplasia which consisted of shallow hip sockets. She was fitted with orthopedic splints and received treatments to reshape her sockets and straighten her legs.

She began running and by the time she was 14 had set a new state record in the long jump in Junior Olympics. Running was her passion and obsession during high school and into college.

Then she really began running. At age 24 she ran 2700 miles across Australia in 97 days (28 miles per day). That feat put her in the Guinness Book of World Records.

Her next goal was to run the perimeter of the United States, so at age 25 on July 21, 1987 she began. 438 days later she completed her goal. She had run 11,134 miles with an average of 25.5 miles per day. Her commitment and endurance is utterly amazing and phenomenal to say the least.

Her accomplishment makes me think about Hebrews 12:1 - *Wherefore seeing we also are compassed about with so great a cloud of witnesses, let us lay aside every weight, and the sin which doth so easily beset us, and let us run with patience the race that is set before us.*

Hebrews 11 identifies many of the patriarchs and matriarchs of faith who inspire and amaze us. Though not in the Guinness book, they are forever etched in God's Book. The faith of Abraham and Sara, Jacob, Joseph and Moses astounds us. The commitment, endurance, perseverance, stamina and faith of our forefathers is remarkable.

Then I think of faithful men and women I know today who are fighting their 24/7 fights. They are battling cancers, injuries, relationship struggles, congenital defects, physical, emotional, mental and financial issues, accidents and the devastating losses of loved ones.

How is it possible? Philippians 4:13 - *I can do all things through Christ which strengtheneth me…* and 2 Corinthians 12:9 - *My grace is sufficient for thee: for my strength is made perfect in weakness.*

Running the Race

Truth for Today – 1 Corinthians 9:24

At thirty years old, she had a full life of championships in running track. Setting records over the last years in the 5,000 and 10,000 meter distances in college as well as national championships, she became world renowned.

But recently at a 10,000 meter World Athletics Championship in Beijing, China, she made new headlines. Barely in front of her were two runners who crossed the finish line to capture the gold and silver awards.

Now, a mere five feet from the finish line and ready to seize the 3rd place bronze medal, she knew she had it captured. She slowed and raised her arms in triumph and the 4th place runner edged her out in a last split second. Her post-race defeat was filled with tears. An early celebration robbed her of a 3rd place finish. She knew that raising her arms had cost her the position.

The Bible speaks of running races. In 1 Corinthians 9:24 we read - *Know ye not that they which run in a race run all, but one receiveth the prize? So run, that ye may obtain.*

Likewise Hebrews 12:1 states - *Wherefore seeing we also are compassed about with so great a cloud of witnesses, let us lay aside every weight, and the sin which doth so easily beset us, and let us run with patience the race that is set before us.*

The young lady experienced a nightmare that we can probably all relate to. The old adage - *Don't count your chickens before they're hatched*, is one we can understand.

The Bible shares specific counsel and encouragement about finishing our spiritual race well.

- 2 Timothy 4:7 - *I have fought a good fight, I have finished my course, I have kept the faith.*
- Philippians 3:14 - *I press toward the mark for the prize of the high calling of God in Christ Jesus.*
- 2 John 1:8 - *Look to yourselves, that we lose not those things which we have wrought, but that we receive a full reward.*

Safe from the Seen and Unseen

Truth for Today – Psalm 91

My son Rick and I were hiking in the Teton mountain range of Wyoming and decided to do an off-trail hike to a glacier.

Rick was about fifty feet ahead of me as we were cutting across a wooded ridge on the way up to the glacier. All of a sudden, he stopped. When I caught up with him he pointed downhill to a grizzly sow with two cubs about 150 feet away. At that moment I knew fear.

I had read several accounts of grizzly attacks and knew the chances of escaping or surviving was minimal. A close encounter with a grizzly bear and her cubs made survival even tougher.

I knew enough about bear behavior to know you do not maintain eye contact with a grizzly. But, it was impossible to look away. The standoff lasted for about 20 seconds until she bit one of the cubs and chased him into the brush. Then, they all disappeared. Everything seemed deathly quiet in those next few seconds!

I knew without a doubt the bear was circling and it would only be a matter of seconds until she came barreling out of the brush at us. But, we got a glimpse of her and the cubs disappearing over a ridge 100 yards away.

Do you suppose sometime during our eternity in Heaven we will learn of the specific times that God protected us? I can't begin to comprehend how many times, seen and unseen, His grace, mercy and protection follows us and keeps us safe.

Psalm 91 provides insight in His protection – *(We) shall abide under the shadow of the Almighty... He shall deliver thee from the snare of the fowler, and from the noisome pestilence... His truth shall be thy shield and buckler... thou shalt not be afraid for the terror by night; nor for the arrow that flieth by day.*

Isaiah 54:17 - *No weapon that is formed against thee shall prosper.*

He has our back!

Security Breach

It was a great trip. The Rocky Mountain National Park, wildlife, scenery, a rodeo and great family time made many memories. We arrived at the airport in Denver for our trip home.

There was a random check of one of our pieces of luggage by an inspector, when our 12 year old daughter jokingly said, "Dad, do you think they'll find your gun?"

I didn't have a gun. She explained to the now agitated inspector that she had been joking, but she still received his tongue lashing.

A friend of mine is now famous in some circles because of doing a similar thing. Joking at an airport security checkpoint resulted in an overnight stay in the local jail.

I would suspect that all of us are guilty at times of speaking without thinking. What we say, who we are communicating with, where we say it, how it is said and when it is spoken all have reactions. Can you think of any times when you wished you could have taken words back? The Bible speaks often of our oral communications.

- Matthew 5:37 - *But let your communication be, Yea, yea; Nay, nay.*
- Ephesians 4:15 - *But speaking the truth in love...*
- Ephesians 5:4 - *Neither filthiness, nor foolish talking, nor jesting, which are not convenient: but rather giving of thanks.*
- Leviticus 19:15 - *Thou shalt not go up and down as a talebearer among thy people.*
- Proverbs 11:13 - *A talebearer revealeth secrets.*
- Proverbs 18:8 - *The words of a talebearer are as wounds, and they go down into the innermost parts of the belly.*
- Ephesians 4:29 - *Let no corrupt communication proceed out of your mouth, but that which is good to the use of edifying...*

On the other hand, the Bible in Proverbs 15 and 17 does give support to enjoying good times together: *A merry heart maketh a cheerful countenance; he that is of a merry heart hath a continual feast; a merry heart doeth good like a medicine.* – Carefulness, context, wisdom and intent make all the difference.

Security

Truth for Today – Revelation 21

Nothing man produces, invents, develops or designs can surpass God's creation. That being said, there are man-made things that are astounding. One of my personal favorites is the Great Wall of China.

The primary purpose of the wall was for security and fortification. Designed to prevent the northern Eurasian nomads from invading the Chinese empire, it was relatively successful for many centuries.

- Tile, lime, stone, dirt, bricks and wood were used in the construction.
- The bricks were mortared with a glutinous rice flour.
- The official length is 13,170.7 miles.
- The earliest portion of the wall was built 2,800 years ago.
- There were an estimated 25,000 watch towers along the wall.
- The average height of the wall is 26 feet and the highest portions are 46 feet.

Man desires security. We build fences, boundaries, and walls to separate us from others. Then we place video cameras to record intruders, motion detectors to alert us, and finally guards and dogs to add extra security. We like to feel safe.

God is interested in security as well. Heaven will have gates and walls. He clearly states that there are certain things that will not be permitted into Heaven. Revelation 21:4 states that death, sorrow, crying and pain are prohibited. Revelation 21:23 tells us there will be no sun nor moon. Revelation 22:5 relates there will be no night.

Revelation 21:27 states - *And there shall in no wise enter into it any thing that defileth, neither whatsoever worketh abomination, or maketh a lie: but they which are written in the Lamb's book of life.*

Security. God's Holy Spirit, His Word, His Grace, His Mercy, His Forgiveness, His Son, the Blood of Jesus and His Love are the security of His children.

Severance

Truth for Today – Hebrews 11

Experiencing success in management and the corporate world generally brings its perks. The benefits of success usually include prestige, power and money. I was no less blessed in my corporate life.

With that money, my spiritual judgment was clouded and I pursued my dream of having acreage, a pond, creek, woods and a new home. I wanted it to be significant enough to impress others. That, sadly, is a transparent and humbling confession.

I provided all that and more for my family and lived the dream. Then God gave Jeni and me an opportunity to go on a short term mission trip to Haiti. My pride and arrogance took a major hit as I viewed the faith and lives of Haitians who lived in abject poverty. How could they be so full of joy with so little? The statistics were staggering as I learned that 80% of Haitians were living on less than $2.00 a day and 50% lived on less than $1.00. My world went upside down.

My heart broke as the Holy Spirit brought revelation and conviction. Life would never be the same after that trip to Haiti in 1985. That was the beginning of a new norm. We sold our dream.

Some have said that I didn't need to sell it all. However, what I had to get rid of was sin and a materialistic bent that wasn't Christ-like.

I think often of the scripture in Matthew 5:29-30 that says, *"if thy right eye offend thee, pluck it out, and cast it from thee: for it is profitable for thee that one of thy members should perish, and not that thy whole body should be cast into hell. And if thy right hand offend thee, cut it off, and cast it from thee: for it is profitable for thee that one of thy members should perish, and not that thy whole body should be cast into hell."*

Was it painful to sever myself from my dream? Of course it was. Was it the right thing to do? For us it was.

The Bible is full of illustrations of men and women who sacrificed themselves for what was right. I don't share my pathetic case to put myself in their category. My "stuff" had to be ripped and torn from my hands. Abraham, Joseph, Moses, Samson, Jesus, the apostles and many others willingly gave up themselves for a greater purpose. I wish learning these life lessons would be easier for me.

She's a Beauty

Truth for Today – Genesis 24

Her long and beautiful eyelashes caught my attention, but it was difficult to get past her odor as I walked past. She was tied in the camel market of northeast Ethiopia. I'm sure that someone would eventually purchase her and add her to his working camel herd.

Camels. I've learned quite a bit about them over the years by watching them along highways or in the deserts of Ethiopia, India and Israel. They are uniquely designed by God to exist in places where horses and cows struggle. Some unusual facts explain their uniqueness in God's creation:

- They are so loved and appreciated in the Arab world that there are over 160 words for "camel" in the Arabic language.
- They are able to eat almost anything. Vegetation, meat, bones, salty or sweet food as they have stomachs of steel.
- Their humps contain fat, not water. Their body fat is in the hump, not in the body, thus making them more able to handle the heat.
- Dromedary camels can carry up to 1000 pounds of cargo.
- Suited for the desert, they have two rows of long and thick eyelashes to keep out blowing sand; a split lip designed to nibble leaves from prickly trees and cacti; thick skin inside their mouth that thorns can't penetrate; glands in the eye to keep their eyes moist in the desert heat; ears covered in long hair to keep out blowing sand; their valvular nostrils can close to prevent moisture from escaping the lungs, thus decreasing water loss.

God truly outdid Himself in creating the camel. The abundance of special features on this animal make her a valuable commodity to the nomads and farmers in the Near East.

The Bible is full of illustrations about camels. They were used as a teaching tool, a beast of burden, and also an indication of great wealth. Job had 6,000 in his possession at the end of his life. Their ability to live and endure in incredibly harsh environments is yet another indication that a creative God exists.

Shingles Belong on a Roof

Truth for Today – Galatians 6:6-10

Jeni and I were driving past our local pharmacy when she said, "They're giving Shingles shots today. Why don't we get one?" I quickly responded, "Shingles are for old people; maybe someday."

Two weeks later I was diagnosed with Shingles. I'm not sure which was worse, the pain of Shingles, or telling Jeni that she had been right and recognizing that I was becoming older.

I got through the Shingles virus in seven weeks and decided it was horrible! About ten months later Jeni encouraged me to get a shot to which I replied, "I've had Shingles once; you can't get them twice." Two months later I suffered through my second set of Shingles. I learned that you can get them twice and even three times. I got the shot! Why is it so difficult to learn from experience?

A researcher was documenting behaviors of Thomson Gazelles in the Serengeti Plain of Africa. He watched a herd of gazelles walking through tall grass to reach a watering hole. As they walked on the trail, a lion grabbed a gazelle. Then the researcher saw other lions in the tall grass. The gazelle herd hastily retreated. But he was amazed that over the next two hours the herd tried two more times to get to the water, on the same trail, with the same results.

The Bible shares a concept about the law of sowing and reaping. It lists dozens of Biblical, historical illustrations, as well as hundreds of cautionary verses about daily life. We can have very predictable results, both good and bad, to our actions by learning from others and from our own experiences.

- Galatians 6:7 - ...*Whatsoever a man soweth, that shall he also reap.*
- Proverbs 22:6 - *Train up a child in the way he should go: and when he is old, he will not depart from it.*
- Proverbs 1:5 - *A wise man will hear, and will increase learning; and a man of understanding shall attain unto wise counsels.*

German wisdom – *Vee get too soon olt und too late schmart!*

Shipwreck

Truth for Today – Acts 27

Estimates vary on how many West Africans were captured and brought by ships to the Caribbean and American slave colonies. But experts generally agree that the numbers range between 12 and 20 million between the 16th and 19th centuries. The Atlantic Slave Trade was a booming economy as people became merchandise and cargo.

Life aboard a slave ship was horrific for the African men, women and children. 15 - 30% of the captives died on board the slave ships from dysentery, scurvy, smallpox and measles.

The eight to ten week passage was long and difficult. Men were typically chained to planks and to one another like cordwood. Women and children were given a bit more space. The ships transported 200 – 400 slaves per trip with about 30 crew managing the ship.

There were a few instances when the African men and women rebelled and overtook their crew. Having killed the crew out of anger and desperation, the Africans were now faced with life on the open sea. With no knowledge of navigation or ship operation, they wandered aimlessly on the ocean until all on board died.

As I read those terrible accounts of slave history, I reflect on what it would have been like for those slaves to sail the unfamiliar ships without a crew. Then I apply it to my life. Are there times I sit in the captain's or navigator's chair with insufficient experience, knowledge and skill? Am I capable of navigating the routes of my Christian journey? Do I need someone with more knowledge, experience and an ability to see into tomorrow?

Though I give Him permission to lead me, I often seek to take over that leadership. At times I over-value my abilities, or merely want to be in charge.

Without the guidance, wisdom and direction of God, my Christian journey would end in disaster and hurt.

Thank you Lord, for being willing to be my
Lord, guide, navigator, escort and companion.

Side Effects

Truth for Today – John 10:10

It happens to all of us sooner or later. An ache, a pain, an unexplained soreness or some other reason that gets us into a doctor's office. The examination is finished and the M.D. writes out a prescription. We take it to the pharmacist and receive the medication.

Opening the package we find a slip of paper that identifies the side effects of the medication. The list is long and it ranges from "may cause itching" to "may result in death".

We weigh out the risk associated with the side effects. How much of a problem is my ache, pain or unexplained soreness? Is getting it fixed worth the risk of three days of itching? Is it worth the risk of death? Generally we take the medication and warily keep an eye on the onslaught of side effects. Usually we are safe.

A problem, the diagnosis and prognosis, the decision to accept the cure and the side effects are something to think about as we ponder the problem of sin.

Sin is a problem that is a contagious plague. It is chronic, continual and progressive. It has been around long enough to establish patterns based on history and experience. Its symptoms are readily identifiable.

Diagnosis and prognosis are available. The cure is identified in the Bible. Jesus Christ, His shed blood, His death and His resurrection are the answer to the plague we call sin. Then the time comes for a decision. Are we willing to accept the cure? Are we willing to say yes to the cure? If so, what are the side effects?

The side effects to salvation are extremely positive. We receive eternal life in Heaven. We forfeit condemnation, conviction and guilt. We become heirs of God and are welcomed into His family. We receive the gift of His Holy Spirit in our lives. The list of side effects is long and the end result eternally peaceful. These side effects are wonderful.

- John 10:10 – *I am come that they might have life, and that they might have it more abundantly.*
- Revelation 21:4 – *And God shall wipe away all tears from their eyes; and there shall be no more death, neither sorrow, nor crying, neither shall there be any more pain: for the former things are passed away.*

Small but Mighty

He was sitting in the grass under a palm tree with his bicycle tire, or rather, various parts of his bicycle tire. Nearby was the rim, the tire and the tube. He had a slow leak and he was methodically checking the tread to find the culprit of his slow leak.

His tough Haitian finger pulled back from a sharp prick and then slowly he pulled out a thorn and handed it to me. It was tiny but tough enough to penetrate hard rubber and find its way into the bike tube. Then he kept searching and found three more. Finally content that all the offenders had been found he fixed the holes and put the bike back together.

I thought of the Apostle Paul as he shared about his infamous thorn in the flesh. 2 Corinthians 12:7 says - *And lest I should be exalted above measure through the abundance of the revelations, there was given to me a thorn in the flesh, the messenger of Satan to buffet me, lest I should be exalted above measure.*

We've all had them. Thorns. A tiny pebble in the shoe. A grain of sand in the eye. Tiny reminders of our humanness. The nagging distraction that all is not right. Something to remind us that in this world there will be tribulation, trial and pain. I am thankful today for the reminders that God has made a Heaven without distractions and earthly reminders. We have daily reminders that this world is not Heaven!

John 14:1-2 - *Let not your heart be troubled: ye believe in God, believe also in me. In my Father's house are many mansions: if it were not so, I would have told you. I go to prepare a place for you.*

"This world is not my home, I'm just a passin' through; my treasures are laid up somewhere beyond the blue; the angels beckon me from Heaven's open door, and I can't feel at home in this world anymore."

Smart-phone Spouse

She is staring intently at the man on the screen of her smart-phone. Then she flicks her thumb to swipe to another screen to view another man. Then again, and again, and again. The world of internet dating sites is growing. On average, each person searching for an internet mate swipes through 20 candidates per day.

76% of singles in the United States have tried internet dating sites, with those activities generating more than $1.2 billion per year. It is big business and it is growing as singles seek the perfect partner.

A recent study in the U.K. suggests that the average woman kisses 15 men, has two heartbreaks, four one-night stands, one live-in lover, been stood up once, and four terrible dates before finding her soul-mate.

Can it be that difficult? Eve had it easier as Adam was her only choice, but more importantly God put that great union together. They were created for one another. Can that concept work all these years later? The Bible provides sufficient principles:

- Matthew 7:7 – *Ask, and it shall be given you; seek, and ye shall find; knock, and it shall be opened unto you.*
- Psalm 37:4 – *Delight thyself also in the LORD: and he shall give thee the desires of thine heart.*
- Mark 11:24 – *What things soever ye desire, when ye pray, believe that ye receive them, and ye shall have them.*
- Matthew 6:33 – *But seek ye first the kingdom of God, and his righteousness; and all these things shall be added unto you.*
- Proverbs 3:5,6 – *Trust in the LORD with all thine heart; and lean not unto thine own understanding. In all thy ways acknowledge him, and he shall direct thy paths.*
- Hebrews 11:1 – *Now faith is the substance of things hoped for, the evidence of things not seen.*
- 1 Samuel 16:7 – *But the Lord said unto Samuel, Look not on his countenance, or on the height of his stature; because I have refused him: for the Lord seeth not as man seeth; for man looketh on the outward appearance, but the Lord looketh on the heart.*

Snowflakes and Chickens

Truth for Today – Proverbs 29:20

It was September and I was traveling east on a central Ohio highway, headed for a meeting. With plenty of time, light traffic and a nice fall day, it made for leisurely travel.

Suddenly I noticed snowflakes blowing across the road. Surprised, I wondered why it was snowing in September and then I realized it couldn't be snow. It must be cottonwood tree fuzz. Then I realized it wasn't cottonwood fuzz as that happens in the spring and I wasn't near any trees.

Perplexed, I saw a semi ahead of me and the white fuzz was coming from the truck and then I knew. I was following a semi load of chickens and it was feathers. I laughed out loud as I thought about how my mind had been deceived. Still smiling as I went around the truck, I looked at the chickens and saw that they were actually ducks.

Ducks! I couldn't believe how easily my mind could be deceived. Snowflakes, cottonwood tree fuzz, chicken feathers, duck feathers! It was a lesson I've not forgotten. Not everything is just as we think, or as we see. Lesson learned – Don't rush to judgment.

It seems like it is easy to sometimes draw conclusions from erroneous, unsubstantiated information. How often do we believe we have all the information on a subject, only to later realize that we did not? I'm thankful for the times in life when God lets me know that I have been, or can be deceived. Lessons learned.

Proverbs 29:20 - *Seest thou a man that is hasty in his words?*
There is more hope of a fool than of him.

Something Extra

Truth for Today – Genesis 1:27

I am an "extra" kind of person. People sometimes comment on the amount of ketchup I use in eating fries, a hot dog or hamburger. They marvel at the volume of chocolate or caramel syrup I put on ice cream. Adding not one, but five maraschino cherries to the top of a sundae is my norm. The extra BBQ sauce, pepper or butter I use in my eating habits makes me an "extra" kind of guy.

Extra makes some things very special. I think of three young men and women I know who have Down's syndrome. I was amazed to find that they each have something "extra". Genetically they carry an extra copy of chromosome 21. Watching their lives and also being touched by their gentle, loving and trusting spirits, I understand why they are special. They definitely have something "extra".

In one of our Haiti Homes of Hope we have a young boy whom I will call Pierre. One day when leaving the home, I shook his hand. I felt a bump on the bottom of his hand. Raising it for a better look, I noticed an extra finger. I looked at his other hand and saw the same thing. I couldn't believe that I had never seen them before or even heard about it.

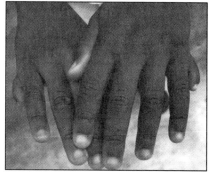

I asked him if they created any problems for him and he said, "Yes, sometimes other children make fun of me." I learned that "extra" for him was not better. We arranged to have them removed for which he was incredibly thankful. He felt normal.

The beautiful thing is that God didn't love him any more or less with or without those fingers. Nor did I. Extra is relative. It can make life better, or it can make life worse. Thankfully, we have a God who absolutely loves to surprise us with His "extra" touches. Are we paying attention to the special attention God is putting into the things in our lives or others around us?

Ephesians 3:20 – *(God who) is able to do exceeding abundantly above all that we ask or think...*

Sorry About That

Truth for Today – Proverbs 30:5

While sitting comfortably in my aisle seat in row 13, the stewardess took my order for a diet cola, and with a smile, gave me a packet of "lightly salted" peanuts. There it was, my .42 ounces of peanuts to last my one hour flight! I knew I could stretch those peanuts out to last the trip.

Carefully opening the bag, I stuck two fingers inside and found a peanut half. Popping it in my mouth I reached for another and could not find it. Looking inside I saw nothing but powder. I poured it out and found four half peanuts and at least .3 ounces of salt! I laughed out loud as I noticed the pile of salt and the printed packet.

I think often about the things in life that do not measure up to expectations. Large bags of potato chips that are half air. Odd shaped containers designed to look large, yet reduce the amount of content. And of course peanut packets that inadvertently are not what they say they are.

It has made me think about the one and only thing that is 100% true, pure and perfect - God's Word as it is recorded in the Holy Bible. It is inerrant, infallible and inspired by God Himself. It is flawlessly accurate and perfectly applicable. We have high expectations about its contents and are never disappointed. Thank you Father for not disappointing us!

Sounds like Greek to Me

Truth for Today – Genesis 11:1-9

With approximately 6,500 languages spoken in the world, it is said that Arabic, Chinese, Japanese and Korean are the most difficult to learn.

To be utterly proficient in Japanese, one must learn three sets of scripts - hiragana, katakana and kanji. It is estimated that there are 50,000 kanji illustrations, which makes me thankful for the 26 letters of our alphabet.

While we can be amazed at the diversity and uniqueness of all of God's creation, rarely do we think about the creation of His various languages. 6,500 of them, plus the wide variety of symbols, sounds, nasal inflections, guttural grunts and drawls that are attached to each language. What a Creator God we serve!

Genesis 11:1-9: *And the whole earth was of one language, and of one speech. And it came to pass, as they journeyed from the east, that they found a plain in the land of Shinar; and they dwelt there. And they said one to another, Go to, let us make brick, and burn them thoroughly. And they had brick for stone, and slime had they for mortar. And they said, Go to, let us build us a city and a tower, whose top may reach unto heaven; and let us make us a name, lest we be scattered abroad upon the face of the whole earth. And the LORD came down to see the city and the tower, which the children of men builded. And the LORD said, Behold, the people is one, and they have all one language; and this they begin to do: and now nothing will be restrained from them, which they have imagined to do. Go to, let us go down, and there confound their language, that they may not understand one another's speech. So the LORD scattered them abroad from thence upon the face of all the earth: and they left off to build the city. Therefore is the name of it called Babel; because the LORD did there confound the language of all the earth: and from thence did the LORD scatter them abroad upon the face of all the earth.*

With 7.3 billion people on earth, God is able to hear all the conversations, and even more importantly understand them all. He is truly an awesome God. Always, always, He is ready to listen!

Stains and First Impressions

Truth for Today – 2 Peter 3:14

After several long flights we landed in Mumbai, India, and then freshened up to go to the United States Consulate. We were escorted into the office of the U.S. Consul General to share information on the work we were doing.

I had been amazed at the beauty of the building, grounds and now the office we were seated in. I looked around at beautiful furniture, exquisite vases, sculpture and the magnificent tapestry on the tiled floor. Seated comfortably, I was listening to the dialogue, but was distracted when I noticed a beautiful ceramic cup on the table beside my chair. Having a love for things of antiquity, I wondered about the age of the cup.

I decided to casually lift it, and as I was prone to do, turned the cup over to look at the bottom to determine age and provenance. As I rotated it, I poured out the remnants of someone's morning coffee onto the beautiful tapestry rug on the floor.

All eyes were on me as the Consul General was quick to assure me that it would be taken care of. So much for first impressions with a person of prominence.

First impressions are difficult to un-do. The experience made me think of what the God of the universe thinks of me.

- Genesis 1:26 - *And God said, Let us make man in our image, after our likeness: and let them have dominion...*
- Genesis 1:31 - *And God saw everything that he had made, and, behold, it was very good.*
- Psalm 139:14 - *...I am fearfully and wonderfully made...*
- Jeremiah 1:5 - *Before I formed thee in the belly I knew thee; and before thou camest forth out of the womb I sanctified thee...*
- John 3:16 - *For God so loved the world, that he gave his only begotten Son, that whosoever believeth in him should not perish, but have everlasting life.*

Stars and Sand

***Truth for Today** – Genesis 22*

A day at the beach, including sun, surf and swimming. We bring back seashells and memories. There are no drawbacks to the day, right? Wrong. Sand. We take it home in our clothing, towels, coolers, car seats and between our toes.

It's then I think about the statement God made to Abraham in Genesis 22:17, where He spoke of the sands of the sea and the stars in the sky. Did you ever wonder which number was larger?

If you are okay with estimates and rough numbers, there are scientists who have made calculations. If you assume average sand grain size, numbers of grains per teaspoon, and numbers of beaches, oceans and deserts, the number would be roughly 7.5×10^{18} or seven quintillion, five hundred quadrillion grains of sand.

When we look at the sky with our naked eye we see thousands of stars. But when the Hubble telescope came on board, millions and billions of stars filled the night sky. Scientists have roughly estimated the number to be 70 thousand, million, million, million. That number equates to many stars per grain of sand.

So, the stars have it over the sands of the sea, right? Yes, but God wants us to know that we've only scratched the surface in learning how to count. His creation and imagination never ceases to amaze us.

Just as stars, galaxies, suns and the universe is so incredibly huge and so vast, at the opposite end of the spectrum we see that His grains of sand are tiny and minute.

Now, let's search beyond the tiny grain of sand to inspect a drop of water. Within ten drops, the number of molecules is larger than the number of grains of sand in the world, or the number of stars known to man. I would suppose that we still have only scratched the surface of comprehending His creation. He is an awesome God!

Sticky Fingers

Truth for Today – John 15

    The plastic part on the toy broke off rendering it useless. Unless of course, I could repair it. I read the instructions on the Super Glue and cleaned the surfaces. One square inch could hold a ton!

    I squeezed on the glue, spread it on the parts, and applied pressure to the two flat plastic parts by holding them between my thumb and index finger. Then I used my middle finger to add additional pressure by pushing down on my index finger.

    Twenty seconds later I started pulling my fingers away from the plastic. But my middle finger was stuck to my index finger's finger-nail. I pulled and tugged but it wouldn't budge. So, my ingenious brain being what it is, I got a razor blade and slid it along the fingernail to separate my middle finger.

    I separated the two fingers, but my middle finger was bleeding and part of my fingerprint was remaining on the fingernail. Not a good idea. It gave new meaning to the word "cleave".

    There are thirty instances of the word "cleave" in the KJV. The two most strategic are in how a husband and wife should bond:

Genesis 2:24 - *Therefore shall a man leave his father and his mother, and shall cleave unto his wife: and they shall be one flesh.*

...and the second is about our relationship with God in Deuteronomy 11:22-23 - *For if ye shall diligently keep all these commandments which I command you, to do them, to love the LORD your God, to walk in all His ways, and to cleave unto Him; Then will the LORD drive out all these nations from before you, and ye shall possess greater nations and mightier than yourselves.*

Cleaving in the original Hebrew means to *"cling to, stick to, stick with, follow closely, join to".*

In the Genesis 2:24 verse the added description of *"they shall be one flesh"* is literal and descriptive. If two things are so totally joined that they become one, it is impossible to separate them. That is the relationship that a husband and wife have, as well as we and our God.

Strange Friendships

***Truth for Today* –** 1 Corinthians 2:16

It was late at night and very dark. Our car headlights lit up the surrounding country side as we turned off the main road onto a dirt road in central Ethiopia. The driver asked, "Would you like to see some hyenas?" Then the headlights picked up the yellow eye-gleam of several hyenas along the side of the road. We parked with our lights shining on the slinking animals as they fed on something we couldn't see.

I don't think that hyenas ever made it to anyone's list of beautiful animals, but they were mesmerizing to watch. Their jaws are powerful enough to bite through bone and muscle. Their slinking posture gives the aura of treachery and deceit. The darkness of night hides their ugly disposition, argumentative nature and physical appearance. I wouldn't trust them in any manner.

However, Yusuf of Harar, Ethiopia is known as Hyena Man. He simply enjoys their company and the notoriety that goes with it. Every night a group of hyenas arrive at his small farmhouse next to the city dump for a feeding. He provides them with mule and camel meat, sometimes hanging it from his mouth for them to munch on.

Though I'm intrigued with his absence of fear for the hyena, the deeper reminder to me is that he loves them and enjoys being with them. All that, in spite of their appearance, disposition, habit of eating decomposing meat, odor and ghastly sounds.

I probably won't change my opinion of hyenas, nor of Yusuf's strange passion, but it does make me think of my acceptance of people outside my comfort zone. Too often, I make judgements about people unlike me.

Lord, help me to have a heart and mind like Jesus.
Help me to never be a respecter of persons.
Help me to not judge by outward appearance.
Help me to be like Jesus to others.

Stubborn Drivers

Several years ago, Jeni and I were making a five hour drive from our home in Indiana to Illinois. The trip took us west on a major highway. A train was stopped on the railroad tracks of a small town. It looked like the train would be there awhile, so I decided to try a side street to find a way around the train.

I found a side street that took us through a park and into the country. I decided to stay on this lesser trafficked road rather than cutting back to the original and busy highway.

Feeling self-satisfied and a bit smug, I drove for ten miles with virtually no traffic. Then Jeni's query, "Are you sure that we're going in the right direction?"

I said, "Absolutely," with an air of authority that began to seal my doom. She said, "Honey, I'm not sure about this road. There's a gas station, why don't you ask to make sure?"

I said, "Trust me," as my eyes casually and discreetly started to look for signs that would indicate I was in fact on the right road.

Seven miles later, I learned that I had been traveling straight south instead of west during my "short cut"! We were traveling away from the main road, not parallel to it.

After a reluctant acknowledgment to Jeni that she had been right, we arrived for our appointment forty-five minutes late.

There have been many other times in my life where I failed to listen to a warning or give credibility to someone's challenging question. What is there about my human nature that does not want to acknowledge error or receive instruction?

I think of the historical story of Balaam. He knew where he wanted to go. He knew when he wanted to go. He knew what he wanted and who he wanted to partner with. God instructed him again and again through various means, but Balaam was self-assured and more stubborn than the donkey he rode on. I think that Balaam and I were both stubborn drivers.

Proverbs 19:20 - *Hear counsel, and receive instruction,*
that thou mayest be wise in thy latter end.

Sunday Worship

Truth for Today – Psalm 23

Ah, Sunday morning. It's time for a leisurely breakfast with family on the deck. Springtime brings out the birds and blossoms. It's truly a day of rest and worship. It's restful, relaxing and an opportunity to count blessings and glorify Him. Then, it's time to head to church and worship God in the midst of other like-minded believers.

All over the world, there are billions across several religions who cannot fathom religious freedom. The Pew Research Center recently finalized an international study on global religious freedom for the year 2012. They published a number of astounding and frightening statistics:

- 74% (5.18 billion people) of the world population, live in countries that have high or very high levels of social hostilities involving religion.
- 29% of countries affecting 64% of the world population have a high or very high level of government restrictions on religion.
- In 2012, 39% of countries used violence to compel people to adhere to religious norms. In 2007, the number had been 18%.
- 25% of countries worldwide had mob violence related to religion. In 2007 the number had been 12%.
- 20% of countries experienced terrorist violence that was religion related. In 2007 it had been 9%.
- Sectarian violence related to religion affected 18% of countries in 2012 but only 8% in 2007.
- 110 countries are identified as harassing Christian believers.

Obviously, not all the persecuted around the world are Christian, but the above statistics indicate an increasing and disturbing trend that violence, harassment, intimidation, persecution and religious cleansing is becoming more of a norm.

Jesus gave us a glimpse of what we should expect in John 16:33 - *These things I have spoken unto you, that in me ye might have peace. In the world ye shall have tribulation: but be of good cheer; I have overcome the world.*

Supply and Demand

Truth for Today – 2 Peter 1:5-9

The debate has been ongoing for centuries around the world. Should governments legislate purity, abstinence and obedience? Does it work, or does it create black markets, illegal usages and crime? Is it possible to force people to make right choices against their will, desires and lusts? Or, if you take the laws away, will humanity gravitate to goodness or to evil? What is the natural default of man?

Such was the dilemma in 1657 when the Massachusetts General Court made liquor of any nature illegal. But alcohol returned, so sin-taxes were imposed on the liquor. Again, rebellion occurred. Americans loved their alcohol such that in 1830 it was found that citizens were consuming 1.7 bottles of hard liquor per week. That was three times the amount consumed in 2010.

Finally after years of haggling, a law was passed in 1920 prohibiting the sale, production, importing and transporting of alcoholic beverages. For 13 years the government sought to legislate obedience and goodness.

During those 13 years, bootlegging and black-market manufacturing of alcohol sky-rocketed to fill the alcoholic appetites of citizens. That led to crime, smuggling, law-breaking, gangs and war among gang lords. The law was repealed in 1933.

The debate on using laws to dictate goodness, morality and obedience in any society will continue. But God tells us that only self-control and His grace will have any real and lasting effect.

- Proverbs 25:28 - *He that hath no rule over his own spirit is like a city that is broken down, and without walls.*
- 1 Corinthians 9:27 - *But I keep under my body, and bring it into subjection: lest that by any means, when I have preached to others, I myself should be a castaway.*
- 1 Peter 4:7 - *But the end of all things is at hand: be ye therefore sober, and watch unto prayer.*
- Ephesians 2:8-9 - *For by grace are ye saved through faith; and that not of yourselves: it is the gift of God: Not of works, lest any man should boast. Not of works, lest any man should boast. Not of works, lest any man should boast.*

Tail Lights

Truth for Today – James 4:13-17

Leaving home at 6:00am for a 45 minute drive to work was mostly relaxing, but some mornings were more difficult than others. There was nothing I dreaded more than mornings with dense fog.

The darkness and the dense fog were a formidable foe on those early mornings. Living in the countryside meant little traffic, but peering through the fog and darkness while looking for headlights before pulling onto a road was tedious. How fast did I need to go to get to work on time? How fast or how slow was safe?

But one of the best things that could happen was seeing the tail lights of another car ahead of me. I could snuggle up behind them at a safe distance and my worries would dissipate like dense fog at sunrise.

Following those tail lights was incredibly easier than trying to find my own way. I found myself relaxing as I let the driver ahead of me navigate the fog, darkness and highway.

It taught me a lesson about how to navigate my life. God certainly is out in front of me. In fact, he created tomorrow and knows what it contains. He has equipped me today for all my tomorrows. The biggest question is the depth of my trust and faith in Him. It's comforting to follow His tail lights.

- Philippians 3:13 - *But this one thing I do, forgetting those things which are behind, and reaching forth unto those things which are before.*
- 1 John 3:20 - *God is greater than our heart, and knoweth all things.*
- Psalm 90:2 - *Before the mountains were brought forth, or ever thou hadst formed the earth and the world, even from everlasting to everlasting, thou art God.*
- James 4:13-15 - *...Whereas ye know not what shall be on the morrow. For what is your life? It is even a vapour, that appeareth for a little time, and then vanisheth away. For that ye ought to say, If the Lord will, we shall live, and do this, or that.*

Take your Time

Truth for Today – Proverbs 24:16

Sometimes, incredibly small things create huge consequences. Consider the old rhyme, "For Want of a Nail."

"For want of a nail the horse-shoe was lost. For want of a shoe the horse was lost. For want of a horse the rider was lost. For want of a rider the message was lost. For want of a message the battle was lost. For want of a battle the kingdom was lost. And all for the want of a horse-shoe nail."

On April 30, 2015 a U.S. RC-135V reconnaissance jet took off from an air base in Nebraska with a crew of 27. Suddenly a fire erupted on board. Soon it was out of control and the plane landed, the men exited and the plane sustained $62.4 million worth of damage.

The cause? A small metal retaining nut had not been tightened which failed to adequately hold an oxygen line above the galley. It had come loose pouring oxygen into the small fire that erupted. One very small untightened nut put 27 men at risk and demolished a huge jet.

According to the U.S. News and World Report, space shuttle Columbia's second flight was delayed when a hydraulic system filter clogged. Five quarts of oil would have prevented the $3 million per day delay. In another case, a punctuation mark left off of a computer software program caused the loss of a very costly satellite. In 1970, a fifty cent piece of wire caused the aborting of the Apollo 13 moon landing.

In Song of Solomon 2:15 we read how the little foxes can spoil the vines and tender grapes, and ultimately rob us of a harvest.

As older adults we have seen many cases where small things can erupt into disaster later. Young people may get tired of the warnings and cautions of their parents and grandparents, but God does want us to learn from others mistakes.

- 1 Corinthians 10:11 - *Now all these things happened unto them for examples: and they are written for our admonition, upon whom the ends of the world are come.*

Taken for Granted

When God shaped the landscape of where we live in Wells County, Indiana, He must have used a level. The highest elevation is 813' and the lowest is 750'. That 63' differential isn't overly noticeable. So, when Jeni and I spent time in the Rocky Mountain National Park, we simply couldn't absorb all that we were able to see.

We were at 10,300' in our car admiring the mountains and valleys, when we rounded a curve and saw a man flagging us down. The highway department was busy repairing the road. Being the first car in line, I lowered my window and began talking to the flag-man. I said, "You have the best job in the world, spending your time in these incredible mountains!" He had a blank look on his face as he slowly turned and looked at the view. Then he said, "I guess I take it for granted. It is pretty nice, isn't it? I never notice it."

1 Thessalonians 2:4 says, "*...we were allowed of God to be put in trust with the Gospel.*" The flag-man's dis-interest in something so phenomenal makes me wonder how often I do that with the Gospel.

There is absolutely nothing on earth as extraordinary or inconceivably more beautiful than the saving grace, mercy, love and salvation of God's Gospel message. Paul states that we have been entrusted with it. It has been placed in our hands!

What did the salvation gift cost God? John 3:16 says, "*For God so loved the world, that he gave his only begotten Son, that whosoever believeth in him should not perish, but have everlasting life.*"

What did the salvation gift cost Jesus? Luke 23:46 tells us, "*And when Jesus had cried with a loud voice, he said, Father, into thy hands I commend my spirit: and having said thus, he gave up the ghost.*"

How much does God care about the unsaved? 1 Timothy 2:4 gives us a glimpse, "*(God) who will have all men to be saved, and to come unto the knowledge of the truth.*"

What happens to those who die without Jesus? Revelation 20:15 – "*And whosoever was not found written in the book of life was cast into the lake of fire.*"

Is there an urgent responsibility on our shoulders to share the Gospel?

Tear It Down

Truth for Today – Colossians 3

Jeni and I experienced our first international short term mission trip to Haiti in 1985. On that trip in 1985, eight of us would be building a small school in St. Louis du Sud.

The first morning at the work site, the missionary gave clear instructions on the right amount of sand, water, gravel, and the size of stones that would be appropriate for the mortar. He then left to take care of other business.

When he returned at noon, he looked at the block wall that I, along with a couple of others had laid in his absence. He said "Tear it down. The wall is bowed because you've used too large of stones in your mortar." I said "Are you kidding?" His response which I will never forget was, "The Haitians deserve the best. Tear it down." We tore down the wall and I learned yet another principle in life.

In January of 2010 a devastating earthquake hit Haiti. Walls, roofs and buildings tumbled down, and approximately 300,000 Haitians lost their lives. Bowed walls, inferior construction, weak concrete and blocks all contributed to the catastrophe. I am thankful we tore down the bowed wall. The Bible teaches us about stewardship:

- Colossians 3:23 - *And whatsoever ye do, do it heartily, as to the Lord, and not unto men.*
- Proverbs 10:4 - *He becometh poor that dealeth with a slack hand: but the hand of the diligent maketh rich.*
- Ecclesiastes 9:10 - *Whatsoever thy hand findeth to do, do it with thy might.*
- Colossians 3:17 - *And whatsoever ye do in word or deed, do all in the name of the Lord Jesus.*
- Luke 6:31 - *And as ye would that men should do to you, do ye also to them likewise.*

Tears

While walking in what is called Jerusalem Old City in the Jewish Quarter, I found an interesting glass item. It was 4" tall and had a magnificent green iridescent color. There were two cavities in the top that ran to the bottom of the piece. The gentleman selling the item told me it was from the 3rd century and was Roman. Then he told me the story.

Mourners often collected their tears in glass bottles at the time of the loss of someone they loved. The glass bottle was then put into the crypt of those deceased. The amount of tears in the bottle and the number of bottles was an indication of how much love the mourners had for their loved one.

I find it interesting to read Psalm 56:8 – *"Put thou my tears into thy bottle,"* as David pleaded with God to watch over him and care for him during his retreat from Saul. David was sure of God's compassion for him in his time of need.

We seem reluctant at times to show our tears as they may be an indication of weakness. However, we are touched deeply when we see tears from someone else. Tears melt hearts and cause others to shed tears. Why is it we associate tears with weakness when it seems David thought God was collecting them? Years ago I was touched by a song – *Tears are a language God understands.*

Often you wonder why tears come into your eyes, and burdens seem to be much more than you can stand. But God is standing near, He sees your falling tears; tears are a language that God understands.
God sees the tears of a brokenhearted soul. He sees your tears and hears them when they fall. God weeps along with man and takes him by the hand; tears are a language God understands.
When grief has left you low it causes tears to flow, when things have not turned out the way that you had planned; but God won't forget you; His promises are true, tears are a language that God understands.

That Was a Bust

Truth for Today – Proverbs 15:22

When I was 13, I made a calloused comment to someone about a classmate of ours who had just been involved in a tragic situation. The comment got back to her and she was devastated. Did you ever wish you could take something back that you had said or done?

In 1986, a non-profit organization in Cleveland, Ohio decided to do a fundraising marketing stunt that would set a world record. They were going to release 1.5 million helium filled balloons from downtown. Unfortunately a rain storm was on its way so they did an early release. The balloons hit a cold front with rain and the balloons dropped to the ground instead of leisurely floating away. The consequences reached epic and horror proportions.

- Drivers in the city were distracted by the spectacle of balloons in the sky and on the ground, and accidents happened.
- An airport runway was shut down for 30 minutes due to the hazard of balloons on the runway.
- Balloons clogged waterways on Lake Erie.
- Balloons landed in a nearby pasture which was home to Arabian horses. They spooked and some were permanently injured resulting in a lawsuit.
- Balloons landed on Lake Erie in mass, hampering the search for two missing fishermen. Finding two bobbing fishermen in a sea of floating balloons wasn't easy. The men's bodies washed ashore creating another lawsuit settled out of court.

It is incredibly difficult for us to "fix" some of our mistakes. There are consequences to actions and we tend to reap what we sow. Learning to control our tongue and actions can reduce our problems immensely, as well as minimizing problems we heap upon others.

- Proverbs 3:5-6 - *Trust in the Lord with all thine heart; and lean not unto thine own understanding. In all thy ways acknowledge him, and he shall direct thy paths.*
- Proverbs 15:22 - *Without counsel purposes are disappointed: but in the multitude of counsellors they are established.*

That's a Big Rock

***Truth for Today** – 1 Corinthian 2:9*

Diamonds are likely the most desirable gem of all gems. $13 billion worth of rough diamonds are mined and produced each year. Ten million people are employed in the pursuit of the jewel that brings emotions of love, tenderness and commitment. In reality, the more common side effects of diamonds are blood, sweat and tears.

The last decade has highlighted the slavery and black-market associated with bringing the gems to market. The high temperature and pressure required to produce diamonds from carbon makes it a rare commodity.

The largest gem-quality diamond ever found was 3,107 carats, 1.37 lbs. and 4.1" long. The value in its final cut state is estimated at $400 million.

As humans, we marvel at the phenomenal beauty that God simply buries in the dirt. We go to war, murder and enslavement to find the jewels in our quest for material wealth and possessions.

But, in the meantime, God has done so much more than create these tiny bits of beauty. Recently, astronomers and scientists discovered a white dwarf star that essentially collapsed and crystallized the carbon. That star became a diamond roughly the size of our Earth. God has in His possession the largest diamond in the universe. It is estimated at 10 billion trillion trillion carats!

Obviously we marvel at the things that are around us, within us, under us or above us. But the Bible says in 1 Corinthians 2:9 - *But as it is written, Eye hath not seen, nor ear heard, neither have entered into the heart of man, the things which God hath prepared for them that love him.*

The whole difference between construction and creation is exactly this: that a thing constructed can only be loved after it is constructed; but a thing created is loved before it exists. – Charles Dickens

That's a Leap

Truth for Today – Job 37

Contestant #1 - He crouched under the goal and looked up. He leaped vertically 24" and hit his goal.

Contestant #2 - He stood in awe beside the Empire State building in New York City. Looking up, he was amazed at the 1250' height of the 103 story building. He tried jumping over the skyscraper and managed a 24" vertical jump and missed his goal by 1248'.

Contestant #1 is a .12" flea. Contestant #2 is a 6' man. Both have a 24" vertical leap. The goal of the flea was the underbelly of a passing German Shepherd dog while the goal of the man was the Empire State building.

If man had the ability to jump like a flea, he could easily jump over the Empire State building. God has built phenomenal things into His creation.

- The common opossum has a specialized protein in its body that counteracts toxic venom from snakes and scorpions.
- Hippopotamuses secrete a red gelatin product on their skin similar to sweat, except it has a sun screen product in it as well as an antibiotic to fight skin infections.
- A snake in Southeast Asia is able to leap up to 325' from one tree to another to evade predators.
- The 2" long Pistol shrimp has a large claw. When the shrimp snaps the claw shut it creates a cavitation bubble that travels at 60 mph and generates a 217 decibel sound that is capable of bursting a human ear drum. When the cavitation bubble bursts it releases a vapor that is measured at 8500° Fahrenheit.
- The Mimic Octopus has an ability to copy the appearance and behavior of up to 15 different types of sea species to scare off predators. It can mimic a sea-snake, lionfish, jellyfish, stingray and sea anemone.

If God has the ability to put these unique traits and abilities into common creatures, what can He do with us? Add His Holy Spirit to the incredible body, soul and mind He created within us, and... *we can do all things through Christ which strengthens us.*

That's Good Enough

It was 90° and humid. The garage needed painted and it was July. Being thirteen years old and dreaming of the swimming hole made scraping old paint off our garage a horrible experience. It seemed that there was no end to the pieces of old paint that needed to be scraped. I was always thankful when dad would say, "That's good enough."

When do we get to a point of "good enough"? Many times we think that 99% is good enough, and generally it is. But would we be satisfied with 99% in these cases? Consider, if 99% were good enough, then...

- 40,000 newborn babies would have been dropped by doctors and nurses last year.
- It would be okay for the U.S. Postal Service to wrongly deliver 1.58 billion pieces of mail per year.
- 4,500 entries in Webster's Third New International Dictionary would be misspelled.
- 24,000 subscribers wouldn't receive their Wall Street Journal tomorrow.
- 1,314 phone calls would be wrongly transferred every minute.

I am so incredibly thankful that our God is perfect. There is no 99% standard for Him. There are no mistakes, dropped communications or delivery errors with Him. He is 100% faithful and perfect, 100% of the time.

Beyond that, I am extremely thankful that He doesn't expect me to be 100% perfect. He does desire us to pursue Him with excellence, and He wants us to be overcomers. However, He knew before we were created that we would be imperfect and that we would need a Savior. His perfection is revealed in our imperfection, so He asked Jesus to pay a price we could never pay.

John 3:16 - *For God so loved the world, that he gave his only begotten Son, that whosoever believeth in him should not perish, but have everlasting life.*

That's Mine!

Truth for Today – Philippians 2

Years ago, friends of ours asked Jeni and me, along with our two children if we wanted to go to central Indiana to search for geodes. We jumped at the chance.

Geodes are incredibly ugly on the outside but their hollow interiors are filled with crystals. We arrived and before long our friend found one and methodically used a hammer to open it to reveal the inside. We were hooked!

Over the course of the next hours, we found dozens. Some were the size of a softball while others were almost 12" across. We filled buckets and placed them in the trunk of my car. When we arrived home we proceeded to unload them. I picked up one particular bucket and moved it off to the side.

My friend said, "What's in that bucket?" I responded, "Oh, those are mine." She said, "Oh, I see, we're getting possessive, aren't we!" Immediately feeling the heat of embarrassment, I put "my" bucket back in the mix and we proceeded to divvy them out equitably.

I was amazed at my reversion back to my childish "sandbox" rules of possession. Is there a natural humanistic tendency built into our DNA? The Bible gives us clear parameters and warnings.

- Luke 12:15 - *And he said unto them, Take heed, and beware of covetousness: for a man's life consisteth not in the abundance of the things which he possesseth.*
- Proverbs 11:24 - *There is that scattereth, and yet increaseth; and there is that withholdeth more than is meet, but it tendeth to poverty.*
- Philippians 2:3,4 - *But in lowliness of mind let each esteem other better than themselves. Look not every man on his own things, but every man also on the things of others.*
- 1 Corinthians 10:24 - *Let no man seek his own, but every man another's wealth.*

The Artist Knows His Work

***Truth for Today** – Genesis 1*

Over the years I have seen a wide variety of counterfeit, fake, forged and replicated items. They range from currency, coins, stamps, exotic vases, flint arrowheads to paintings. Nearly anything of value inevitably is reproduced.

I have seen reproductions guaranteed as authentic by so-called experts. Even the experts can be fooled. Abraham Lincoln once said, *"You can fool all the people some of the time, and some of the people all the time, but you cannot fool all the people all the time."*

What if we put the original Mona Lisa next to an excellent reproduction? Could you tell the difference? Could an art expert tell them apart?

If Leonardo da Vinci were alive and had to determine the genuine article, he would have no problem. He created the painting and knew every stroke, blend of color, depth of paint and nuance. His authentication would be 100% accurate. Quite possibly he painted a personal detail into the painting that only he could notice and identify.

God as our Creator is intimately familiar with each of us. He knows every physical, mental, emotional and spiritual attribute within us. He has planted His unique personal touch inside us that cannot be replicated. He alone knows us in our entirety. Do we trust Him to take care of every aspect of our life?

The Ayes Have it!

***Truth for Today* –** Proverbs 22:9

We were just concluding a board meeting when the board president said, "All in favor say aye." After the affirmation he said, "The ayes have it."

That prompts thoughts about the statement of "The ayes have it". How often do our eyes tell a story?

Possibly our eyes speak much more loudly than our voice. We can see joy, sadness, guilt, shame, anger, disappointment, hopelessness, grief, pleasure, frustration, displeasure, approval, disapproval and desperation in others eyes.

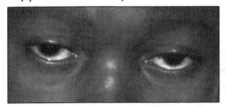 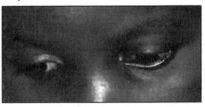

The above photos are the eyes of twelve year old children who live on the streets of Port au Prince, Haiti. For years, these eyes have seen too much. Eyes that have wept buckets of tears. Eyes that have witnessed battles for life and death. Eyes that watched the ebbing of life from their parents eyes.

The eyes have it. When I met these two children and looked into their eyes I saw emptiness. Hopelessness. Fear. Shame and guilt. Intense sadness and hurt.

As Christ-minded believers we have the ability to see things that the Holy Spirit opens our eyes to see. With that visibilty and depth perception we become responsible.

When Jesus looked into the eyes of the woman caught in adultery; the woman at the well; Zaccheus; the widow who had just lost a son; the blind, crippled, maimed and leprous, Jesus saw their needs. Action was right behind the visual image. The eyes have it.

> Proverbs 22:9 - *He that hath a bountiful eye shall be blessed; for he giveth of his bread to the poor.*

The Bird Wins

Truth for Today – Genesis 3:1-20

One of the birthday presents in front of me was long, flat and had potential. As I peeled off the paper I saw my dream. A BB gun! Finally, I was old enough to have my perfect gift.

Along with the BB gun came a verbal list of "do's and don'ts" from my dad. He did a good job of instructing me to "Never, ever shoot a purple martin."

A purple martin is a phenomenal bird. The largest of the swallow family, with a forked tail, it was a literal dive bomber as it swoops and dives with its wings tucked to its side. They are difficult to attract and difficult to keep. Once occupying a bird house, they generally come back to it year

after year. My dad had spent a lot of time in getting and keeping them. He didn't want me doing anything to damage that.

The martins had a tendency to land on telephone wires within 10 feet of my gun. That was an incredible temptation for a boy with a new gun. I gave in to the temptation. The martin fell from the wire, fluttered and landed in a large evergreen shrub. Though I searched and searched, I could not find it. My dad came home from work and Numbers 32:23 became reality – *"Be sure your sin will find you out."* The crippled purple martin made an emergence from the bush as my dad walked to the house. There was a consequence to my sin.

Where there is no consequence for sin, there is fertile ground for future sin and transgression.

- Galatians 6:7,8 - *Be not deceived; God is not mocked: for whatsoever a man soweth, that shall he also reap. For he that soweth to his flesh shall of the flesh reap corruption; but he that soweth to the Spirit shall of the Spirit reap life everlasting.*

The Door is Closed

Truth for Today – 1 John 5

Our plane landed forty-five minutes late and Jeni and I were stuck in aisle 28 as the passengers ahead of us slowly retrieved their carry-on luggage. We were getting anxious as we knew we had too few minutes to get to our connecting gate.

We began running and uttering quick prayers as soon as we got off the plane pulling our roller bags. Out of breath, we were 50' away from our gate when I saw the door to our jet-way close.

I ran up to the airline clerk and pleaded, "Please let us board, I have meetings I need to get to!" Her response was short and sweet, "Sorry, but the door is closed." There was no recourse other than to wait for another plane.

Standing there dismayed, we watched as the jet-way door began opening and a stewardess came through to get a key she had forgotten at the counter. The clerk looked at me, smiled and said, "It looks like the door is open." She took our tickets and we were escorted by our heroine stewardess to our seats.

It's easy for me to say, "God is good all the time", "God heard and answered my prayer" and "Isn't He an amazing God", when things actually come together in a way that I like.

What would have been my reaction if the door had not opened? What if I had to wait four hours for another flight only to find out that there were no available seats and I would miss my meetings? What then?

Is God good all the time? Are all our prayers answered, or only those that get the results we think we need or want?

- 1 John 5:14,15 - *And this is the confidence that we have in him, that, if we ask any thing according to his will, he heareth us: And if we know that he hear us, whatsoever we ask, we know that we have the petitions that we desired of him.*
- Isaiah 65:24 - *And it shall come to pass, that before they call, I will answer; and while they are yet speaking, I will hear.*

The End

Truth for Today – Acts 1:7-8

As my dad's wheelchair was being pushed past my mom and I on his way to surgery, he put his thumb and index finger together in an *"everything is okay"* sign. Those were his last words to us, even though they were non-verbal. He never communicated again prior to his death but his "okay" spoke volumes about his faith and life. A person's last words tell us a lot about their lives.

- *How were the receipts today at Madison Square Garden?* - P.T. Barnum
- *Okay, okay... I'll come. Just give it a moment.* – Pope Alexander VI
- *I'm going away tonight. I want you to look after my wife and little man. I'm on fire. I'm burning up. Burning up.* - James Brown
- *This is not the end of me.* – Henry Campbell-Bannerman
- *I just wish I had time for one more bowl of chili.* – Kit Carson
- *I think I'll sleep now.* – George Washington Carver
- *I have tried so hard to do right.* – Grover Cleveland
- *Lady, you shot me.* – Sam Cooke
- *You got me.* – John Dillinger
- *One last drink, please.* – Jack Daniel
- *I'll sleep well tonight.* – Henry Ford
- *I'd rather be fishing.* – Jimmy L. Glass
- *It was the food! Don't touch the food!* – Richard Harris
- Jesus Christ's last words at his death as recorded in Luke 23:46 - *And when Jesus had cried with a loud voice, he said, Father, into thy hands I commend my spirit: and having said thus, he gave up the ghost.*
- Jesus Christ's last words at his ascension in Acts 1:7-8 - *And he said unto them, It is not for you to know the times or the seasons, which the Father hath put in his own power. But ye shall receive power, after that the Holy Ghost is come upon you: and ye shall be witnesses unto me both in Jerusalem, and in all Judaea, and in Samaria, and unto the uttermost part of the earth.*

The Food Chain

Truth for Today – Job 41

The ocean is full of life. There are an estimated 28,000 different species of fish worldwide. Add to that the sponges, eels, worms, crustaceans and amphibians. The cycle of life in the sea depends on the food chain that exists.

But, in the ocean, the Great White shark is at the top of the food chain. Growing up to 20 feet in length and weights of 5000 pounds, they can cruise along at 15 miles per hour. Their color scheme makes them nearly invisible from below and from above. Several rows of razor sharp, sawing and ripping teeth, numbering in the thousands, make them the masters of the sea. Instances are rare of the Great White losing out to another predator.

In Africa, the lion is considered at the top of the food chain. Some would say the Cape Buffalo is a close second, while others would say the leopard and elephant are at the top of the list.

In the air, there are the raptors. The eagles, hawks, owls and falcons dominate the food chain. They are considered "apex predators." Their excellent eyesight, hooked beak and eight hooked talons keep them safe from other predators.

Being at the top of the food chain creates a predictable balance in the cycle of life. The apex predators keep the rodent and other populations under control. Remove the top predators from any environment and life turns upside down.

There are instances when top predators lose their battle. It may be rare, but it does happen. Nothing in life is certain, it seems. But, there is one thing that is absolutely certain. God loses no battles. There is nothing or no one who can conquer God. He is in charge and in the end He wins.

I've been reading in the Bible, about the ending of the age.
And one thing that's for certain, it grows closer every day.
But I am not concerned about, the way it's gonna end.
Because I've read the back of the book and know we're gonna win.

The Good and the Bad

Truth for Today – 1 Corinthians 6:12

God's creativity extends into the horticulture world. Though impossible to find accurate numbers, the estimated number of different plant varieties around the world is 400,000. Just one example of the many thousands is a tall green plant with pointed leaves and jagged edges with an Old English name of *haenep*.

Historically, it first shows up as imprints on some of the earliest Chinese pottery, and Palestinian Jews wrote of it in the 2nd century.

The usages for its fibers are diverse, including mulch, animal bedding and litter. The oil from the plant seeds are used in oil based paints, moisturizing agents in skin-cream, for cooking and for manufacturing plastics. The seeds by themselves are used in bird seed mixes. Other valuable uses are in the manufacturing of paper products, textiles, clothing, biodegradable plastics, cement production, insulation, health food and bio-fuel. Research is under way to use it in electrodes for super-capacitors. It can be used to make a milk-like tea, salads, flour, tofu and nut butters. Our Creator God is amazing and imaginative!

Thomas Jefferson and George Washington raised it on their plantations as did many others as a cash crop. Up until the 1940's it was commonly known as *hemp* and used for many products including rope. Today it is a regulated plant more commonly known as *Cannabis* or *Marijuana*.

Nearly anything in God's creation can be used for good or evil. With free will we have opportunities to exercise self-control and wisdom as we seek to follow Biblical principles. Cannabis has received justifiable bad press for its psychoactive drug components but part of the success of our country was borne on the back of this ill-fated plant and its usefulness in industry. God asks us to listen to His Spirit as we make decisions in our lives.

- 1 Corinthians 6:12 - *All things are lawful unto me, but all things are not expedient: all things are lawful for me, but I will not be brought under the power of any.*
- Proverbs 25:28 - *He that hath no rule over his own spirit is like a city that is broken down, and without walls.*

The Greatest Acts of All Time

Truth for Today – 2 Corinthians 11:14-15

The talent and ingenuity of magicians around the world is pretty phenomenal. Sleight of hand tricks or whatever else they are able to accomplish in their vocation, is simply amazing.

They are seemingly able to turn paper or glass into currency; turn an empty hat into a hat full of doves or rabbits; converting a rabbit into a dove; water into ice in a few seconds; one dollar bills into hundred dollar bills; and a Hummer into a Fiat. How do they do that?

We don't need to go to the internet to read about astounding feats, we can simply open our Bibles.

- Exodus 7:12 - Pharaoh's magicians threw their magic wands on the ground and they turned into serpents.
- 2 Corinthians 11:14 - Paul shares that satan can transform himself into an angel of light.
- 2 Corinthians 11:15 - Paul also speaks about satan's messengers being able to turn themselves into ministers of righteousness.
- Matthew 7:15 - Jesus cautioned us on satan's ability to turn ravenous wolves into docile sheep.
- Genesis 20:2 - With a few convincing words, Abraham turned his wife into his sister.

But, there are two actions that are the most remarkable and incredible. Those two things are supernaturally miraculous. The first is God's ability to turn anything that is evil, sinful, and unbelievably bad into something that is pure, virtuous and excellent. He is able to do that with accidents, loss, disease and abuse, and then use it for His good and the betterment of His Kingdom.

The second is God's ability to convert the most atrocious, wicked, brutal, vicious, evil, immoral, decrepit and sinful man or woman into a Godly, loving and beautiful person.

Our God doesn't use sleight of hand, deception or trickery to accomplish it. In a moment, in the twinkling of an eye, He is able to astound us with His absolutely awe-inspiring acts. He is an awesome God!

The King Can Crow

Truth for Today – Luke 14

So much for the urban myth that roosters only crow at the crack of dawn. In Haiti, you can hear them at midnight and every hour before dawn. In fact, I'm not sure that I've ever even heard them at the crack of dawn.

In any respect, roosters seem to be kings of their world. The bright colors of their feathers make them believe they are royalty. Then there is the ever present strut that can be somewhat intimidating and certainly arrogant looking.

I ran across this particular rooster in southwest Haiti. He had an air about him that did not match his appearance.

God usually uses His creation to teach me about myself. I wonder how many times I have been puffed up, arrogant, proud of my strut, and full of myself. Just as I look at this rooster and think, "If you only had a clue…" I wonder how many people have looked into my life and thought the same thing.

In our humanness we have a tendency to elevate ourselves at times. Again, the Bible clearly helps us see ourselves.

- Luke 14:11 - *For whosoever exalteth himself shall be abased; and he that humbleth himself shall be exalted.*
- Romans 12:3 - *For I say, through the grace given unto me, to every man that is among you, not to think of himself more highly than he ought to think.*

The King is Coming

Truth for Today – 1 Timothy 2:1-8

As I listen to the news and read the newspapers, I see the weaknesses of many country leaders, including presidents, dictators, kings, queens, premiers, and tyrants.

We have ringside seats to corruption, power struggles, sleaze, bribery, fraud, dishonesty and outright shenanigans. What do those things do in affecting our trust levels of men and women of authority and power? How is it possible to have respect for those in high governmental offices?

Even as we read the Old Testament accounts of country leaders 3000 years ago, we see the heart of man has always defaulted towards evil. Jeremiah 17:9 says, *The heart is deceitful above all things, and desperately wicked: who can know it?*

Abraham Lincoln said, *"Nearly all men can stand adversity, but if you want to test a man's character, give him power."* Obviously, not all leaders deserve the broad label of evil, so perspective needs to be maintained while looking at reality.

What is our role as believers in being in subjection to those in governmental and political leadership? Romans 13:1 says, *Let every soul be subject unto the higher powers. For there is no power but of God: the powers that be are ordained of God.*

1 Timothy 2:1,2 – *I exhort therefore, that, first of all, supplications, prayers, intercessions, and giving of thanks, be made for all men; for kings, and for all that are in authority; that we may lead a quiet and peaceable life in all godliness and honesty.*

I would suggest that it is difficult to be in subjection to governmental authorities who are not governing Biblically.

That being said, I am thankful the God of the universe answers to no one. Wrongs someday will be made right. Evil, wickedness and injustices will be handled by Him. Though the Bible says that God has placed governmental leaders on the throne, He has reserved final judgment of the universe for Himself. After all, He is God!

The Last Muffin

Truth for Today – Ecclesiastes 11:3

It had been an early morning flight out of Fort Wayne, Indiana into O'Hare in Chicago. I had not had breakfast, so upon arrival in Chicago I got in line for a coffee prior to my next flight.

As I stood in the slow moving line, the gentleman in front of me stepped up to the counter and ordered a coffee and muffin. The young lady behind the counter started filling his order.

Then, almost in slow motion, the man dropped to the floor at my feet. I looked at his face and saw his rolled back open eyes. I grabbed his wrist and found a very slight pulse. I yelled, *"Is there a doctor or nurse here?"*

People gathered in a circle around the two of us on the floor but no one came forward. Someone dialed 911 while I loosened his collar and tie. There was still no response. I looked at the food counter and saw his coffee and muffin. I pulled his wallet and saw his name and address and knew that there would be grief in that city. I called his name, again and again, all to no avail.

Finally after a long few minutes of what seemed like an eternity, the emergency medical personnel arrived. I stood up to join the ever-widening circle of onlookers. I said to the lady beside me, "I'm surprised that there were no doctors or nurses in the crowd." She said, "I'm a nurse but I don't get involved with these things. They are lawsuits waiting to happen!" I learned several lessons that day:

1. Be ready. Our life may be over today.
2. There will be unfinished muffins when we die. Make sure that the important things that need taken care of, are taken care of.
3. Risk is part of life. When we accept risk, we can make a difference in someone else's life.
4. Lost opportunities generally bring guilt and shame.
5. And last but not least, several days later, I called the gentleman's home to see how things turned out. His wife said, *"He passed away and is in Glory."*

Jesus is coming again. Maybe today!

The Rich Poor Woman

Truth for Today – Luke 16

She was in her forties and knew about poverty and loss. She had given birth to five sons. Her husband had left years ago for a better life and another woman in Port au Prince. But she did what mothers everywhere do. She tried to make a life for her five sons.

Then she saw the life draining out of her oldest as well as the next two. They worked hard to keep their family together and to provide some amount of food to exist. Their hard work was at the expense of their health. She learned of three families who would take her oldest three, so she sent them away. She knew grief and loss.

After several years, she has only seen them one time. But in spite of the grief and loss, she now understands that their lives likely went from bad to worse as they became domestic servants or slaves. She feels the shame of giving her sons away. She continues to work hard to keep her remaining two sons healthy. The harsh realities of poverty are in every country around the world.

Even in the humblest of homes in Haiti, the love of God changes things like light invading darkness. A dirt floor, thatched roof, and only a little bit of food doesn't diminish the faith of a Christ filled believer. I was incredibly touched by the strong faith of the mother I've described. Her love for her sons is exceeded only by her love for Her Savior.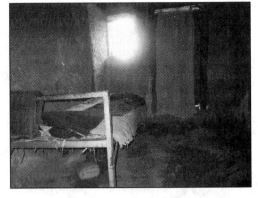

I'm reminded of Lazarus in Luke 16:24-25, *"And he cried and said, Father Abraham, have mercy on me, and send Lazarus, that he may dip the tip of his finger in water, and cool my tongue; for I am tormented in this flame. But Abraham said, Son, remember that thou in thy lifetime receivedst thy good things, and likewise Lazarus evil things: but now he is comforted, and thou art tormented."*

The Same But Different

Truth for Today – Romans 15:6

As I think of the imagination God had during His days of creation, I think of the almost countless types of birds, animals, fish, cells, bacteria, stars, colors, natural wonders, sunrises and sunsets. That is variety at its best and assures me that our God loves diversity.

In Christianity, there are many divisions, schisms, splits and separations around the issues of diversity, unity and uniformity. It is difficult to sort out. What is diversity? What is unity? What is uniformity?

Diversity is the difference we see in mammals and reptiles; zebras and eagles; bacteria and a galaxy; and a male and female.

Unity is the ability for diverse creation to exist in an ecosystem and universe in a manner that intertwines them together. Remove one or two members and the universe changes and is different. Removal of a member can threaten the survival of those remaining.

Uniformity is an environment where everything seems to be identical. Uniformity is not unity and it most certainly is not diversity.

A friend of mine has a beautiful family. They are close, caring, Godly and tight enough that nothing will tear it apart. They are not identical or uniform, but they are united. They are diverse.

They have seven children. There are two boys and five girls. That is diversity. The oldest five are biological children, the younger two are adopted. That is diversity. The fifth child has Down's syndrome. That is diversity. The youngest two are Haitian and black. That is diversity.

Diversity does not mean that a family, group, or universe cannot live in unity. God's creation is filled with diversity and the world we have is not spinning out of control. It works in the universe and it works in families and it can work in churches.

- 1 Cor. 1:10 - *Now I beseech you, brethren, by the name of our Lord Jesus Christ, that ye all speak the same thing, and that there be no divisions among you; but that ye be perfectly joined together in the same mind and in the same judgment.*
- Romans 15:6 - *That ye may with one mind and one mouth glorify God, even the Father of our Lord Jesus Christ.*

The Significant Ear

Truth for Today – 1 Corinthians 12

She was five months old, tiny, and changed Jeni's and my life forever. She was our first foster child and was a part of our family for over three years. In a world of 7.3 billion people, how could one insignificant child make such a profound difference? Is it possible that irrelevant, small things are much more significant than we could ever imagine? Possibly those seemingly unimportant things are not insignificant at all?

I love how 1 Corinthians 12 lays out how the body of Christ is made up of many members. Paul uses the analogy of our physical body to help us understand the significance of the members of our spiritual body.

He speaks of the foot, hand, eye, nose and ear and how they are part of the body. All have importance in spite of some having more beauty or strength than others.

We could talk about the intricacies of each member of the body, but for a moment let's explore the ear.

There are three parts to it. The outer, middle and inner ear. The outer ear brings vibrations to the ear drum. The ear drum focuses those vibrations to a focal point for the middle ear to process. The middle ear passes those vibrations to the inner ear which sends those signals to the brain via nerve fibers. Thus, simplistically, we hear.

The middle ear has three tiny and fragile bones. The hammer bone (maleus) collects the vibrations from the eardrum and sends them to the connecting anvil bone (incus). The anvil sends them to the connected stirrup bone (stapes) which sends the vibrations to the inner ear.

Who would call those three tiny bones insignificant? They are unseen and I'm sure, not a thing of beauty. Without them, we would miss out on many beautiful aspects of God's creation. The World Federation of the Deaf estimates there are 70 million deaf in the world. They know the significance of hearing loss.

How do we process our significance? Do we believe God has gifted each of us in unique and powerful ways? We are made in His image and likeness and filled with value and usefulness.

The Ultimate Museum

Truth for Today – Revelation 21

Exploring the Smithsonian National Museum of Natural History is a phenomenal experience. The breadth and depth of the exhibits defies description.

One particular area which captured my interest, is the "Hall of Geology, Gems and Minerals." Of particular interest were the 15,000 individual gems and jewels in inventory from around the world. Beginning with Afghanite to Zoisite, one can only imagine the multitude of colors, refractive light and value housed in the gallery. Including the Hope Diamond and the Star of Asia Sapphire, the value of the collection has to be unbelievably high.

In spite of the breathtaking beauty, exorbitant worth, countless colors, carats, multiple facets, size and sheer numbers, the Gem Gallery pales drastically from the words we read about Heaven in Revelation chapter 21.

Descriptive adjectives include... *new, holy, great, glory, precious, jasper, crystal, pure gold, pure glass, sapphire, chalcedony, emerald, sardonyx, sardius, chrysolyte, beryl, topaz, chrysoprasus, jacinth, amethyst, pearls.* Other places speak of the mansions, streets paved with pure gold, fabulous singing with nothing negative or evil present.

When I explored the Smithsonian's inventory of gems and jewels, I was restricted by time. The museum would close. We needed to get back to the hotel. Vacation would be ending. There simply wasn't enough time to see it all or experience it to the levels I would have liked. Besides the gems and jewels, there was the Native American exhibit, the Dinosaur exhibit, the Ocean Hall and the many other exhibits I wanted to view.

One of the phenomenal blessings of Heaven will be the absence of time. No pressure to hurry. No admission costs to the jewel studded foundations and doors. No need to take off shoes as we do tours of mansions. No lines to wait in. No rope barriers to prevent us from viewing exhibits. I'm sure it will be a hands-on experience with no signs about trespassing and touching. Heaven is a beautiful place!

The Value of Silver

Truth for Today – Mark 10:45

The road was narrow and crowded with farmers and their various animals. There were also many slaves and servants carrying a variety of products to market for their masters. Suddenly, a large ox broke away from its owner and charged a slave, goring him with one of its horns. The slave fell to the ground, and bled to death.

According to Exodus 21:32, the owner of the ox had to pay the slave owner thirty shekels of silver for compensation, as well as stoning the ox. That was the value of a slave.

In Matthew 26:14-16, we read - *Then one of the twelve, called Judas Iscariot, went unto the chief priests, And said unto them, What will ye give me, and I will deliver him (Jesus) unto you? And they covenanted with him for thirty pieces of silver. And from that time he sought opportunity to betray him.*

It is commonly thought that the thirty pieces of silver were Tyrian shekels used at the time of Christ to pay temple taxes. The chief priests had access to the silver coins and used them to pay Judas.

It's interesting to ponder the fact that Jesus Christ, the Son of God had the same value as a slave or man-servant. Thirty shekels or pieces of silver.

Followers of Jesus would have attached far more value to Him than that of a slave. But, was Jesus a man-servant or slave? Consider the facts:

- His Father gave Him away to serve others. John 3:16 - *For God so loved the world, that he gave his only begotten Son...*
- Though willing to serve, Jesus still pleaded with His Father to set Him free of his tasks. Luke 22:42 - *Father, if thou be willing, remove this cup from me...*
- Jesus came to earth to serve, not to reign as a master. Mark 10:45 - *For even the Son of man came not to be ministered unto, but to minister, and to give his life a ransom for many.*

Lord, help me to have the servant mind,
heart and willingness of my Savior.

Things are Moving

Truth for Today – Acts 16:23-40

I was at Chicago's O'Hare airport on Tuesday, January 12, 2010 waiting for a flight. Suddenly I heard a loud, spontaneous groan coming from a crowd as they gathered in front of a television monitor. It was then I saw the headlines about a devastating earthquake in Haiti. Having many friends and employees there, I was crushed and filled with apprehension. It was devastating to the people of Haiti.

The earth began to move in Leogane, just 15 miles west of Port au Prince. As the 7.0 magnitude earthquake continued to send its rolling waves outward, buildings began to crumble and fall. The houses and structures of Port au Prince, Leogane, Jacmel and countless villages crashed down on residents. The damage was immediate, catastrophic and devastating, but it was only just beginning.

By January 24th, 12 days later, there were 52 aftershocks measuring greater than 4.5 magnitude, which continued to do more damage. The numbers are varied from many sources, but it is generally agreed that an estimated 200,000 to 300,000 men, women and children lost their lives, 300,000 residences and commercial buildings were destroyed, and 1.5 million people were displaced.

Over the next several months I was able to hear many testimonies from Haitians about how the disaster unified the country and increased their faith. One might assume that tragedies can diminish faith, but that was not the case. Many came to a personal faith in Christ, countless had opportunities to help orphans and those who were injured. Though the ground moved in dramatic ways, the Spirit of God moved in a much more phenomenal way.

Romans 8:28 - *And we know that all things work together for good to them that love God, to them who are the called according to his purpose.*

Things are not What They Seem

Truth for Today – Job 19:1-3

A friend of mine shared a story with me that was indicative of the wonderfully chaotic life he leads with his family.

"I had a bicycle that had a flat tire. I pumped it up and found it flat again a couple of days later. I pumped it up and a couple of days later it was flat again. I finally caved in and decided to replace the tube. I took the old tube, pumped it up and looked for the hole and couldn't find one. I remarked at dinner that evening about how the tube would hold air now that it was off the bike. That was when one of my young daughters quietly confessed that she liked to hear the hissing sound of air seeping from the tire when she'd stick something in the valve."

Things are not always what they seem. A small nail hole in the tube? The rim leaking air? No... it was something else. Many times we draw conclusions with what seem to be the obvious answers.

Have you ever drawn a conclusion about someone based on how they looked, how they acted, what they said, what someone else said about them, where they went, or who they went with? And then later, as you heard more details or facts, your earlier conclusion changed?

Rushing to judgment or premature conclusions is not Biblically sound. I think of the Bereans in Acts 17:11 – *...they (the Berean people) received the word with all readiness of mind, and searched the scriptures daily, whether those things were so.* Proverbs 25:8 teaches us to be slow to rush to judgment or we may have regrets and be embarrassed by our hasty conclusions or words.

Rarely do we have all the facts as we observe the lives of others. I pray that no one judges my life without knowing all the facts. It makes me thankful to know God knows all and is a righteous judge.

This Far and no Further

Truth for Today – Revelation 20:10

As a boy growing up I loved dogs. That is, until I was bitten by the infamous Rip, a German Shepherd. On that day, everything changed. That encounter turned me, as a dog-lover into a dog non-lover (synonymous with dog-hater).

Along with Rip, there were two other dogs that I hated to be anywhere close to. One was a dog who belonged to my mom's cousin Mel. The other was a dog who belonged to my uncle Harry.

The dogs had things in common. They were both German Shepherds. They were both snarling beasts whenever anyone drove into their yard. Fangs, lips curled back, wild eyes, hair on their backs standing up, growls and snarls. In my young mind, they were ferocious monsters.

The other thing they both had in common was that they were tied with chains to their dog house. My bravery increased greatly when I heard the rattle of those chains and saw the built-in safety and security. I could get out of the car and actually walk to the house. My fear diminished as I thought of the heavy and stout chains holding those wild beasts in check.

I marvel at times as to how much we fear satan. His reputation precedes him. The Bible shares a few thoughts about him:

- 1 Peter 5:8 - *Be sober, be vigilant; because your adversary the devil, as a roaring lion, walketh about, seeking whom he may devour.*
- 2 Corinthians 11:14 - *...for satan himself is transformed into an angel of light.*
- John 10:10 - *The thief cometh not, but for to steal, and to kill, and to destroy.*

But in 1 John 4:4, we see the battle is won *...greater is He that is in you, than he that is in the world.* Satan is defeated! He is bound. Satan is the loser! The chains holding him back are strong! *Rev. 20:10 - ...the devil that deceived them was cast into the lake of fire and brimstone.*

Thorny Love

Truth for Today – Mark 15

The church was in the middle of a remote pasture full of brush and bushes. It had been a long afternoon. The Indian sun had been hot and many people packed the primitive church in India.

The small congregation was anxious to hear about Jesus. On that afternoon and early evening, they heard many things that included the sacrificial love of Jesus and His willingness to put others first. As is true in nearly every sermon about the Gospel and the crucifixion, speaking of the crown of thorns which Jesus endured, would likely have been included.

In hearing the Gospel message, the small group would be made aware of the pain that Jesus endured for undeserving strangers and those who were unworthy of His love and sacrifice.

As the last song was sung and the final prayer offered, it was now time to leave. The small group emerged to face a darkening night.

John, from the U.S., headed down the trail. Suddenly a small hand grabbed his hand and led him to the waiting truck. When they arrived, John looked down at the little boy who had walked him through

the thicket. It was then he saw that the boy was barefoot and had sacrificially walked on the thorns alongside the trail so John would find his way on the path.

Thorny love, self-sacrifice and love in action. The small boy possibly didn't understand his actions were like those of Jesus. The thorns were just one small part of the pain which Jesus willingly and lovingly absorbed for us. He also endured rejection, torture, betrayal, pain, abandonment, being forsaken by His own Father and carried an enormous load that was not His to carry.

Tick Tock...

Truth for Today – John 3

"There's only room for 400, so seating is limited."
"You'll have to wait 45 minutes for a table."
"We are closed on Saturday's."
"You have to be 42" tall to go on this ride."
"Sorry, you need to be age 60 to get the senior's breakfast."
"Sorry, you need to be under the age of 8 to get the child's meal."

The restrictions of life go on and on. God also sets parameters for who can live in Heaven.

- John 14:6 - *Jesus saith unto him, I am the way, the truth, and the life: no man cometh unto the Father, but by me.*
- John 3:3 - *Verily, verily, I say unto thee, Except a man be born again, he cannot see the kingdom of God.*
- Mark 8:34 - *Whosoever will come after me, let him deny himself, and take up his cross, and follow me.*

So, who can enter the gates of Heaven? 1 Timothy 2:4 says, *(God) who will have all men to be saved, and to come unto the knowledge of the truth.*

Sadly, the parameters God has set regarding being born again, being a Jesus follower, and being a believer is restrictive. That creates urgency as to how important it is that all men hear the Gospel.

The total population of the world is approximately 7.3 billion. As we begin to reduce that number by those who do not believe or follow Jesus, we find the number of those going to Heaven plummeting dramatically. Jesus said in Matthew 7:13-14: *Enter ye in at the strait gate: for wide is the gate, and broad is the way, that leadeth to destruction, and many there be which go in there-at: Because strait is the gate, and narrow is the way, which leadeth unto life, and few there be that find it.*

There would be many ways to calculate the number of those who are saved and those who are not. Some calculations would indicate that every minute, 70 people die without Jesus and without a hope of Heaven. Put your finger on your pulse. Every heartbeat becomes an urgent and crushing reminder of another lost soul dying without Him.

Together Forever

Truth for Today – John 14:3

John and Bobby were very close. John had been a night watchman for the Edinburgh, Scotland City Police until he died in 1858. His death was very difficult for Bobby.

John's remains were carried to Greyfriars Kirkyard, the Edinburgh graveyard where he was buried. Bobby followed the procession and sat on the gravesite for the next 14 years.

Bobby was a Skye Terrier and became very famous, to the extent the city erected a memorial statue and fountain on his behalf. Bobby passed away on January 14, 1872 but lives on in infamy due to his devotion and faithfulness to his master.

In 2005 in Argentina, Miguel brought home a German Shepherd named Capitan. A year later, Miguel passed away in a hospital and his remains were taken to a funeral home miles away from his home town. From there he was taken to a cemetery.

The next Sunday, Miguel's family went to the cemetery to visit the gravesite. They were shocked to see Capitan at Miguel's grave. The cemetery director told the family that he had seen the dog make two laps around the cemetery until he located and sat by Miguel's grave. Capitan stays by his master's side every day and has done so for years. It is yet another testimony of devotion and faithfulness.

The stories remind me again and again of God's faithfulness to His creation.

- Hebrews 13:5 - *He hath said, I will never leave thee, nor forsake thee.*
- Matthew 28:20 - *I am with you always, even unto the end of the world. Amen.*
- Romans 8:38-39 - *For I am persuaded, that neither death, nor life, nor angels, nor principalities, nor powers, nor things present, nor things to come, nor height, nor depth, nor any other creature, shall be able to separate us from the love of God, which is in Christ Jesus our Lord.*

Tomorrow

Truth for Today – Proverbs 3

It was a clear and moonless night. Living in the country provides darker night-time skies than living in the city or suburbs. I enjoy laying in the grass and gazing into the heavens.

My imagination seems to roll during those times, as I look at the twinkling and shooting stars, constellations and the endless depths of the infinite darkness. I try to envision where Heaven and my Father might be. I think about the second coming of Jesus. Heaven-gazing stirs the imagination. As I look, the thought crosses my mind, "It's like looking into tomorrow."

Looking into tomorrow. Now, that's an interesting thought. God did give various men the opportunity of getting a glimpse into tomorrow and beyond. The book of Revelation is all about God providing a peek into the future for John.

The minor and major prophets were given glimpses into the tomorrows of the children of Israel. We have visions, premonitions and insights into the future at times, but only God is purely and wholly perfect in knowing tomorrow.

Most people wish they could have the gift of prophecy and know more about tomorrow. It would have a huge impact on the stock market, choices and decisions we make, where we go to college, where we work, what we do, who we do it with and when.

But, sadly we must live in today, a world of chaos. It is full of chance, coincidence and disorder. Or is it? Is there predictability? Is there an order in the universe and in our lives?

How many times have you had a troubling situation arise for which you needed an answer? It was then you were amazed that just yesterday God had given you a Bible chapter during your devotions, which was just what you needed today. God's people everywhere are full of illustrations of God's providence, insights and how He pours Himself into the details of our lives.

Proverbs 3:5-6 – *Trust in the Lord with all thine heart; and lean not unto thine own understanding; in all thy ways acknowledge Him and He shall direct thy paths.*

Trading Options

Truth for Today – Matthew 21

When I think about how our Jesus left the golden streets and the beauty and majesty of Heaven for the dirt of our Earth, I am humbled. Then I think of all the trades He made for sinful and fallen man.

He gave up His heavenly throne for a cross; His golden crown for a crown of thorns; huge multitudes of adoring angels for crowds clamoring for His crucifixion; His Deity for flesh; His relationship with His Father for men and women who would desert and abandon Him; and His blood for our sins.

As we approach the time of year when Jesus was abandoned, accused, tortured, rejected, crucified and resurrected, I think of His triumphal entry into Jerusalem, which only began the ending of His short life of ministry.

Revelation 19:11 tells us of something else He gave up in Heaven... *And I saw heaven opened, and behold a white horse; and He that sat upon him was called Faithful and True.*

Jesus traded His white horse for a donkey as He rode into Jerusalem. Matthew 21:5 - *Behold, thy King cometh unto thee, meek, and sitting upon an ass.* The list of trades goes on and on as the Bible describes the price Jesus was willing to pay for us.

Jesus was quick to let go and quick to grab hold. I am humbled today as I think of His willingness to be a servant, slave and the lowest of the low. How quickly do I get upset when the stock market goes down; or I get cut off in traffic; or I get a cold; or my espresso was lukewarm; or...? Am I quick to let go of earthly things, and quick to grab hold of Heavenly things?

- Hebrews 13:5 - *Be content with such things as ye have: for he hath said, I will never leave thee, nor forsake thee.*
- Luke 9:58 - *And Jesus said unto him, Foxes have holes, and birds of the air have nests; but the Son of man hath not where to lay his head.*

Trouble on the Ice

Truth for Today – Matthew 18:11-14

During winter, the grazing for deer becomes more difficult. Living near the shores of the 2,600 acre Albert Lea Lake in Minnesota, the deer population was hungry. Finally one brave doe stepped foot on the ice. Maybe she was wondering if there was greener grass on the other side.

Then another tentative step and another. Finally a second young doe followed. Their excitement and strength took them far from the shore. Then it happened. One of the does fell and then the second doe fell. Neither could gather the strength nor hoof-hold to rise. They floundered on the ice, gradually losing their strength.

Someone noticed and put out a call for help. Two young men with a hovercraft went to check it out. The deer tried to get up and escape, but finally they relaxed, quietly exhausted from their efforts.

The men attached ropes and slowly pulled them to shore. Removing the tow ropes, the deer escaped into the trees surrounding the lake.

I wonder what it was like when the one sheep left the flock of 100? No doubt he was enjoying freedom and independence in his quest for greener pastures.

Matthew 18:11-14 describes it well - *For the Son of man is come to save that which was lost. How think ye? If a man have an hundred sheep, and one of them be gone astray, doth he not leave the ninety and nine, and goeth into the mountains, and seeketh that which is gone astray? And if so be that he find it, verily I say unto you, he rejoiceth more of that sheep, than of the ninety and nine which went not astray. Even so it is not the will of your Father which is in heaven, that one of these little ones should perish.*

The illustrations of the two deer as well as the lost sheep speak of some basic principles:

- Animal and human nature desire independence and something different than the norm.
- Inherently we get ourselves into trouble.
- Ultimately we need a savior.

Thank you Jesus...

True Riches

Truth for Today – 1 Kings 10

Friends of ours were expecting another child. We all know the anticipation that comes when we know there will be an addition to a family. The vast majority of the 384,000 births happening every day around the world are predictably normal. However, some of the births are abnormal in some way. We hear about complicated deliveries, premature births or unwanted children.

Of those births, there are a few where the child has special needs or challenges. Such was the case for our friends, when Hannah was born with Down's syndrome.

A year or so after Hannah had been born, I asked Hannah's father how it was going. He said – *"We don't count ourselves worthy of receiving our daughter Hannah."* I was incredibly touched by his response.

In our human nature we have perceptions as to what true riches or treasures might be. Is it dollars in the bank, stock portfolios, multiple cars or homes, exotic vacations, gold, diamonds and jewels? How do we define true riches? The scripture provides clues...

- Luke 12:33,34 – *Sell that ye have, and give alms; provide yourselves bags which wax not old, a treasure in the heavens that faileth not, where no thief approacheth, neither moth corrupteth. For where your treasure is, there will your heart be also.*
- Luke 15:7 – *I say unto you, that likewise joy shall be in heaven over one sinner that repenteth, more than over ninety and nine just persons, which need no repentance.*
- Luke 15:8-10 – *Either what woman having ten pieces of silver, if she lose one piece, doth not light a candle, and sweep the house, and seek diligently till she find it? And when she hath found it, she calleth her friends and her neighbours together, saying, Rejoice with me; for I have found the piece which I had lost. Likewise, I say unto you, there is joy in the presence of the angels of God over one sinner that repenteth.*

What are our treasures? I'm guessing they are not gold or silver.

Trust and a '53 Ford

Truth for Today – Matthew 18:21-35

Dad needed a second car and bought a used 1953 Ford at auction with only 9000 miles on it. He was elated at the bargain he got for the six year old sedan and ran the car for several years.

Growing up on a farm in the 50's and 60's meant that I was driving tractors from the time I was eight. It also meant driving trucks by the age of twelve and learning how to drive a car at fourteen.

When I was fifteen, some older friends of mine called and wanted to know if I wanted to play basketball at a barn a quarter mile away. Though I did not have my driver's license as yet, I asked Dad if I could take his Ford. He said, "You don't have your license." I kept up the pressure and he gave in with the caution, "Make sure you are careful with my car."

I was careful and arrived arrogantly at the barn. The basketball goal was inside the barn, but a combine was parked on the playing floor. After putting the combine in neutral, it was easy for eight boys to push the combine out of the barn.

I would like to forget the rest of that day. Finished with basketball, we needed to get the combine back in the barn. Eight boys couldn't push it up the incline. One of the boys had the idea that we could push it in with a car. My dad's '53 Ford was the chosen vehicle.

Someone found a 4" x 4" wooden post and placed it on the Ford's front bumper and the rear axle of the combine. I got in the driver's seat, started the car, put it in low gear and started pushing. The combine began to move! Suddenly there was a horrible racket as the post slipped and pushed its way into the radiator of my dad's car. That pushed the radiator into the fan blade of the motor, which promptly sheared the motor mount bolts from the frame of the car.

After a quarter mile walk home I learned what it was to lose trust with my dad and also learned the difficulty of winning it back.

Galatians 6:7 - *Be not deceived; God is not mocked:*
for whatsoever a man soweth, that shall he also reap.

Trust Me!

Truth for Today – Psalm 23

Our secretary came into my office holding her hand. She had just slammed her car door on one of her fingers. She was in pain. The fingernail was already black and blue and her finger was throbbing.

I told her that if we could drill a tiny hole in her fingernail it would relieve the blood and pressure under the nail. She was ready for anything, so, I went to the tool crib and got a tiny 3/64" diameter drill bit. She laid her finger on the desk top and I slowly rotated the bit between my thumb and index finger applying a small amount of pressure downward. The blood came out and she was almost immediately relieved. I was her new hero.

Six months later, our accountant came into the office holding his hand, in obvious pain. It was the same situation. I told him what I had done for the secretary and he said, "No way!" I said it worked really well with her, and then I said, "Just trust me."

He agreed, so I went to the tool crib and repeated the scenario. I began the gentle drilling process and after 15 seconds he screamed and jerked his hand out. The drill was stuck in his finger!

A little investigation revealed that the drill I was using was dull which pushed his finger gently down under the pressure. When the drill finally broke through the fingernail, it released the pressure, his finger came up and the drill went in. I was not his hero! The words of "Just trust me" still haunt me.

Trust. How is it earned? How is it kept? Is it possible to regain trust once lost? I'm sure my accountant would never let me operate on him again and rightfully so. My fingernail drilling confidence is gone and I don't trust myself.

Is God trustworthy? The Bible clearly tells us that He is perfectly trustworthy. Even if we blame Him for the consequences of our poor choices and lose trust in Him, He is still perfect.

- Psalm 9:10 - *And they that know thy name will put their trust in thee: for thou, LORD, hast not forsaken them that seek thee.*
- Psalm 56:3 - *What time I am afraid, I will trust in thee.*

Trusting Dad

As I was walking through a Haitian village I noticed a dad shaving his son's head. The boy was wedged between his dad's knees and his

hand was locking the boys head in place. The sharp thin razor blade was accurately moving, sliding and doing its work. The little boy was smiling.

I loved the visual image of a dad taking care of his son. The entire process spoke to me of "trust". The care, precision, the smile, and trust caused me to reflect on my personal relationship with God.

Do I squirm when God locks me into a position with no wriggle room? I like the independence of doing things myself and having the freedom of choice. Though God gives us free choice, there have been times when I know He has protected me from myself.

Do I trust God enough to let Him mold and shape me? Am I willing to let Him round off my rough edges? Am I willing to let Him take the time to do it well? Do I resist when He desires to change me?

I've found that the Bible leaves me little wriggle room for being independent. I've learned that God has my best interests at heart. I've learned that if I let Him take His time with me, it will be worth it. Lord, here I am.

- Isaiah 55:8 - *For my thoughts are not your thoughts, neither are your ways my ways, saith the Lord.*
- Isaiah 29:16 - *Surely your turning of things upside down shall be esteemed as the potter's clay: for shall the work say of him that made it, He made me not? Or shall the thing framed say of him that framed it, He had no understanding?*

Try to Pry

Truth for Today – Romans 8

I grew up with a rat terrier dog named Tippy. Beyond her first love of dealing with rats, Tippy loved to chase balls. When she retrieved the ball, the game began of me trying to pry the ball out of her mouth. It was nearly impossible. Her jaws were locked. She was able to exert approximately 200 lbs. per square inch of pressure on the ball.

The rat terrier's cousin, the pit-bull terrier, can apply 235 psi. A mountain lion comes in at 350 psi; a wolf at 406 psi; a great white shark exerts 670 psi which is similar to an African male lion at 691; a Kodiak bear applies 930 psi; a Bengal Tiger at 1050 psi. The list of gorillas, alligators, hyenas and hippos produce even more than the tigers. However, at the top of the biting list is a saltwater crocodile at 7,700 psi.

In thinking about the saltwater crocodile and its incredibly strong bite, is there any way to escape its grasp? Poking an alligator or crocodile in the eye with your thumb can make it open its jaws. So, even with its incredible bite, it is still possible to get free.

God's animal kingdom always inspires me in a spiritual way. When I learned of what His animals are capable of in the biting department, I had to think of Romans 8. There we are taught that it is impossible to be freed from the grip of His love. How great is that?

Romans 8:35-39 - *Who shall separate us from the love of Christ? Shall tribulation, or distress, or persecution, or famine, or nakedness, or peril, or sword? As it is written, for thy sake we are killed all the day long; we are accounted as sheep for the slaughter. Nay, in all these things we are more than conquerors through him that loved us. For I am persuaded, that neither death, nor life, nor angels, nor principalities, nor powers, nor things present, nor things to come, nor height, nor depth, nor any other creature, shall be able to separate us from the love of God, which is in Christ Jesus our Lord.*

Romans 5:8 - *But God commendeth his love toward us,
in that, while we were yet sinners, Christ died for us.*

Tug of War

Truth for Today – Luke 10:29-37

When my cousins would get together we would play many outdoor games. "Tug of War" was a special game which everyone could play. A long line of cousins on one end of a rope would pull against an opposing line on the other end.

No one would budge for a time, and then as a few would get tired, one group would gradually gain ground. The back and forth would continue until one group would win.

The Bible talks about a spiritual Tug of War that is going on every day in every part of the world. Galatians 5:17 - *For the flesh lusteth against the Spirit, and the Spirit against the flesh: and these are contrary the one to the other.*

Sadly the reality of the tugs of war around the world pits the strong against the weak. That is a principle that is common in nearly every country. *The strong and powerful commonly exploit the weaknesses of the weak and vulnerable.*

In Burundi, Chad, Congo, Rwanda, Sierra Leone, Somalia and Sudan, boys as young as ten years old have been exploited and forced to fight as child-soldiers.

There are an estimated 10 million children exploited, trafficked and forced into prostitution around the world.

Though women and girls comprise one-half of the world population, millions are considered property and chattel.

Millions of poverty-ridden men, women and children around the world are kept under the power and rule of the rich.

An entirely different principle is the opposing force in the spiritual tug of war. *Agape love walks alongside the vulnerable and willingly absorbs their weakness.* There's no exploitation with agape love!

The story of the Good Samaritan in today's reading gives us a glimpse into God's heart for the last, least, lost and lonely.

Mark 12:30 - *Thou shalt love the Lord thy God with all thy heart, and with all thy soul, and with all thy mind, and with all thy strength.*

Twice Adopted

***Truth for Today* –** Esther 2

The country of Colombia in South America has a reputation for the size, beauty and clarity of their magnificent emeralds. Colombia accounts for 80% of the world's production.

Colombia has another reputation among those watching human rights issues. "Los Desechables" (the disposables).

Massive amounts of disposable Colombian children live on the streets or under them in the sewers. They live their short and desperate lives trying to survive by sniffing glue or getting high on crack cocaine. They are trying to escape the trafficking and exploitation that is their entrance into the local or international brothels, or the syndicates and cartels dealing with weapon smuggling, counterfeiting and narcotics.

One of their greatest fears are the "death squads"; groups of armed men with a mission to rid the cities of "Los Desechables". Unknown, vast numbers of children have been taken from the streets, routinely murdered and dumped in unmarked landfills and other nameless holes in the ground. They are eradicated like cockroaches.

It was into this society and environment that an unwanted little girl was born. Though placed in an orphanage, the hope of long-term care inevitably assured her of a future on the streets or under it.

But, she was found by an American adoptive family who whisked her out of her life and into another. In her new life, she heard about Jesus and gave her life and heart to Him. As she shared her testimony of faith and salvation, she said something that touched everyone. *"I was adopted twice. The first was when my adoptive family loved me and added me to their family. The second was when my Jesus loved me and added me to God's family."*

The environment and society that all of us are born into is a fallen world. By default we are seemingly all destined to being destroyed. Only intervention by God provides a life of peace and eternal joy.

Thank you Lord for giving us an opportunity to be saved from our future and giving us the chance to be a part of your family.

Two Becoming One

Truth for Today – Genesis 2:21-25

Anyone married for longer than a month is aware that maintaining a healthy marriage can be challenging. Two people with different personalities, talents, experiences, backgrounds, likes and dislikes are bound to have difficulties. One study identified the nine most common reasons for marital strain.

1. How to spend free time
2. Money issues
3. Household chores
4. Politics
5. Intimacy
6. Kids and pets
7. Religion
8. Jealousy
9. Stress

The antidotes for combatting marital stress are Biblical and commonly known, but refresher courses are helpful.

- 1 Corinthians 13
- Colossians 3:12-19
- Ephesians 5:21-33
- Genesis 2:24
- 2 Corinthians 6:14
- 1 Peter 4:8
- Ecclesiastes 4:12
- Ephesian 4:2-3
- Mark 10:9
- Luke 6:37
- Ephesians 4:26
- Proverbs 3:27

A man doesn't own his marriage; he is only the steward of his wife's love. - Edwin Louis Cole

Unexpected Surprises

***Truth for Today* -** Genesis 1:1-25

It was 30 minutes to sunset in San Diego, California. Jeni and I really wanted to see the sun set over the Pacific. Leaving our hotel, we merged into five lanes of traffic and headed west on the interstate. Traffic, for this Midwestern driver, was horrible. After 15 minutes of driving, I decided to give up on the sunset and head back to the hotel.

Discouraged, and now heading east, I looked in the rear view mirror and got a glimpse of gorgeous red and orange reflections immersed in a darkening blue sky. Needless to say, I got off at the next exit and headed back west with just a few minutes remaining for what I knew would be a beautiful sunset.

Pulling off at the Sunset Cliffs exit, I headed west and parked. I jumped over the beach railing to the top of a rock and asked Jeni to toss me the disposable camera from the car. As I looked down I saw trash on the boulder strewn beach and was disappointed to have my dream of a fabulous beach and sunset photo diminishing. I snapped a quick snapshot of the sunset, frustrated at my unrealized expectation.

Oh well... such is life. We arrived back home in Indiana and sent the camera in for film developing. When the photo of the sunset was in front of me I was flabbergasted. No trash was visible, there was a great sunset, and suspended over the sun was a spread-winged seagull. I thanked God for surprising me with such a great and undeserved gift.

Isn't that just like our Father who is always wanting to surprise us in ways we didn't imagine? Thank you Lord for your imagination! God is always ready to turn disappointments into surprises. Wait for Him. Ephesians 3:20 says it well - *Now unto him that is able to do exceeding abundantly above all that we ask or think...*

Lord, help me to wait for your surprises. Teach me patience. Fill me with expectations that can only be fulfilled by you. Help me to never settle for second best as I wait for your abundance and excellence. Wait for it...

United or Unity?

At first glance the two words seem identical, "united and unity". We hear the word "united" often at wedding ceremonies, as the concept of two becoming one is taught. We look at a map of our country and read the words, "United States of America".

Though two people can become married and be united, statistics indicate that 50% of marriages end in divorce. That is not unity.

There were thirty-four states making up the United States of America in 1861. They were united, but they were not in unity as the Civil War would prove.

Two cats tied together by their tails are united, but quickly we would find out they are not in unity.

Two ice cubes sitting side by side in a bowl are united, but they are not one. When they melt, they are in unity.

Sometimes it seems that God's family is united, but not in unity. Diversity in doctrine, interpretation of scripture, culture, language, worship, traditions and opinions divide God's people. As in a marriage, when there is unity, there is peace.

Can we imagine what would happen if there were true unity in God's family? It will happen in Heaven. We can pray that we do not spend too much time trying to be united when God really wants unity.

- 1 Corinthians 1:10 - *Now I beseech you, brethren, by the name of our Lord Jesus Christ, that ye all speak the same thing, and that there be no divisions among you; but that ye be perfectly joined together in the same mind and in the same judgment.*
- Psalm 133:1 - *Behold, how good and how pleasant it is for brethren to dwell together in unity!*
- Ephesians 4:3 - *Endeavouring to keep the unity of the Spirit in the bond of peace.*
- Ephesians 4:13 - *Till we all come in the unity of the faith, and of the knowledge of the Son of God, unto a perfect man, unto the measure of the stature of the fulness of Christ.*

Unwelcome Missionary

Truth for Today – 1 Timothy 2:3,4

We are all touched by the statistics related to the number of people around the world who are un-saved, un-churched and without Bibles. We pray for them and we help where we can, but what is our level of faith and commitment in getting the Gospel and Bibles to the world?

Do we believe that getting a Bible into the hands of someone who doesn't know about Jesus is eternally life-changing? Do we believe that missionaries are effective in getting the Gospel to places where it has not been? If so, again, what is our level of faith and commitment in helping to make it happen?

Recently I had the opportunity to spend time with a husband and wife missionary who are in their 40th year of missions and ministry in India. One of his quotes hit me like a sledgehammer... *"Churches and pastors in the U.S. aren't always excited to see us in their church because we signify $ going out rather than $ coming in."*

His statement challenged me as I thought of my impure priorities and motives at various times in my life. The Bible clearly helps us understand God's heart for the unsaved.

- 1 Timothy 2:4 – *(God) who will have all men to be saved, and to come unto the knowledge of the truth.*
- John 3:16 - *For God so loved the world, that he gave his only begotten Son, that whosoever believeth in him should not perish, but have everlasting life.*
- Ezekiel 33:11 - *As I live, saith the Lord God, I have no pleasure in the death of the wicked.*
- 2 Corinthians 5:21 - *For he hath made him [to be] sin for us, who knew no sin; that we might be made the righteousness of God in him.*
- 1 Timothy 6:10 - *For the love of money is the root of all evil: which while some coveted after, they have erred from the faith, and pierced themselves through with many sorrows.*

Lord, deliver me from myself and the impure
motives and priorities I sometimes have.

Use of a Ruse

Truth for Today – Judges 7

As military leader and judge of Israel, Gideon had a flaw. His faith and courage was weak. But would we have been different? In the valley of Moreh, he looked out over his enemy. They were *"like grasshoppers for multitude; and their camels were without number, as the sand by the sea side for multitude."* However, Gideon had his warriors - 32,000 of them, and they gave him courage.

But, God asked Gideon to send home 22,000 men, and then another 9,700, leaving him with 300 to fight the battle. We know the results. Gideon's men surrounded the Midianite camp, blew their trumpets and broke their clay pots revealing the light inside. The enemy was over-run during the ensuing confusion.

Fighting wars and battles is about strategy. Our military leaders learn tactics, maneuvers, past successes and failures to prepare for future battles. One of the greatest tactics is learning "deception."

- Feigned Retreat – Pretending your troops are retreating while luring the following enemy into an ambush.
- Fictional Troops – Exaggerating your troop size so the enemy loses courage.
- Smoke Screen – Using fog or smoke to hide troops for an ambush.
- Trojan Horse – Using a decoy or ploy to get access to your enemies camp.
- Strategic Envelopment – Distracting the enemy with a small group of forces so the larger force can surround them.

As believers, we've come to learn the tactics of satan and his demons. They've had thousands of years of learning strategy and maneuvers in fighting billions of battles with God's people.

- 2 Corinthians 11:14 - *Satan himself is transformed into an angel of light.*
- Ephesians 6:11 - *Put on the whole armor of God, that ye may be able to stand against the wiles of the devil.*

The greatest tactic in our battles against
satan is getting to our knees quickly.

Waiting Treasures

Truth for Today – Matthew 6:19-21

Hundreds of years ago, the royal family of the southernmost state of India had wealth. They placed their treasures in a vault for safekeeping under a Hindu temple in Thiruvananthapuram. Over the years many worshippers and travelers added to the wealth.

In 2011, authorities opened the closed underground vault that had been sealed 150 years ago. What they found was staggering. The gold, jewels, diamonds and artifacts are conservatively valued at over $22 billion. Some of the inventory is identified as:

- Gold coins dating back thousands of years
- Nine-foot long gold necklaces weighing almost 6 pounds
- One ton of gold
- Sacks full of diamonds
- Thousands of antique jewelry pieces studded with diamonds and emeralds
- Precious stones and jewels wrapped in silk bundles

Currently there is a controversy as to who the treasure belongs to. The Hindu temple? The secular government? The descendants of the royal family? The ruling gods of the temple?

The treasure causes me to reflect on how many treasures remain undiscovered by me in my life. Busyness and wrong priorities rob me of beauties yet discovered, of wisdom yet untapped, of deep and unfound truth in the Word of God, and of depths of relationships left dormant.

I am also challenged in thinking how the assets buried beneath the temple were not used for the last, least, lost and lonely of India. But, as I judge that, I think of the assets I have and whether greater good could come from what I own.

At the end of the day, I think the greatest treasure of all time is nearly untapped. God's Word and Wisdom in the Bible and the answers to unanswered universal questions lay within. Healing for the multitude of problems, discouragements and difficulties of life are waiting to be found. It is waiting as undiscovered treasure.

Walk on Water

I was 10 years old when we took our first trip to Florida. My mom and dad bought me a set of goggles, snorkel and fins. As an experiment I tried to use the fins to walk on the swimming pool water. The fins were large, webbed and wide. Trying multiple times by stepping, jumping or running in, I had the same result. I immediately sunk to the bottom of the pool. I gave up.

The experience causes me to reflect about Jesus being able to walk on water. The story had always intrigued me, but now it seems like a greater miracle than ever. Does that mean it is impossible to walk on water?

The Common Basilisk Lizard lives in Central and South American rain forests. They can weigh up to 1 pound and reach a length of 30". Another name for the lizard is *Legarto de Jesus Cristo* or *Jesus Christ Lizard*. The lizard can run on water at speeds of 7 mph for a distance up to 60'.

God had a great imagination during those days of creation. He created a lizard that would be a reminder about Jesus to all who would see it. Walking on water is not impossible. The Basilisk lizard proves the point. What about man? Has any man other than Jesus Christ been able to accomplish such a miracle?

Matthew 14:28-30 - *And Peter answered him and said, Lord, if it be thou, bid me come unto thee on the water. And he said, Come. And when Peter was come down out of the ship, he walked on the water, to go to Jesus. But when he saw the wind boisterous, he was afraid; and beginning to sink, he cried, saying, Lord, save me.*

There have been only two men since creation who have walked on water, Jesus Christ and Peter. There are three points we can learn from Peter's experience:

- Faith is powerful. We can move mountains or walk on water.
- Phil. 4:13 - *I can do all things through Christ which strengtheneth me.*
- Peter teaches us of our weak human nature, flesh and doubt.

Warfare

Truth for Today – 1 Peter 5

We have seen the images of warfare and how it evolves over the course of time. During the Middles Ages, the Revolutionary War as well as the U.S. Civil War, men lined up in rows and columns and moved toward one another to do battle. Men were mowed down by cannonballs and musket-balls with little effort. In battles against Native American Indians, the U.S. Cavalry and Infantry found themselves in a different war. The Indians understood the benefits of a hit and run strategy, as well as reconnaissance and guerilla tactics.

WWI took trench warfare to new levels, while also including armored tanks and mustard gas as resources. WWII became a two pronged war in Europe and the Pacific with broadening scope: On the ground; in the air; and on the seas. Korea was a new venue with the cold being an enemy that decimated the U.S. Army. Then of course the guerilla warfare of Viet Nam became yet another evolution. The desert wars in the Middle East became yet another type of warfare to learn.

Not only does our military need to acclimate to the climates of the countries they fight in, they must also know the techniques of their enemy. In the process, new weaponry is developed to fit the time and place where the battles would be fought.

Wilhelm Mauser helped develop and mass produce pistols and rifles in the early 1870's to fill the military needs of Germany. His Mauser factories produced huge amounts of weapons for several countries. In the 1940's a new design of Mauser emerged for a specific use. A Mauser rifle was retro-fitted with a curved barrel. The curved barrel could shoot around corners utilizing a periscope.

Any Christian believer knows well that satan understands tactical warfare and that his techniques and weapons change with time. While the old styles of his tactics and weaponry may still work, he is able to adapt to any culture in any time. God encourages us to keep on our toes!

1 Peter 5:8 - *Be sober, be vigilant; because your adversary the devil, as a roaring lion, walketh about, seeking whom he may devour.*

Watch and Learn

Truth for Today – Romans 8:28

We've heard the old proverb - *"When life gives you lemons, make lemonade."* I suppose there would be many more axioms we could quote, such as, *"God turns the tragedy of crucifixion into a glorious resurrection."* Or possibly, *"Without rain, there's no rainbow."* The list goes on.

How do we process the daily ups and downs of life? Are we filled with optimism or pessimism? Are we known as positive or negative thinkers?

I was intrigued by a photo I've seen recently of a man standing in front of his home which was demolished by a tornado. The photo showed him smiling next to a sign that said - *"Home for Sale - Price Reduced - Some Assembly Required."* I love his attitude of rising above his situation. It made me smile.

Dog owners who have had dogs which required surgery or had other issues know about dog-cones. It's a plastic cone that fits around the dog's neck and then extends out to a larger diameter beyond the dog. It limits the dogs view as well as prevents the dog from reaching their wounds.

Sounds like a "bad" thing, right? Limiting a dogs rights? However, recently I watched a video of a dog with a cone. Several other dogs were aggressively eating dog food on a sidewalk and desperately trying to get their share. The dog with a cone approached, lowered his head and covered all the dog food with the cone which permitted him to eat all the food undisturbed. I loved it. He was definitely learning how to make the most of a bad situation.

> *Lord, help me to believe that you are able*
> *to bring good from bad situations.*

Watch Where you Step

Truth for Today – Genesis 3

I personally am very afraid of dogs, both large and small, tail-waggers or not. A fear that had its root in being bitten when young, by a German Shepherd named Rip.

I can understand fears that are grounded in a traumatic experience. An experience such as a four year old child falling in the deep end of a pool and having a fear of water makes sense. Or a toddler getting pecked by a parakeet and being afraid of birds is understandable. But what is it about snakes?

A third of humans suffer from *ophidiophobia*, which is to be abnormally afraid of snakes. Very few people have actually had traumatic confrontations with them. There simply seems to be a natural fear or even aversion to the slithering reptiles.

The Black Mamba snake in sub-Saharan Africa is highly venomous. The toxicity of the venom is very rapid acting and can kill an adult human in as little as 20 minutes. They are the fastest snakes in the world, traveling at speeds up to 14 mph. They are extremely aggressive and will charge someone within 75' of them. Once attacking the victim, they will strike with venom up to a dozen times.

Whether venomous or constrictors, many people fear snakes. Could it be there is a natural animosity built into us since Adam and Eve's encounter in the Garden of Eden?

Genesis 3:13-15 - *And the Lord God said unto the woman, What is this that thou hast done? And the woman said, the serpent beguiled me, and I did eat. And the Lord God said unto the serpent, Because thou hast done this, thou art cursed above all cattle, and above every beast of the field; upon thy belly shalt thou go, and dust shalt thou eat all the days of thy life: And I will put enmity between thee and the woman, and between thy seed and her seed; it shall bruise thy head, and thou shalt bruise his heel.*

The original Greek for *"enmity"* in verse 15 is *"enemy, hostility and hatred"*. I am thinking the fear and repulsion we feel about snakes has a Biblical and spiritual root. I suspect that God ordained it that there would be a mutual disconnect between man and the serpent.

Watching but not Listening

Truth for Today – Proverbs 11:14

Jeni and I were excited for the opportunity to visit the island of Kauai. We both love the natural beauty you can find in the hard-to-get-to areas. We had heard about Polihale Beach on the western side of the island.

We were intrigued by the potential of seeing the Na Pali cliffs jutting into the Pacific, the pounding surf and seven miles of beach. We had read that the road to the beach was difficult. The area is secluded and quite a distance from civilization. We also read that the rental car company's insurance policy is void if you go to Polihale Beach. You're on your own which is just what I wanted.

Finally getting to the last two mile stretch before the beach, I noticed the first small wisps of sand drifting across the road. Soon, the wisps became larger. After I went through a three inch deep by five foot wide "drift", Jeni said, "Maybe you should turn around. We don't want to get stuck out here!" Of course my response was, "Don't worry, I'm used to driving through Indiana snow drifts. This is easy."

Shortly thereafter, a larger drift appeared across the entire road. I sped up to gain momentum. Soon I was spinning my wheels and settled solidly on top of lots of sand. I looked at Jeni and she smiled, but to her credit, said nothing. I learned that day the difference between a sand drift and a snow drift.

Getting out of the car, I started scooping sand away from my wheels. The wheels were off the road surface and the bottom of the car was resting on the sand. It was a long wait until others wanting to get to the beach arrived. I was blocking their path so they were all anxious to help me get out of my predicament. They weren't overly interested in my thoughts about snow drifts in Indiana.

Why is it difficult to sometimes hear and receive counsel? Is it because we believe we are already wise, experienced and know what's best? Is it pride? Sometimes a real life experience of "I told you so", or, "You should have listened to me" can help.

Proverbs 11:14 - *Where no counsel is, the people fall:*
but in the multitude of counsellors there is safety.

Weakling

Truth for Today – John 15

Walking the 40 acres of the LSM Agriculture Park in Haiti, I was observing the research and development of a wide variety of products. Beef, goats, citrus, tilapia, corn and poultry. Close to the forage

operations, I noticed a white plastic pipe sticking 8' out of the ground. As I got closer to the boundary marker used to identify a future lane, I noticed a weed growing out of the top of the pipe.

The pipe was hollow and I realized how vulnerable this weed was as it searched and reached for the light. It was standing 8' tall and stabilized by something other than itself.

Without the soil below, the pipe surrounding it, rainwater channeled down the pipe, or the sun overhead, this weed would wither and die. It was supported by something other than itself.

I realized that I am so like that weed. Without the breath of life,

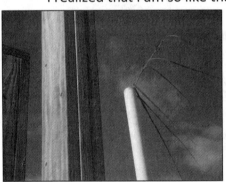

His Word, His Son, His grace and mercy, I would cease to exist. I cannot live without His gifts and blessings. My life becomes easier when I realize that God cares more for me than the flowers and birds. I know that He has things in place to protect and sustain me.

John 15:4,5 - *Abide in me, and I in you. As the branch cannot bear fruit of itself, except it abide in the vine; no more can ye, except ye abide in me. I am the vine, ye are the branches: He that abideth in me, and I in him, the same bringeth forth much fruit: for without me ye can do nothing.*

Weights

Truth for Today – Hebrews 12

As a Merino sheep living in New Zealand, life couldn't get much better. Plenty to eat, other sheep to spend time with, periodic wool cuts and safety. Only one thing was missing, freedom.

One particular sheep decided to try independent living. Escape! In fact, he became so adept at avoiding capture by living in caves, that he was independent for six years. One of the unique things of a Merino sheep is that they do not shed their wool. So, over the course of his six years of freedom, his wool coat became larger, heavier and hotter. He could barely see through the wool which created the speculation as to why he was finally captured.

His wool was sheared and amazingly found to weigh 60 pounds, enough to make 20 large men's suits.

As I thought about this sheep, I thought of a Bible verse in Hebrews 12:1 - *Wherefore seeing we also are compassed about with so great a cloud of witnesses, let us lay aside every weight, and the sin which doth so easily beset us, and let us run with patience the race that is set before us. Looking unto Jesus the author and finisher of our faith.*

As human beings, our default is to be independent, self-centered, selfish and self-indulging. Generally we don't think about the consequences of having an independent nature. Loneliness, the difficulty of handling life's problems by ourselves, and having no one to help us cope are the costs associated with being a loner. As people we can use humor, anger, defensiveness and arrogance to keep others out of our space. It works. But, what of the consequences?

Consequences for the sheep was his difficulty in eating, seeing, getting around on his weak legs, and staying cool. Consequences for us are the accumulated sins, weight of issues and baggage that we may carry, as they accumulate and weigh us down. We are in a race and becoming sleek and lean is the answer. Jesus wants us dependent on Him.

What Are You Saying?

Truth for Today – Malachi 3:6

In today's culture it's very difficult to be politically correct so that we don't offend other cultures, races or ways of life. Words and phrases mean something different today than they might have meant 50 years ago, or in some cases just 10 years ago. For instance consider these phrases:

- *"He's cool"* - 50 years ago, it was about temperature. 20 years ago it was about being level-headed. Today, it's about someone being in style.
- *"That's bad"* - 50 years ago, it was about not being good. Today it's about something that is cool, in-style, radical or beautiful.
- *"He's gay"* - 50 years ago, the word meant happy, full of life, exciting and free. Today it denotes an alternative life-style.
- *"That's awful"* - 100 years ago the word meant something that was awesome or full of awe. 50 years ago it meant horrible. Today it is an adjective signifying something "exceedingly great" as in "an awful lot of money."
- *"The cell"* - 100 years ago it meant jail or prison. 50 years ago it defined a tiny element of our physical body. 20 years ago it denoted a terrorist group of militants. Today it's a small electronic tool we put to our ear.
- *"That's fantastic"* - A century ago it meant that something was too ridiculous to be true. Today it indicates something that is awesome or incredible.
- *"He's a holy terror"* – 25 years ago it defined the stage called "the terrible two's." Today it defines terrorism swathed in religion.

But in God's world, the meanings of words do not change. God knows what He means when He defines marriage. He knows what the word "repent" means. The word obedience doesn't change with God, not do His promises change. He is an awesome God.

Malachi 3:6 - *For I am the Lord. I change not...*
Psalm 33:11 - *The counsel of the Lord standeth forever...*

What If?

Truth for Today – Ephesians 1

She was born with spina bifida, a congenital condition in one out of 1000 births. Some of her lower vertebrae were exposed at birth due to the incomplete closing of the embryonic neural tube. Though the hole was closed, the lasting damage to the spinal column left life-long challenges. In her case, it greatly affected her ability to walk.

Her condition alone, in the best of circumstances, is traumatic, but this little baby was then placed in an orphanage in Ukraine. There she was found by a family from the U.S. who loved her and brought her into their family.

Now, anyone who knows her is quickly aware of her independence, determination, guitar playing and gorgeous winning smile. One day when she was barely in school, a conversation occurred between this little girl and her mom.

"I was in an orphanage, right?"
"Yes you were."
"Mom, if you hadn't adopted me, would I still be in the orphanage?"
"Maybe, unless another family would have adopted you."
"Well, if no one did adopt me, then I would have been there forever?"
"Probably so."
"No one would ever have told me about Jesus, right?"
"Probably not."
"Then I would never have been able to go to heaven..."

As I think of this conversation, I think of the *"what if's"* of our lives.

- What if this little girl had not been adopted?
- What if this family had chosen to not adopt?
- What if Jesus would have been disobedient in Gethsemane when He asked His Father to *"Remove this cup from me?"*
- What if Jesus would have walked away from His opportunity to show love to us?

Thank you Lord for adoptive families, who search for the last, least, lost and lonely, and give them forever families, and Jesus.

What is a Family?

Truth for Today – Psalm 82:3

She was young and unable to fend for herself. Her back was shaped almost like an "S" due to a spinal deformity. Her family had deserted her and she was alone. Then, a pod of sperm whales swam close to her and permitted the bottle nose dolphin to join them.

The scientists observing were amazed to see the adoption taking place as the dolphin was permitted to nuzzle and rub itself against the bodies of the massive whales.

Lisa Rogak in her book "One Big Happy Family" shares a variety of stories about animals adopting other species. Fascinating stories such as the boxer dog Tilly which adopted an abandoned baby goat. While protecting it and grooming it, a friendship was born.

Or another story about a baby squirrel that was brought into a mother cats litter of kittens. The squirrel nursed alongside the rest of the litter.

An orphaned baby monkey became attached to a dog, literally. The monkey regularly rides on the dogs back and the dog is very protective of the monkey.

Imagine a large male pig with tusks gently caring for a one week old lamb. These images of adoption and nurturing seem to portray what the Garden of Eden might have been like before sin entered the world. We may have much to learn from the animal species.

Psalm 82:3 speaks of God's plan for the last, lost, least and lonely - the 153,000,000 orphans of the world. *Defend the poor and fatherless: do justice to the afflicted and needy.*

In 2004, U.S. citizens adopted 24,000 orphans from abroad. It has steadily decreased since then, to 6,441 in 2014. God has a plan but sadly, there seem to be efforts underway that thwart those plans.

Lord, remind me to pray and find ways to
care for the orphans of the world.

What is His last name?

Truth for Today – Isaiah 9:6

We all have a "given" name. In some countries it is called a first name and in others a forename. We likewise have a "last" name which is sometimes called a surname or family name. So in the case of Jesus Christ, "Christ" is not His last name, family name or surname. Christ in the original Hebrew was equated with the word "messiah" or "anointed". In Greek, again it is literally "anointed" and "messiah".

In the scripture there are many words to identify who Jesus was and is. Jesus THE Christ, Advocate, Almighty, Alpha and Omega, Amen, Arm of the Lord, Author, Finisher, Beginning, End, Beloved, Blessed and only Potentate, Branch, Bread of Life, Bridegroom, Bright and Morning Star, Captain, Carpenter, Chief Shepherd, Chief Cornerstone, Chiefest among ten thousand, Chosen, Commander, Counselor, Dayspring, Day Star, Deliverer, Door, Elect, Emmanuel, Everlasting Father, Faithful, Faithful Witness, Finisher of the Faith, First and Last, First Begotten, Firstborn, Foundation, Forerunner, Friend of Sinners, Gift of God, Glory of Israel, God with us, Good Master, Governor, Great Shepherd of the Sheep, Heir, High Priest, Holy One of God, Hope, Horn of Salvation, Image of God, Jehovah, Judge, Just One, King, King of Israel, King of the Jews, King of Saints, King of Kings, King of Glory, King of Zion, King over all the Earth, Lamb of God, Lawgiver, Leader, Life, Light, Light of the World, Light of the Gentiles, Living Bread, Living Stone, Lion of the tribe of Judah, Lord, Lord of Lords, Lord of All, Man of Sorrows, Master, Mediator, Messenger, Messiah, Mighty God, Mighty one of Israel, Mighty to Save, Minister of the Sanctuary, Morning Star, Most Holy, Most Mighty, Nazarene, Offspring of Israel, Only Begotten, Overseer, Passover, Plant of Renown, Potentate, Power of God, Physician, Priest, Prince, Prince of Life, Prince of Peace, Prince of the kings of the Earth, Prophet, Propitiation, Rabbi, Rabboni, Ransom, Redeemer, Resurrection and the Life, Redemption, Rock, Rock of Offense, Root of David, Root of Jesse, Rose of Sharon, Ruler, Salvation, Sanctification, Sanctuary, Savior, Scepter, Seed of David, Servant, Shepherd, Son of God, Son of Man, Teacher, True Vine, Truth, Vine, Way, Witness, Wonderful, Word. - Those are a lot of last names! HE IS THE CHRIST!

What is Truth?

Truth for Today – 2 Timothy 3:16-17

- A firefly isn't a fly. It's a beetle.
- A prairie dog isn't a dog. It's a rodent.
- India ink isn't from India. It's from China and Egypt.
- A horned toad isn't a toad. It's a lizard.
- A lead pencil doesn't contain lead. It contains graphite.
- A peanut isn't a nut. It's a legume.
- A koala bear isn't a bear. It's a marsupial.
- A guinea pig isn't from Guinea and it isn't a pig. It's a rodent from South America.
- Shortbread isn't a bread. It's a thick cookie.
- A funny bone isn't a bone. It's the spot where the ulnar nerve touches the humerus.
- A bald eagle isn't bald.
- A cucumber isn't a vegetable. It's a fruit.
- A Mexican jumping bean isn't a bean. It's a seed with a larvae inside.
- Sweetbread isn't a bread. It's the pancreas or thymus gland from a calf or lamb.

Pilate asked the question, *"What is truth?"* We can become confused on a daily basis as to what we hear in the news regarding religion, politics, international issues and almost anything else. Almost nothing is as it appears to be.

We accept well known sayings as being pure scripture when in actuality they are not. Sayings like, *"Spare the rod and spoil the child"; "Money is the root of all evil"'; "God moves in mysterious ways",* are samples.

So, what is truth? Not surprisingly, the absolute purest form of truth is the Bible itself. It is the measuring stick that is perfect and absolute. It has never changed, nor will it. Reading it, memorizing it and absorbing it are essential for believers to know truth. It is also the most vital tool we can put into the hands of unbelievers. I'm challenged today to be more diligent in searching out God's Word and Truth.

Lord, help me to find time to know You better.

What Kind of Creature is That?

Truth for Today – John 3

Nick left his house after dark. He knew the ramifications of being seen, especially if anyone knew where he was going. Not that he intended to do anything immoral or illegal. He simply was looking for answers to a few life issues. He had heard of a man who possibly could help him, so he went there.

Nick looked the man in the eyes and said, *"We know that thou art a teacher come from God: for no man can do these miracles that thou doest, except God be with him."* The teacher named Jesus said, *"I say unto thee, except a man be born again, he cannot see the kingdom of God."*

Nicodemus said, *"How can a man be born when he is old? Can he enter the second time into his mother's womb, and be born."*

Nicodemus obviously had a difficult time comprehending the concept of being "born again". What could it possibly mean? If Nicodemus had been a tiger hunting guide in India, or a tiger skinner, he maybe would have understood.

When a tiger is skinned, more than one hunter was surprised to see that the stripes of a tiger are also in the flesh. If you shaved the hair from a tiger, the skin would have the same markings. In other words, a tiger is a tiger from nose to tail, inside and out. He cannot change.

Jeremiah said it another way, *"Can the... leopard change his spots?"* He went on to say, *"Then may ye also do good, that are accustomed to do evil."*

Being born again is becoming someone brand new. Spotless, clean, new, flawless and unblemished. 2 Corinthians 5:17 says, *"Therefore if any man be in Christ, he is a new creature: old things are passed away; behold, all things are become new."*

The concept of being born again and converted requires a miraculous change. It is something supernatural and something that can only happen by faith and the grace, mercy and love of God.

2 Peter 3:13 – *"...be diligent that ye may be found*
of him in peace, without spot, and blameless."

What You Can't See Can Hurt You

Truth for Today – Romans 4:8

It was 1963 and he was 24 years old. He had a lifetime of living ahead of him, and his 1963 Ford Thunderbird was just the thing to do it with. Then he crashed the T-Bird into a truck.

He had multiple injuries but the most severe was a broken hip. Medical care focused on the hip and the other injuries were then treated and subsequently healed.

The years came and went. 40 years after the accident he set off a metal detector in a court house. An X-ray indicated a metal rod in his left arm. Since it wasn't creating any problems it was decided to let it be. Then, when he was 75 years old, it started to hurt. The surgeon removed a seven inch metal rod. It was the turn signal lever from his 1963 Thunderbird and a souvenir from his accident 51 years earlier.

The story prompts me to think about hidden things. Things such as sin. Things which can do ongoing or future damage. Things which have eternal consequences. Numbers 32:23 says, *"Be sure your sin will find you out."* Hidden things will be exposed.

- Romans 14:12 - *So then every one of us shall give account of himself to God.*
- Luke 12:3 - *Therefore whatsoever ye have spoken in darkness shall be heard in the light; and that which ye have spoken in the ear in closets shall be proclaimed upon the housetops.*
- Proverbs 28:13 - *He that covereth his sins shall not prosper: but whoso confesseth and forsaketh them shall have mercy.*
- Psalm 90:8 - *Thou hast set our iniquities before thee, our secret sins in the light of thy countenance.*
- 2 Kings 17:9 - *And the children of Israel did secretly those things that were not right against the LORD their God.*
- Isaiah 29:15 - *Woe unto them that seek deep to hide their counsel from the LORD, and their works are in the dark, and they say, Who seeth us? and who knoweth us?*

Romans 4:8 - *Blessed is the man to whom the Lord will not impute sin.*

What's That you Say?

***Truth for Today* –** Matthew 7:1-5

The church was quiet and waiting for the pastor to begin his sermon. He began, and then I heard it. Someone whispering. It seemed to be someone behind me two or three benches.

I was a visitor in the church and knew few people. The sermon continued and the whispering continued. Looking at a few people near me, I was amazed that no one else seemed to be troubled.

As the whispering persisted, my frustration and distraction increased. The accusations in my mind began. Why aren't they being reverent? Obviously they are not paying attention.

With a quick glance I found the culprits. A young man was whispering to an older man. Then I recognized them as a father and son I had recently met. They were visiting from another country. The young man knew English and his father did not. The son was translating the sermon to his dad. I was touched and humbled at the same time. As the sermon continued, I was no longer frustrated nor distracted. What did I learn from that Sunday morning?

- I am prone to judging things without knowing all the facts.
- I had permitted my personal judgment to rob me of a blessing.
- Others were not distracted because they knew the situation and more facts than myself.
- While accusing others of not paying attention, I had been the guilty party.

As people we have a tendency to cast judgment without knowing all the facts. Invariably when I think I have my fault under control, another situation arises, helping me understand my weakness.

- John 7:24 - *Judge not according to the appearance, but judge righteous judgment.*
- Luke 6:37 - *Judge not, and ye shall not be judged: condemn not, and ye shall not be condemned: forgive, and ye shall be forgiven.*
- James 4:12 - *There is one lawgiver, who is able to save and to destroy: who art thou that judgest another?*

What's That You're Writing?

Truth for Today – John 8:1-11

He was in the 6th grade and had a crush on the girl in the next row. While the teacher taught, he was busy writing a note. But when he tried to pass the note to his girlfriend, the teacher noticed. She said, "What's that you're passing?"

The teacher grabbed the note and asked the embarrassed boy if she could read it to the class. She smiled as she read it to herself and then said, "No, I better not." The class giggled and laughed. Even 53 years later, I've always wondered what the note said.

The 6th grade note with an unknown message reminds me of John 8:1-11. A woman had been caught in the act of adultery. The leaders of the community were demanding that she should be stoned, but they wondered how Jesus would handle it.

Their harsh, legalistic and judgmental attitudes demanded justice. But Jesus merely wrote things in the dirt while they ranted. Then he asked those who were without sin in their lives to cast the first stone. They left, beginning from the oldest to the youngest.

What did he write? Who knows? The scripture doesn't say. Could it have been that he wrote specific sins in the dirt that individual men recognized as their own? Jesus would have known their hearts and their sins, and of course the men would have recognized their own sins. Could it have been that Jesus was exposing their hidden truths?

Certainly the scripture cautions us in our rush to judgment, or our desire to mete out justice, while adhering to the letter of the law.

- Romans 2:1-3 - *Therefore thou art inexcusable, O man, whosoever thou art that judgest: for wherein thou judgest another, thou condemnest thyself; for thou that judgest doest the same things. But we are sure that the judgment of God is according to truth against them which commit such things. And thinkest thou this, O man, that judgest them which do such things, and doest the same, that thou shalt escape the judgment of God?*

Lord, help me to wait for Your Holy Spirit to take care of judgment and justice; and help me to clear my heart before challenging another.

When Pigs Fly

***Truth for Today** – 1 Timothy 6:7-9

While in Haiti with my U.S. friend Ralph, he told me about hog-wings. I knew about buffalo-wings, but had not heard of hog-wings. He said that some restaurants serve them in the U.S. The meat is from the most tender part of a pig's leg shank. They are slow cooked and basted often in barbecue sauce. The meat literally falls off the bone and is delicious. My mouth was watering, as I put it on my list of "foods to savor" when I got back home.

The next day, Ralph and I were in a Haitian open market in Les Cayes and I took a photo of Haitian hog-wings.

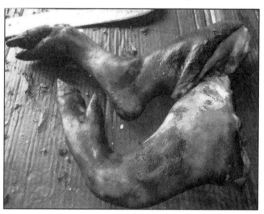

As I looked at them laying on the cardboard, I did a mental "delete" of them from my "food to try someday" checklist.

Haiti is the poorest country in the western hemisphere and most people do not have choices about food. Sadly, refrigeration, sanitation, and appropriate cooking techniques are not readily accessible to a Haitian. If you are even able to find pork, Trichinosis and other parasites are prevalent.

I am humbled as I think about the blessings I have in the U.S.A. and how quickly I judge the blessings of others. This meat, though inhabited by parasites, slow cooking in the hot Haiti sun, and spending its day as a prime landing strip for flies would have been a welcome addition to many Haitian's. Sadly, they can't even afford this phenomenal feast. I repent of what I perceive to be my worldly, self-deserved entitlements.

Where are You Going?

***Truth for Today** – Luke 15

I was five years old. It was a different era in the early 1950's than it is in the 21st century. It was small town, mid-western America when almost everyone knew everyone else.

Dad needed something at one of our local downtown stores. He parked our 1949 Chevrolet in a parking space along the main street. He told me to "Stay put and I'll be back soon."

After waiting, I rolled down the window of the big black sedan and crawled out. As I was walking on the sidewalk, a friend of my dad stopped me and said, "Where are you going?" To which I replied, "I'm looking for my dad and I know where I'm going!"

I've thought about that event many times since it was told to me. Usually I think about it when I make a decision that had less than desirable results. It's then I think about my statement, "I know where I'm going." Why is it that we are slow to learn the wisdom of following God rather than waiting for Him to catch up? Why is it that we go our own way and do our own thing and then expect Him to clean it up?

But, aside from all of that, I also think often about the statement, "I'm looking for my dad." The spiritual analogy of that is simple yet so profound. God's entire human creation is looking for their Father. Many have no idea that the emptiness in their lives and hearts is the absence of their Dad.

Those who have found Him (or rather were willing to be found by Him) know the peace and joy that comes with being secure in His arms. Today, I wish my five year old memory would have captured that sweet moment when I finally found my dad. I'm sure he scooped me up and hugged me, but I'd guess there was a scolding in there somewhere!

Luke 15:5-6 - *And when he hath found it, he layeth it on his shoulders, rejoicing. And when he cometh home, he calleth together his friends and neighbors, saying unto them, Rejoice with me; for I have found my sheep which was lost.*

Where's the Sunlight?

Truth for Today – Philippians 4:11-12

Here is a totally random question. What happens when worms, moles or other burrowing critters try to surface, only to hit the bottom of an asphalt or concrete parking lot? Do they burrow down and try again, and again, and again? That would be an incredibly frustrating exercise in futility as a multi-acre parking lot would seemingly go on forever.

The question makes me think about people who are trapped in situations from which there seems to be no escape.

Consider spouses trapped in a marriage, with cycles of emotional, physical or mental abuse. Or possibly individuals who have chronic pain. What about people who have significant physical challenges limiting their ability to perform routine daily tasks?

People who suffer from mental illness sometimes feel captive in a body not their own. Possibly there's a couple who are infertile, while desperately desiring children. Perhaps we all have things we would desire changing, but cannot.

The Bible encourages each of us to have a contented spirit. If we focus on things we cannot change, we are led to frustration, anger and desperation. Desperation can bring dire consequences to ourselves or others.

It's no wonder God encourages us to have a thankful and contented spirit.

- Philippians 4:11-12 - *Not that I speak in respect of want: for I have learned, in whatsoever state I am, therewith to be content. I know both how to be abased, and I know how to abound: every where and in all things I am instructed both to be full and to be hungry, both to abound and to suffer need.*
- Hebrews 13:5 - *Let your conversation be without covetousness; and be content with such things as ye have: for he hath said, I will never leave thee, nor forsake thee.*
- 1 Timothy 6:6 - *But godliness with contentment is great gain.*
- 2 Corinthians 12:10 - *Therefore I take pleasure in infirmities, in reproaches, in necessities, in persecutions, in distresses for Christ's sake: for when I am weak, then am I strong.*

Who Was the Rescuer?

Truth for Today – Matthew 26

The dog was swimming when caught by a riptide. A man saw the dog being swept out further and further to sea and jumped in to rescue him. Soon the man was grabbed by the tide and was farther out than the dog which he had intended to rescue. The dog eventually made it to shore, but the rescuer was in trouble. A policeman, who was also a triathlete, swam to the would-be rescuer, calmed him and brought him safely to shore. The rescuer had been rescued.

The tow truck had quit running and coasted to the side of the road. Minutes later, another tow truck arrived and proceeded to tow the stranded tow truck to a repair shop. The rescuer had been rescued.

At 58 years old she had one passion. She loved cats. When a cat ran up one of her trees, she tried to coax it down. The cat simply didn't cooperate, so she started climbing. At 60', she lost her nerve. She couldn't reach the cat and she couldn't climb down. Finally the fire department sent a ladder truck to rescue her. The rescuer had been rescued.

These three stories teach me about the power our Lord Jesus has. God asked Him to rescue the entire human race from themselves. Jesus was the ultimate rescuer. Equipped in every way, He obediently came to earth, ready to rescue and serve.

Some might say that He was the one who needed rescued or intervention, to protect Him from the scribes and Pharisees who continually sought to entrap Him. Not so. He handled those tight situations perfectly by Himself.

Others might say He needed help when satan tried to tempt Him in the wilderness to accept riches, power and glory. Again, with His Word, He found a way out.

After being betrayed by Judas, He was captured, interrogated and sentenced to death. Surely He would need help to escape the Roman soldiers and Jewish leaders. He knew that he could ask for twelve legions of angels to rescue Him, but He didn't ask.

No one needed to roll the stone away from His grave to free Him. He was God. He is still God. He is our God. He is our rescuer.

Who's in Charge?

Truth for Today – Job 38

She was born at 5:27am this morning and was 6 lbs. 11 oz. of gorgeous life. She will share this birth date with 384,000 other children around the world born on this day. If born in Monaco, she will have a life expectancy of 89 years, but only 48 years if born in Sierra Leone.

He passed away this morning at 4:48am after a year-long battle with cancer. He was 73 years old. On this day, he will join eternity with 156,000 other dying people around the world.

If we woke up this morning with good health, we probably will not be joining the 156,000 entering eternity today. We will most likely retain our place to share another day with our 7.3 billion co-earthlings.

Life and death. Fate? Destiny? Who is in charge of the breath of life and heartbeats? The Bible provides the answers:

- Job 12:10 – *(God) in whose hand is the soul of every living thing, and the breath of all mankind.*
- Psalm 115:3 - *But our God is in the heavens: he hath done whatsoever he hath pleased.*
- Proverbs 16:9 - *A man's heart deviseth his way: but the LORD directeth his steps.*
- Romans 14:8 - *For whether we live, we live unto the Lord; and whether we die, we die unto the Lord: whether we live therefore, or die, we are the Lord's.*

He's got the whole world in His hands...

Worth it All

Truth for Today – Colossians 3:23-24

My dad spent almost two years in the Luzon, Philippines and New Guinea during World War II. Though it was incredibly difficult and left him marked for life, he made a statement to me that I will never forget. *"I wouldn't pay a plug nickel for my time in the army, but I wouldn't take a million dollars for the lessons I learned."* He said it was worth it.

My five foot, 100 pound mother delivered me full term at 7 lbs. 5 oz. in a difficult delivery at 5:30am on Sunday, November 6, 1949. The problem? I was born breech. I'm hoping she considers the pain of that day as being worth it.

Rarely, on the day after a birth, will a new mother say, "Wow, I'm ready to do that again!" But, if you give them a couple of months, the pain and memories become a bit distant.

I wonder how it went for the children of Israel as they suffered the torture of their 40 years in the wilderness. Their complaining spirit during those years without a home are recorded for all posterity to read. As they entered the Promised Land with all of its benefits, security and resources, I would suspect there were statements like, "It was worth it all."

A girl had suffered three years of sexual abuse and finally after counseling and time, was able to say something profound. "I never thought I would get to the day when I'd say, it was worth it. Today I can see how God is using it all for His good."

Perhaps we can gain courage and perseverance by singing through the lyrics of a popular song...

> *Oft times the day seems long, our trials hard to bear;*
> *We're tempted to complain, to murmur and despair;*
> *But Christ will soon appear to catch His Bride away,*
> *All tears forever over in God's eternal day.*
>
> *It will be worth it all when we see Jesus,*
> *Life's trials will seem so small when we see Christ;*
> *One glimpse of His dear face, all sorrow will erase,*
> *So bravely run the race till we see Christ.*

Would You Repeat That?

Truth for Today – Psalm 1

It was a small bar in a rough and tough neighborhood in a large city. As I drove past, I noticed a sign in the window. It intrigued me such that I drove around the block and came back to read it again. Ah, this was good enough for a photo.

COLD ICE - Is there a word we could use, meaning "stating the obvious"? How about superfluous, redundant, unnecessary, and excessive, along with the usual phrases of "duh" and "really".

Without seeming to be sacrilegious, that sign reminded me of the Bible and of a thousand sermons I have heard. Repetition, repetition, repetition. Covering the same material again and again.

How many times have I heard the beautiful story of Christmas, Easter, and Good Friday, as well as the many funerals and marriage ceremonies?

How many times have I read the stories of creation and the fall, or about Noah, Daniel, Moses and the Exodus?

Do I ever tire of hearing about the Sermon on the Mount or the repetition of Jesus healing the blind, deaf, maimed and dying?

What about the Acts of the Apostles, or the book of prophecy of John in Revelation? Repetition? Redundant? Once is good enough? Never! Tell me again and again and again!

2 Timothy 3:16 - All scripture is given by inspiration
of God, and is profitable for doctrine, for reproof,
for correction, for instruction in righteousness.

Wrong Solution

Truth for Today – Psalm 37:4

Living in the Midwest, I knew only too well the aggravating habits of the groundhog. Also known as the woodchuck, the groundhog is a rodent. They will move approximately 2.5 tons of soil in burrowing their tunnels. Their underground homes will have multiple entrances and exits, making their capture difficult.

We once had a groundhog who made his home under our small garage which had a dirt floor. The floor became spongy and some of the tunnels caved in, but our persistent and uninvited tenant simply burrowed another tunnel. I think he maybe later died of old age. My experience gave me sympathy for a friend of mine.

He noticed that groundhogs had invaded his old barn and he was in a quandary as to what to do. He had a desire to restore the barn, but the groundhogs were getting in the way of his vision. He tried multiple times to rid himself of the varmints, but failed.

Then, someone told him about a sure-proof method. So, he followed the instructions to the letter. He entered the barn and poured five gallons of water into a groundhog burrow and let it settle. Then he poured one gallon of gasoline into the hole. Since gasoline floats on water, the gas flowed through the burrows on top of the water instead of soaking into the ground.

Then he dropped a match into the burrow. The fumes from the gasoline ignited above ground and started the hay in his overhead haymow on fire. It wasn't long until the barn was gone and in all likelihood, the groundhogs as well.

My friend suffered the loss of a barn, as well as the ongoing humiliation of what had happened. When I asked him about using his story, he replied – "Sure. I'm amazed at how often we try to do things just right, only to have them turn out so wrong."

- James 4:10 - *Humble yourselves in the sight of the Lord, and he shall lift you up.*
- Proverbs 3:5 - *Trust in the LORD with all thine heart; and lean not unto thine own understanding.*
- Psalm 37:4 - *Delight thyself also in the LORD: and he shall give thee the desires of thine heart.*

You Can't Fix That!

Truth for Today - Genesis 39

He was a repairman fixing a copy machine at the Post Office. His tools were laid out and he was elbow deep in rollers and belts. Those were the days of using black carbon toner which was poured from a plastic bottle into a tray. The carbon toner was a fine powder that did a lot of damage to clothing, fingers and anything else it touched.

I asked him if he had ever had a memorable moment with toner dust. He laughed and said...

"I remember once when I'd finished repairing a machine, I was going to use my hand vacuum to suck up the residue powder. Accidentally I had it on "blower" instead of "vacuum". You can't imagine the mess as I blew jet-black carbon dust all over the office, desks and people! You can never undo or fix those kinds of things!"

That caused me to think about how a little carelessness can do great damage. When I think of communications, I think of words or statements I've made that have hurt people. How quickly a word or two can do long-lasting damage. Reputations can be damaged, tarnished or ruined by innuendo, gossip or jesting. Many times it is just as the copy machine repairman said – "You can never undo or fix those kinds of things!"

Jesus said it this way in Matthew 12:36 - *But I say unto you, That every idle word that men shall speak, they shall give account thereof in the day of judgment.*

Luke 12:3 - *Therefore whatsoever ye have spoken in darkness shall be heard in the light; and that which ye have spoken in the ear in closets shall be proclaimed upon the housetops.*

You Can't See Me!

Truth for Today – Numbers 23:19

He was desperately in need of money. Who knows what for? But the need took the Iranian man to his local wizard. He had heard that the wizard could make people invisible and the thief had an idea.

He paid the required $450 to the wizard for the invisibility spells and headed to a bank. He walked up to a customer and pulled the man's money out of his hand. Then he did the same to another and another. The angry customers quickly pulled the man down and held him until the police arrived.

The thief said, "I've been tricked by the wizard." The police couldn't find the sorcerer who apparently *had* turned "invisible".

How easily are we deceived in similar situations? We might say "no way", but reality might prove otherwise. Though few of us would fall for the invisibility scam, are there other ways we are deceived?

Most people desire to be attractive to others, as well as desiring love, romance and intimacy. That becomes the foundation of how advertisers package, advertise and market their wares to a buying public. Are we swayed by their tactics?

If a celebrity or sports star adds his name or face to a product, does it make a difference? Do we equate a brand name to excellence? Is the product any better or any worse than its competition?

What is that old saying? "When it seems too good to be true, it probably is." Advertising is strategic in getting consumers to buy a product. How susceptible are we to messages, subliminal or blatant?

Can we believe God when He says that Heaven is a phenomenal place? What about the concept of having streets paved with gold? Or, how valid can it be that we will see or hear things in Heaven that were not known on earth? Is it possible that everyone in Heaven will have their own mansion?

- Psalm 119:160 - *Thy word is true from the beginning: and every one of thy righteous judgments endureth for ever.*
- Numbers 23:19 - *God is not a man, that he should lie; neither the son of man, that he should repent: hath he said, and shall he not do it? or hath he spoken, and shall he not make it good?*

You Do What?

As a country with a population of 1.25 billion, it is extremely difficult to find passionate, born again, Christian believers in India. At less than 1.5% of the population, and facing militant opposition at times, they are not readily identifiable.

I met a young man in a coffee shop in northern India. Our conversation turned to religion, and I soon learned of his deep faith in God as well as his personal testimony. Sensing he was a professional, I asked him what he did. I will never forget his answer, "My work is engineering, but my vocation is evangelism."

As I talked to the man, I thought of the apostle Paul as he shared the difference between making tents and being an evangelist.

Acts 18:3-6 – *And because (Paul and Aquila were) of the same craft, he abode with them, and wrought: for by their occupation they were tentmakers. And he reasoned in the synagogue every sabbath, and persuaded the Jews and the Greeks. And when Silas and Timotheus were come from Macedonia, Paul was pressed in the spirit, and testified to the Jews that Jesus was Christ. And when they opposed themselves, and blasphemed, he shook his raiment, and said unto them, Your blood be upon your own heads; I am clean; from henceforth I will go unto the Gentiles.*

The Indian's faith was passionate, vibrant and on-fire. Ronald A. Heifetz said it this way, *"If you find what you do each day seems to have no link to any higher purpose, you probably want to rethink what you're doing."*

Ephesians 4:1 challenges us with the thought – *"I therefore, the prisoner of the Lord, beseech you that ye walk worthy of the vocation wherewith ye are called."* The Bible is consistent in teaching us to do it well:

- Colossians 3:17 - *And whatsoever ye do in word or deed, do all in the name of the Lord Jesus, giving thanks to God and the Father by him.*
- Colossians 3:23 - *And whatsoever ye do, do it heartily, as to the Lord, and not unto men.*

You Meant What?

Truth for Today – Colossians 2

Thirty years ago, six families decided to take their twenty young children to sing hymns at local health care facilities. It was a great opportunity to spend time together teaching outreach to our children. Our family was one of those six families making memories.

Many things have changed over the course of these last thirty years. For instance, most of those twenty children now have families of their own. We, as couples, have continued on with our tradition of singing, in spite of all of us now being in our sixties.

An experience recently, reminds me of another thing that has changed. While singing to about twenty elderly people at a nursing home, a 93 year old lady whispered something to me. I leaned down and asked her to repeat it and she said, "You old folks still sing pretty good!" I laughed out loud as the significance of her statement sank in. I am guessing that our singing over the years has changed.

Perceptions, opinions and words are all relative. In this case, the elderly lady had diminished eyesight, hearing and possibly her mental acuities. The term "old" has different meanings, relative to our age. The term, "sing pretty good" is relative to our hearing and mind. Again, our perceptions and opinions generally are relative.

When God lays out His parameters, commandments and cautions, they are not relative to time, culture, gender, age or ethnicity. His Word and instruction are applicable to all people, at all times, in all places.

It may be easy to diminish a Biblical instruction by saying it is not applicable in the 21st century. Caution should always be used when dropping something that has been a solid principle for centuries. Once dropped, it is nearly impossible to retrieve later.

- 1 Thess. 5:21 - *Prove all things; hold fast that which is good.*
- 2 Thess. 2:15 - *Therefore, brethren, stand fast, and hold the traditions which ye have been taught, whether by word, or our epistle.*
- Revelation 1:25 - *But that which ye have already, hold fast till I come.*

You'll Have to Wait and See

Truth for Today – Revelation 21

It was a cold Saturday morning in December of 1959 and I was ten years old. Dad and mom got my sisters and I out of bed, and told us to get ready as they had a surprise for us.

The immediate question was, "What is it?" And of course the inevitable answer was, "You'll have to wait and see!"

A quick breakfast and we piled into our 1957 Pontiac Star Chief. Now the question changed to, "Where are we going?" Then the same reply of, "You'll have to wait and see!"

Anticipation of something special is torture for a ten year old. Dad knew where we were going and what we were going to see and do. But he didn't give us a clue, just simply saying, "You'll have to wait and see!"

It reminds me of the verse in 1 Corinthians 2:9 - *Eye hath not seen, nor ear heard, neither have entered into the heart of man, the things which God hath prepared for them that love him.*

The Bible gives us hints about Heaven. There will be streets of gold, beautiful singing, mansions everywhere, and no tears or death. The thought fills me with excitement and anticipation.

When I go to our local health care facility for the elderly, I hear the same things again and again from God's children.

- "I can't wait to go to Heaven."
- "I don't know why I'm still here."

Anticipation of something special is torture for a ten year old. Anticipation of something special is torture for an eighty-five year old. Age doesn't change anything.

Oh, back to the 1959 surprise! We drove 15 miles to a neighboring town. Twenty questions later, Dad pulled into a parking lot and we piled out of the 1957 Sky Chief.

It was then we saw a locomotive and passenger cars. It was a half day train ride and we as kids were not disappointed. In fact it was better than anything we could have imagined. I saw things, heard things and smelled things I never had before. It exceeded my long-awaited anticipation. Heaven will be infinitely and abundantly more!

Your Sin Will Find You Out

Truth for Today – James 5:12

I had grown tired of using my dad's 1953 Ford to go to places 17 year old boys like to go. After all, in 1967, you just didn't run around in a 4 door, green, 14 year old sedan. So, dad and I went shopping and I found a 1964 Ford Mustang with a four speed transmission; 289 cu.in. engine; and mag wheels with red walled tires.

When we bought it, the local dealer gave us a 30 day warranty to cover any problems. He had been a friend of my dad for years and dad trusted him.

About three weeks into my 30 day warranty, the clutch went out on the car. Dad and I took it to the dealer. The dealer said to my dad, "We had a 30 day warranty on the car and I will honor that. But, you do need to know that our shop is right beside the outdoor drive-in restaurant that kids frequent. I've seen this car go through this drive-in many times and listened as your son popped the clutch and laid rubber on the highway while leaving. However, I will still honor my warranty. I just thought you needed to know." I learned several things that day.

- God doesn't let sin slide. Numbers 32:23 - *...be sure your sin will find you out.*
- Just because you are able to do something, it doesn't mean that it is wise. 1 Corinthians 10:23 - *All things are lawful for me, but all things are not expedient: all things are lawful for me, but all things edify not.*
- If you are going to promise something, you need to follow through with action. James 5:12 - *But above all things, my brethren, swear not, neither by heaven, neither by the earth, neither by any other oath: but let your yea be yea; and your nay, nay; lest ye fall into condemnation.*
- Our reputation needs to be kept pure. Romans 12:17 - *Provide things honest in the sight of all men.*
- We are all being watched. Matthew 10:26 - *...for there is nothing covered, that shall not be revealed; and hid, that shall not be known.*

Your Voice Carries

Truth for Today – Ephesians 5:15

    Jeni and I were already aboard the plane, and watching other passengers find their seats. A frail elderly man came down the aisle and sat directly behind us. Soon a flight attendant brought his fragile wife in a small cart and helped her into the seat beside her husband.

    They were 92 years old and had been married 68 years. As we were waiting to take off, their non-stop conversation was revealing:

(He) Why did you have to bring that bag? - *(She) Because I need it.*
Why do you need it? - *Because I have my lipstick in it.*
Why do you need your lipstick? - *Because I need to match.*
What for? These 150 people don't care whether you match or not? - *Well I care.*
Won't make no difference if you match, if this plane crashes. These 150 dead people won't care at all. - *Well, if it crashes, I hope I'm dead.*
Well if that's what you want that's fine with me, but I want to live awhile. What time is it? - *It's 1:20.*
You're wrong. It's 1:30. - *Your watch is fast. It's 1:20.*
You're definitely right all the time, aren't you? - *Well, your watch is so dirty; it's no wonder you can't tell what time it is.*
Where's our daughter? - *She's sitting up there somewhere.*
I'd like to see where she's at. - *Get up and look...*
I can't, my seatbelt is on. - *They tell me that I talk loud and my voice carries. I better be careful what I say.*

    Believe me, they were the best in-flight entertainment I've ever had! On the other hand I wondered what their marriage of 68 years had been like. What kind of image, perception and impression are we sharing and leaving with others?

    I had judged them based on that five minutes... then I found out they were going to the funeral of their son. My judgment changed...

You're Afraid of What?

Truth for Today – Ephesians 2:8-9

I developed a fear of dogs after being bitten when I was ten. It doesn't matter if they are large or small, friendly or snarling, my palms sweat and my heart-rate increases. Fears can be debilitating.

As people we have a tendency to fear certain things. We fear heights, being on water, the dark, snakes, spiders, public speaking and flying. Generally it comes from an early experience in life.

Two of the most common fears are a fear of rejection and a fear of failure. Most of us experience both, but generally one of the fears will dominate most of our life.

If we are relationship driven, we tend to have a fear of rejection. If we are non-relationship driven, then we tend to be goal oriented and experience a fear of failure. Anxieties and stress can escalate for those with a fear of rejection, when conflicts arise with others.

Fear of failure can move us towards perfection or even obsessive compulsive behaviors. A fear of failure can cause us to become angry at those who interfere with our success. Blame and judgment of others can also happen.

A fear of rejection can prompt us to enable bad behavior in others, or to excuse sin. It can likewise cause us to seek out relationships with others that can be inappropriate, or even sinful in our quest to be accepted.

Both fears have damaging consequences in our relationship with God. Both can take us down a legalism path in seeking perfection before a just God. God knows our strengths and weaknesses and shares insights with us in how to cope with these fears.

- Ephesians 2:8-9 - *For by grace are ye saved through faith; and that not of yourselves: it is the gift of God: Not of works, lest any man should boast.*
- Romans 8:38-39 - *For I am persuaded, that neither death, nor life, nor angels, nor principalities, nor powers, nor things present, nor things to come, nor height, nor depth, nor any other creature, shall be able to separate us from the love of God, which is in Christ Jesus our Lord.*

You're Different

Truth for Today – Jeremiah 1:5

With 7.3 billion people on earth, it is difficult to imagine that each are unique. However, with so many variable characteristics, features, colors and sizes, it appears that even between identical twins there are differences.

Though we are prone to submit to peer pressure so we can be like others, we still seek to maintain a personal identity. To what length are we striving to be different?

A grandmother holds the current world record for longest fingernails. In 1990 she began letting them grow. When she broke the world record, the nails on her left hand measured a total of 10 feet 2 inches and on her right hand 9 feet 7 inches. That's a total of 19 feet 9 inches of fingernails. Now, that is truly unique.

God has designed His universe for His purpose and pleasure. We are created as humans in His image and likeness. Variations in characteristics still render us unique. I doubt we can imagine how boring our world would be if all people and all cultures were alike.

What does the Bible say about the uniqueness we have and what God thinks about that?

- Jeremiah 1:5 - *Before I formed thee in the belly I knew thee; and before thou camest forth out of the womb I sanctified thee, and I ordained thee a prophet unto the nations.*
- Psalm 139:14 - *I will praise thee; for I am fearfully and wonderfully made: marvellous are thy works; and that my soul knoweth right well.*
- Exodus 4:11 - *And the Lord said unto him, Who hath made man's mouth? Or who maketh the dumb, or deaf, or the seeing, or the blind? Have not I the Lord?*
- John 9:2-3 - *And his disciples asked him, saying, Master, who did sin, this man, or his parents, that he was born blind? Jesus answered, neither hath this man sinned, nor his parents: but that the works of God should be made manifest in him.*
- Matthew 10:30 - *But the very hairs of your head are all numbered.*

You're Odd (a bonus day)

Truth for Today – Luke 18

Can you picture this conversation between two houseflies as they watched a grasshopper? "Can you imagine? He has his ears on his front legs."

Or possibly a conversation between two grasshoppers as they were looking at a housefly? "He's so strange and odd! His taste buds are on his feet!"

In reality, both statements are accurate. Some grasshoppers and crickets have ears on their front legs, and houseflies taste with their feet.

As human beings, how often do we consider someone different than ourselves, as being odd, strange and less of a person? Do we look at someone's color of skin, size or shape of a nose, too much hair or not enough, size and proportion of the body, voice inflections, hair color, physical or mental challenges as being inferior to ourselves?

Do we discriminate due to where someone lives or what their income level might be, the car they drive, the home they live in, or where they send their children to school? The Bible clearly lays out parameters for us, in how we gauge someone else.

- Romans 14:10 - *But why dost thou judge thy brother? or why dost thou set at nought thy brother? for we shall all stand before the judgment seat of Christ.*
- Luke 18:11 - *The Pharisee stood and prayed thus with himself, God, I thank thee, that I am not as other men are, extortioners, unjust, adulterers, or even as this publican.*
- Romans 2:11 - *For there is no respect of persons with God.*
- James 2:2-4 – *For if there come unto your assembly a man with a gold ring, in goodly apparel, and there come in also a poor man in vile raiment; And ye have respect to him that weareth the gay clothing, and say unto him, Sit thou here in a good place; and say to the poor, Stand thou there, or sit here under my footstool: Are ye not then partial in yourselves, and are become judges of evil thoughts?*
- James 2:9 - *But if ye have respect to persons, ye commit sin.*